Library of
Davidson College

LITERARY CRITICS AND REVIEWERS IN EARLY
NINETEENTH-CENTURY BRITAIN

Literary Critics and Reviewers in Early 19th-Century Britain

PETER F. MORGAN

CROOM HELM
London & Canberra

© 1983 Peter F. Morgan
Croom Helm Ltd, Provident House, Burrell Row,
Beckenham, Kent BR3 1AT
Croom Helm Australia, PO Box 391, Manuka,
ACT 2603, Australia

British Library Cataloguing in Publication Data

Morgan, Peter F.
 Literary critics and reviewers in early nineteenth-century Britain
 Britain.
 I. Title
 820.9'007   PR451

ISBN 0-7099-1774-0

Printed and bound in Great Britain by
Biddles Ltd, Guildford and King's Lynn

CONTENTS

Introduction
1. JEFFREY AND THE EDINBURGH REVIEW 1
   Part One.   Jeffrey's criticism 1
   Part Two.   Jeffrey's attitude towards
               Wordsworth 22
   Part Three. Jeffrey's relation with Caryle 40
   Part Four. Caryle and Macaulay as reviewers 59

2. QUARTERLY REVIEWERS 75
   Part One.   Scott 75
   Part Two.   Southey on poetry 89
   Part Three. Southey on prose 105
   Part Four. Croker 111
   Part Five. Lockhart 122

3. THE WESTMINSTER REVIEW: MILL AND POETRY 132
   Part One.   Early life 132
   Part Two.   Central years 146
   Part Three. Later years 165
Index 178

ACKNOWLEDGEMENTS

I am grateful for permission to reprint material, in all cases slightly modified, from Humanities Association Bulletin, Neophilogogus, Scottish Literary Journal, Studia Germanica Gandensia, Stuides in Scottish Literature, and Wordsworth Circle. The section on "Southey and Poetry" is reprinted by permission of The University of Tennessee Press. From Richard B. Davies and Kenneth L. Knickerbocker, eds.: TENNESSEE STUDIES IN LITERATURE, No. XVI. Copyright © 1971 by The University of Tennessee Press. The typing of the manuscript was ably executed by Bill Bowen; Ida Noel's support was invaluable.

INTRODUCTION

The aim of this volume is to present a perspective on the literary criticism of the early nineteenth century. This perspective has been laboriously developed through a number of studies which have been published separately over the years in various journals. The connection between these studies has always been in the mind of the author, but it has not been evident to their readers. This is the material reason for bringing them together here.

Study of the remarkably varied, romantic and comic poetry and prose of Thomas Hood (1799 - 1845) drew the author's attention to the importance of the periodical as a factor in the literature of the early nineteenth century. Hood contributed to the London Magazine which flourished in the early 1820's, as well as later to the Athenaeum and to the New Monthly Magazine, before editing Hood's Magazine in the last years of his life.

Hood, like the periodicals with which he was associated, is significant in a twofold way. That is, he was a creative writer in his own right. He was also remarkably successful in imitation of the manner of others. In particular, he imitated Keats in his romantic verse. Thus, with others, he mediated the Keatsian mode, so that it became available to the Victorians through him, as well as directly from Keats himself. As these phrases indicate, Hood is also of interest as a writer belonging to the transition between Romantic and Victorian. An illustration is the first stanza of 'Ode: Autumn,' published in the first London Magazine, February 1823:

Introduction

> I saw old Autumn in the misty morn
> Stand shadowless like Silence, listening
> To silence, for no lonely bird would sing
> Into his hollow ear from woods forlorn,
> Nor lowly hedge nor solitary thorn; --
> Shaking his languid locks all dewy bright
> With tangled gossamer that fell by night,
> Pearling his coronet of golden corn.

These features of originality and also as a channel of communication characterise not only a single writer, such as Hood, but more broadly the journalism to which he contributed. That is, the periodicals make a directly original (often critical) contribution. They also make a contribution through the mediation (also often critical) of work which originates elsewhere. Through them it is possible to perceive not only original strands in the literary fabric, but also synthetic ones. It is possible to perceive as well the process of literary involvement in the broader culture, not only as it occurs at one moment, but also as it develops over a period of time, in this case the particularly significant period from the romantic heyday to the onset of the Victorians.

The study of Hood taught the author that scholarship is an inexhaustible domain, even where a single author of the second rank in concerned. How much more one appreciates its inexhaustibility with regard to the vast periodical field. This appreciation, inwardly felt, is enhanced as one admires the bold attempts of the learned bibliographers to chart what the pioneer Michael Wolff calls 'the golden stream.'[1] One thinks particularly of the contributions in the Victorian period of Walter Houghton in the Wellesley Index and of John North in the Waterloo Directory, and one is struck by the appropriately Wellingtonian overtones of their titles. Earlier one thinks of William S. Ward's listing of Literary Reviews in British Periodicals 1798-1820, of David Reiman's massive anthology The Romantics Reviewed, and of John O. Hayden's critical survey The Romantic Reviewers.

My own incursion into this important field was limited, like that of the last three scholars named, by a preoccupation with literary criticism, though in such an area it was impossible to ignore the broader political and cultural contexts. I narrowed the endeavour further by a concentration on the criticism of contemporary poetry and fiction, for the sake of the narrowing itself and

Introduction

also because these constituted crucial contributions in themselves and I felt that a study of the changing reaction to them would be of value. I focussed on the leading quarterly reviews and monthly magazines: the Edinburgh Review, the Quarterly Review, and the Westminster Review; Blackwood's Magazine, the London Magazine, and Fraser's Magazine. Again, the reason was focussing for its own sake, but also because these periodicals represented sustained and influential critical response. Moreover, a chronological pattern of influence and development can be traced through them, starting from the inauguration of the Edinburgh Review in 1802.

An initial but quite extensive survey produced an analysis that may perhaps be compared to that of Hayden in the work referred to above. That is, one examined the multiple comments on the oeuvre of an author in a certain number of periodicals and discovered a response which ranged narrowly between the two poles of 'favourable' and 'unfavourable'. This analysis appeared unsatisfactory because of the shallowness of the conclusions. They were shallow partly because of the limitations of the material examined. For example, it often took the form of off-the-cuff or incidental comments. It was also difficult to decipher the meaning of the terms 'favourable' and 'unfavourable' or their equivalents as they appeared in the shorthand of the scholarly investigator scribbled over that of the critic or the reviewer himself.[2]

An approach which bypassed this critical obstacle was that illustrated to a degree by John Clive in his study of the Edinburgh Review, by George L. Nesbitt in examining the Westminster Review, and by Leslie Marchand with regard to the Athenaeum. These scholars made an attempt to identify the ethos of the particular journal. The ethos was also suggested by the delvings of Alan Lang Strout into the correspondence of the house of Blackwood and hence into the interpersonal life which lay behind the publication of a journal, strongly evidenced in the 'Noctes Ambrosianae' of Maga. I sensed the ethos myself through an examination of the correspondence of Taylor and Hessey, publishers of the London Magazine, culminating in Taylor's lament over the dispersal of 'our formerly gay Party.'[3] The esprit de corps of the contributors to a journal might develop an appropriate style expressive of a shared philosophical

xi

Introduction

outlook, as in the quarterlies generally, as observed by Macaulay;[4] or of mood, often exuberant, sometimes satirical, as in the magazines, especially <u>Blackwood's</u> and <u>Fraser's</u>, the latter noted by Carlyle in <u>Sartor Resartus</u> as 'A vehicle all strewed (figuratively speaking) with the maddest Waterloo-Crackers.'[5] The style is thus expressive of a periodical spirit, rather than a finely honed instrument of sober or clinical examination of the subject under review.

The special figurative style of the reviewer might reveal him playing the professional role of judge (above all, Jeffrey in the <u>Edinburgh Review</u>), prosecuting counsel, teacher, doctor or surgeon; the domestic role of cook (for example, Lockhart in considering Tennyson) or butcher; in a world of savage fantasy the role, not uncongenial to <u>Blackwood's</u>, of torturer, ogre, murderer or cannibal.[6]

Gregariousness expressed itself less overtly in the discreet quarterlies than in the magazines, with their pseudonymous contributors: Elia, the Opium-Eater and Janus Weathercock in the <u>London</u>; the participants in the 'Noctes Ambrosianae' in <u>Blackwood's</u>; Oliver Yorke, the editor of <u>Fraser's</u>: these leading significantly to Thackeray's role as Yellowplush in <u>Fraser's</u>, Carlyle's personae in <u>Sartor</u>, and Dickens as Boz.

With regard to the quarterlies, I myself did not feel willing, let alone able, to make a study of the <u>Quarterly</u>, analogous to Clive's of the <u>Edinburgh</u>, much as that is still needed; or a study which would update that of Nesbitt; or the still absent study of <u>Maga</u>. I felt that I should continue to strive for the broader view, though this had to take a different form from that provided by Hayden. His survey, though useful, possessed limitations which I have suggested.

I was led further along the particular path which I have followed by spending many years at the University of Toronto where, on the one hand, access to the more recondite material was limited, and, on the other, emphasis was heavily on the major authors who could be intensively studied as representative of the British literary tradition. Under this salutary influence I moved away from the quite impersonal analytical approach, in order to focus on the leading contributors and their views. These men led in terms of both contemporary and modern reputation, as well as because of their substantial contributions to the journals. Thus my

Introduction

focus fell on Jeffrey, editor of the <u>Edinburgh Review</u>, with its most distinguished contributors of the next generation, Carlyle and Macaulay. It fell on Lockhart, son-in-law and later biographer of Scott, and second editor of the <u>Quarterly Review</u>, with his contributors Southey and Croker, literary and political mainstays of the review for many years, as well as Scott himself. Attention fell finally on John Stuart Mill, editor of and leading contributor to the <u>Westminster Review</u>. The first intention was to study these authors as critics in the reviews, and this was relatively easily encompassed in the cases of Jeffrey and Croker, virtually all of whose critical work was done there. I also began with a study of Jeffrey, who can be regarded as the father of the review form itself, of review criticism in general, and of the review article. These dominated the literary scene throughout the nineteenth century, not only in England but throughout the Western world. Virtually all of Jeffrey's formal criticism, as I have just indicated, took the shape of contributions to the <u>Edinburgh Review</u>, and he himself published representative selections from it in 1844. I studied Jeffrey's critical writings in themselves, and his attitude to Wordsworth in particular. This was followed by an examination of his relation both critical and personal to Carlyle as a contributor, and then by a comparative study of the contributions of Carlyle and Macaulay. Carlyle's contributions constitute a small but significant entity in his <u>oeuvre</u>, significant as marking the start of his career as man of letters, thanks to Jeffrey. It was of interest to study Macaulay's work of the same kind, as showing a young man making a similar <u>debut</u>. However, Macaulay found the Whig setting of the <u>Edinburgh Review</u> infinitely more congenial than did Carlyle, so much so that Macaulay's subsequent fame rests both on the essays, published there, and on the History of England.

In the case of these <u>Edinburgh Reviewers</u>, criticism constituted a major part of their contributions, so it was relatively easy to examine and analyse. Oddly enough, and perhaps significantly, the <u>Quarterly Review</u> showed a different pattern. Scott, Southey, Croker and Lockhart were major contributors, but what they provided was heterogeneous in character. If anything they eschewed the role of judge so dear to the <u>Edinburgh Reviewers</u> and referred to in the motto of the

Introduction

Edinburgh, 'judex damnatur cum nocens absolvitur.' So in these cases my search for critical judgment took me beyond the pages of the Quarterly, to examine the substantial opus of Scott; that of Southey; Lockhart, especially the lives of Burns and Scott and the novels; and Croker, with the edition of Boswell's Life of Johnson. One admires the energy and range of all these men, their deep sense of writing out of a well-rooted literary tradition. Perhaps especially in the Quarterly Reviewers one observes the lack of compartmentalisation in approach: that is, they do not make a point of setting themselves up as critics.

    John Stuart Mill was the major contributor as critic to the Westminster Review. Stimulated by the scholarly bounty of my distinguished colleague J.M. Robson, editor of Mill's collected works, I felt the urge to explore in greater depth Mill's attitudes towards poetry and the poetic. In fact what I endeavoured to do was to trace the poignancy of his lifelong effort to move beyond the hostility and the indifferentism of the earlier reviewers. Thus my study of Mill has a broader biographical base than the work on the other critics, though it is convenient in the middle section to focus on his contributions to the periodicals: the London Review, the London and Westminster Review, and also the Monthly Repository. In fact, Mill does move periodical criticism along from the rather threatening, almost histrionic stance of Jeffrey, Macaulay and Carlyle, as well as from the negative attitude or the absence or concealment of attitude on the part of their Tory counterparts. Mill's work has a more modern tone. He still feels the urgent need to judge, but judgment is accompanied by both the analytical intelligence and the sympathetic imagination.

    I have tried to develop rational schemes descriptive of the critical contributions of these eminent reviewers, and I have met with different problems in the different cases. With Jeffrey there appears to be a clear shift in attitude about 1811, discernible yet hard to explain.[8] With Carlyle and Macaulay I confine myself by and large to their contributions to the Edinburgh Review. With the Quarterly Reviewers I feel that consistent accounts have been produced. It is not only because of the extent of my investigation that Mill appears as the most subtle of these writers about literature. There is a mercurial quality to his thoughts which reveals him as a man of the

Introduction

modern age.
    As I have said, this study has been undertaken on the basis of a consideration of the significance of the critics as periodical writers. In focussing on the criticism I have borne in mind the context in which it appeared, and how this context, the review, made it especially available and significant to contemporaries, as well as strongly influencing the mode of presentation and the style itself. I hope that a contribution has been made to the history of criticism in its social context.

NOTES

    1. In *Editing Nineteenth Century Texts*, ed. J.M. Robson (University of Toronto Press, Toronto, 1967), p. 37.
    2. Compare J.H. Alexander, *Two Studies in Romantic Reviewing* (2 vols, Universität Salzburg, Salzburg, 1976), vol. 2, p. 369: 'The Lady of the Lake was received extremely favourably on its appearance in 1810. Of the twenty reviews, thirteen were favourable (five of these enthusiastic), three were neutral, and four were critical (two of them very hostile).' The reviews are then listed. Alexander's is a valuable detailed account of reviewing in the periodicals up to the *Edinburgh*, as well as of contemporary criticism of Scott's poetry.
    3. *Keats-Shelley Journal*, vol. 7 (1958), p.68.
    4. See my note 'Macaulay and the Periodical Style,' *Victorian Periodicals Newsletter*, no. 1 (1968), p. 27.
    5. *Sartor Resartus*, bk. 1, ch. 2.
    6. I noted these images in VPN, no. 7 (1970), p. 10.
    7. John Morley observed Macaulay's 'perfect accord with his audience' and called him and Mill 'the two masters of the modern journalist,' *Fortnightly Review*, n.s. vol. 19 (1876), p. 495, reprinted in his *Critical Miscellanies* (3 vols, Macmillan, London, 1886), vol. 1, where the phrases quoted occur on p. xi.
    8. Though David Erdman tries to do so on the basis of a letter from Coleridge which is no longer extant: 'Coleridge and the "Review Business",' *Wordsworth Circle*, vol. 6 (1975), p. 18. See also Ralph Waldo Emerson, *Journals* (15 vols, Harvard University Press, Cambridge, Mass., 1960-82), vol. 10, p. 558.

Chapter One

JEFFREY AND THE <u>EDINBURGH REVIEW</u>

PART ONE. JEFFREY'S CRITICISM

Jeffrey edited the <u>Edinburgh Review</u> from 1802 until 1829. At this time he became Dean of the Faculty of Advocates and soon after entered Parliament. As a leading Whig he piloted the Scottish portions of the Reform Bill through the House. Later he was appointed Judge, but he retained his interest in the <u>Edinburgh Review</u> and in literature. He helped Carlyle and Macaulay in the advancement of their careers, and in private letters and talk he applauded the novels of Dickens.

With the <u>Edinburgh Review</u> Jeffrey inaugurated a major phase of English literature and journalism. The review provided substantial and thoughtful comments on the literature and general cultural life of the time. It was good that the coverage took place in this form. In this way the outstanding literary achievements of the day were mediated to a growing public. However, the attitude of Jeffrey and the <u>Edinburgh</u>, though Whig, and therefore opposed to Tory government, was at the same time cautious and in favour of gradual change in the Establishment, both politically and in culture. The <u>Edinburgh</u> expressed itself vigorously and caustically in attacks on the radical so-called 'Lake school.' An attempt at indicating that the attitude was not entirely unscrupulous is made below. I also make some effort to achieve an understanding of the great romantic poet, Wordsworth, in relation to a significant element in his milieu.

It is the contention of this first chapter that critical principles underlie Jeffrey's career as literary contributor to the <u>Edinburgh Review</u> and that these principles remain constant. An

1

attempt is made to identify them, but at the same time to show the fluctuations which take place in them. Particularly, Jeffrey's view of the English literary tradition and of contemporary poetry in relation to it seems to change about 1811, and I hope to indicate this change which I denominate as being from 'simple' to 'complex'. In this survey I occupy a middle ground between the arguments of Russell Noyes who champions Wordsworth as faultless bard against Jeffrey the malevolent critic (<u>Wordsworth and Jeffrey in Controversy</u>, Bloomington, 1941), and the views of James A. Greig who unquestioningly adopts Jeffrey's positions (<u>Francis Jeffrey of the Edinburgh Review</u>, Edinburgh, 1948). I aspire to occupy the same judicious middle ground as René Wellek (<u>A History of Modern Criticism...The Romantic Age</u>, New Haven, 1955). I amplify my discussion, as he was unable to do in the course of his massive survey, with quotations which illustrate the skill of Jeffrey's critical thought and expression through the medium of the review.[1]

i

Jeffrey is indeed concerned with principles. At all times he believes that the principles of literature were established irrevocably a long time ago. He declares in the <u>Edinburgh Review</u> that 'Poetry has this much...in common with religion, that its standards were fixed long ago, by certain inspired writers, whose authority it is no longer lawful to call in question' (I, October 1802, 63).[2] And again, 'In matters of taste...there are no discoveries to be made, any more than in matters of morality...the elements of poetical interest are necessarily obvious and universal - they are within and about all men; and the topics by which they are suggested are proved to have been the same in every age, and every country of the world' (VII, October 1805, 2, 3). Jeffrey states that Wordsworth especially is ignorant of 'the few settled and permanent maxims, which form the canon of general taste in all large and polished societies' (XXIV, November 1814, 3).

Thus Jeffrey appeals to principles, but in the period before 1811 he emphasizes that these principles have been adhered to by great writers through the succeeding centuries; to the English tradition belong Shakespeare, Milton, Dryden,

Pope, Johnson and Crabbe. Now Southey, Wordsworth, Coleridge and Lamb with hardly credible presumption expend their admittedly remarkable talents in setting themselves against the whole tradition. Jeffrey even goes so far as to set Wordsworth and his school against 'all existing authority' (XI, October 1807, 228).

In the early years of the <u>Edinburgh Review</u> Jeffrey usually rests content with opposing the new school to the great English writers. Their inspiration comes not from the main tradition but from the byeways represented by the 'old ballads,' Wither and Henry More, the quaintness of Marvell and Quarles, the cold ingenuity of Donne, the naïveté of Ambrose Philips, the homeliness and harshness of Cowper. This statement, originating in the review of October 1802 (I.64), can be illustrated from at least two further places:

> ...the Wordsworths, and the Southeys, and Coleridges, and all that misguided fraternity,...with good intentions and extraordinary talents, are labouring to bring back our poetry to the fantastical oddity and puling childishness of Withers, Quarles, or Marvel [<u>sic</u>] (XII, April 1808, 133).

> While gravely preferring the tame vulgarity of our old ballads, to the nervous and refined verses of Pope or Johnson, they lay claim, not to indulgence, but to admiration; and treat almost the whole of our classical poets with the most supercilious neglect; while they speak in an authoritative tone of the beauties of George Wither and Henry More. With such ludicrous auxiliaries, they wage a desperate war on the established system of public taste and judgment (XVII, February 1811, 434).

In Jeffrey's view the main inspiration of this group, however, is not to be found in less important English writers, but on the Continent, in the anti-social principles and sick sensibility of Rousseau, the irregularity of 'the German dramatists' (XVII, February 1811, 437), especially Kotzebue and Schiller.

ii

In the years before 1811 Jeffrey thus derives from universal principles a long literary tradition which he believes has been flagrantly violated by some modern poets. What are these principles as Jeffery sees them at the various stages of his critical career? They underlie his discussions of the language, emotional tone, and subject of poetry. He seems to be most upset by the language of Southey and Wordsworth which he sees as affectedly naive as well as enthusiastic. His attention is of course drawn to this aspect of their work by Wordsworth's intensely irritating theory, uncompromisingly set forth in the Preface to the second edition of <u>Lyrical Ballads</u> (1800). Jeffrey asserts that the low language supposedly advocated by Wordsworth is unsuitable to all poetic occasions. However, he objects to it not only on aesthetic grounds but also, more basically, on grounds of social propriety. There are, after all, two classes of society, the vulgar and the refined. Whose sentiments are 'the most proper object for poetical imitation?' There can be no doubt.

> It is needless for us to answer a question, which the practice of all the world has long ago decided irrevocably. The poor and vulgar may interest us, in poetry, by their <u>situation</u>; but never, we apprehend, by any sentiments that are peculiar to their condition, and still less by any language that is characteristic of it. The truth is, that it is impossible to copy their diction or their sentiments correctly, in a serious composition; and this, not merely because poverty makes men ridiculous, but because just taste and refined sentiments are rarely to be met with among the uncultivated part of mankind; and a language, fitted for their expression, can still more rarely form any part of their 'ordinary conversation' (I, October 1802, 66-67).[3]

Jeffrey here clearly presents poetry as not being merely socially orientated, but also as having a class basis. However, his position changes. What appears to bring about this change is the effect on him of thinking anew about the poetry of Burns and Crabbe. The former depicts humble life with 'that delicacy, as well as justness of conception, by which alone the fastidiousness of an ordinary reader can be reconciled to such representations' (XIII, January 1809, 260). Crabbe also deals with the poor, but unlike Wordsworth he writes 'in the good old taste of Pope and Dryden' (XII, April 1808, 146). Jeffrey vindicates 'The Village Register' in the following terms:

> there is a justness and force in the representation which is entitled to something more than indulgence; and though several of the groups are confessedly composed of low and disagreeable subjects, still, we think that some allowance is to be made for the author's plan of giving a full and exact view of village life, which could not possibly be accomplished without including those baser varieties. He aims at an important moral effect by this exhibition; and must not be defrauded either of that, or of the praise which is due to the coarser efforts of his pen, out of deference to the sickly delicacy of his more fastidious readers (XII, April 1808, 141).

Crabbe objectively shows the poor, but he does not use their language, nor does he show their sentiments except for an acceptable moral purpose.

Two years later Jeffrey goes further still in admitting subjects from humble life more easily into the realm of poetic acceptability:

> where subjects taken from humble life can be made sufficiently interesting to overcome the distaste and the prejudices with which the usages of polite society too generally lead us to regard them, the interest which they excite will commonly be more profound and more lasting than any that can be raised upon loftier themes; and the poet of the Village and the Borough be oftener, and longer, read, than the poet of the Court or the Camp. The most popular passages of Shakespeare and Cowper, we think, are of this description (XVI, April 1810, 34).

The only persons from humble life whom Jeffrey now excludes from poetic treatment are the disgusting: 'The only sufferers, then, upon whom we cannot bear to look, are those that excite pain by their wretchedness, while they are too depraved to be the objects of affection, and too weak and insignificant to be the causes of misery to others, or, consequently, of indignation to the spectators' (XVI, April 1810, 38). Evidently, the range of Wordsworth's poetic compassion is still too great for our critic. Jeffrey always prefers a refined, cultivated language, though he now admits that a remarkable poet can extend it beyond the boundaries of the refined and cultivated classes. He allows these boundaries to be extended, but not to be destroyed.

The discussion of Jeffrey's attitude towards Wordsworth's language has led us to a consideration of his attitude towards the poet's human subject matter. The emotional tone which Jeffrey deplores in the new school he deplores especially because he believes that poetry is primarily emotional rather than intellectual: 'It is the business of poetry to delineate Feeling' (I, January 1803, 399), as all beautiful objects 'please upon the same great principle of sympathy with human feelings' (XVIII, May 1811, 30-31). Further, 'The end of poetry...is to please...without any laborious exercise of the understanding' (XI, October 1807, 216). Indeed, 'Poetry...deals only in obvious and glancing views' (XXXVI, February 1822, 438).[4] Here is another difficulty that Wordsworth presents, particularly in such a poem as 'Ode: Intimations of Immortality from Recollections of Early Childhood,' which lacked its helpful full title when Jeffrey dismissed it as 'illegible and unintelligible' (XI, October 1807, 227). In an extravagant mood on one occasion Jeffrey even goes so far as to suggest that poets in general 'ought fairly to be confined to the established creed and morality of their country, or to the <u>actual</u> passions and sentiments of mankind; and that poetical dreamers and sophists who pretend to <u>theorise</u> according to their feverish fancies, without a warrant from authority or reason, ought to be banished the commonwealth of letters' (XXXVI, February 1822, 438).

The feeling which Wordsworth and his fellows express when their 'meddling intellect' is at rest Jeffrey finds to be not only vulgar as opposed to refined, but also babyish and feeble rather than manly and strong. Wordsworth in particular furnishes himself 'from vulgar ballads and plebeian nurseries' (XI, October 1807, 218): 'Even in the worst of these productions, there are, no doubt, occasional little traits of delicate feeling and original fancy; but these are quite lost and obscured in the mass of childishness and insipidity with which they are incorporated' (XI, October 1807, 231). Indeed, the authors of <u>Rejected Addresses</u> have caught perfectly Wordsworth's 'maukish affectations of childish simplicity and nursery stammering' (XX, November 1812, 438). These are characteristics of 'Alice Fell' which its author 'in policy' withdrew from the 1820 edition of his poems on account of the ridicule of 'the small critics.'[5] Wordsworth himself came to feel the need for 'more elegance and dignity.'[6]

Jeffrey turns with relief from Wordsworth's 'childish and absurd affectations...to the manly sense...of Mr Crabbe' (XII, April 1808, 137). Manliness is also a virtue in Burns, like his unaffected adherence to nature and the tradition (XIII, January 1809, 276). Further, manliness is the most appealing quality of Byron, as Jeffrey declares in his review of the first two cantos of <u>Childe Harold's Pilgrimage</u> in February 1812, 'There is, indeed, a tone of self-willed independence and originality about the whole composition - a certain plain manliness and strength of manner, which is infinitely refreshing after the sickly affectations of so many modern writers; and reconciles us not only to the asperity into which it sometimes degenerates, but even in some degree to the unamiableness upon which it constantly borders' (XIX, February 1812, 467). In spite of the generally favourable tone, a hint can be detected here of the moral objection which Jeffrey makes more strenuously to Byron after the publication of <u>Childe Harold's Pilgrimage</u>, Canto IV (1818). With regard to Wordsworth's feeling, Jeffrey at last finds 'Laodamia' admirable because it possesses the 'classical and manly' qualities inculcated by the <u>Edinburgh Review</u> (XL, March 1824, 81).[7]

Jeffrey is concerned not merely with feeling but also with the decorous relationship between feeling and subject, a topic already touched upon in connection with the poet's language and the people he deals with. Naturally Wordsworth offends in the general field of feeling and subject. He courts 'literary martyrdom' by

> connecting his most lofty, tender, or impassioned conceptions, with objects and incidents, which the greater part of his readers

will probably persist in thinking low, silly, or uninteresting. Whether this is done from affectation and conceit alone, or whether it may not arise, in some measure, from the self-illusion of a mind of extraordinary sensibility, habituated to solitary meditation, we cannot undertake to determine (XI, October 1807, 218).

When not discussing Wordsworth, as we have seen, Jeffrey can take a positive approach to the question of the sensitive relation between poetic feeling and subject. A theoretical basis for his views, in this as in other respects, is to be found in his article on Alison on Taste, dated May 1811. Here Jeffrey states that the language of poetry is largely founded on the analogy between our internal feelings and external objects, though he recognises the uniqueness of the poet in recognising such analogy: 'The great charm, indeed, and the great secret of poetical diction, consists in thus lending life and emotion to all objects it embraces; and the enchanting beauty which we sometimes recognize in descriptions of very ordinary phenomena, will be found to arise from the force of imagination, by which the poet has connected with human emotions, a variety of objects, to which common minds could not discover their relation' (XVIII, May 1811, 24).[8]

This theoretical basis is elaborated upon in Jeffrey's review of Hazlitt's <u>Characters from Shakespeare's Plays</u>, dated August 1817. Here Jeffrey ponders Shakespeare's unique contribution, and his musings receive complex expression. He softens and sentimentalises the analogy. Jeffrey is grateful to Hazlitt for indicating

> that familiarity with beautiful forms and images - that eternal recurrence to what is sweet or majestic in the simple aspects of nature - that indestructible love of flowers and odors, and dews and clear waters - and soft airs and sounds, and bright skies, and woodland solitudes, and moonlight bowers, which are the material elements of Poetry - and that fine sense of their undefinable relation to mental emotion, which is its essence and vivifying soul - and which, in the midst of Shakespeare's most busy and atrocious scenes, falls, like gleams of sunshine on rocks and rivers - contrasting with

all that is rugged and repulsive, and reminding us of the existence of purer and brighter elements - which HE ALONE has poured out from the richness of his own mind, without effort or restraint (XXVIII, August 1817, 473).

Reviewing John Wilson's <u>Poems</u> five years before, Jeffrey had defined poetry even more selectively: 'the very essence of poetry [is] to be enraptured with such things [as] a sleeping child, or a lovely cataract...female purity and moonlight landscapes, and fine dreams, and flowers, and singing birds' (XIX, February 1812, 374). As we have just seen, Jeffrey finds such an essence distilled in the work of Shakespeare; now he notices its absence from the work of Wilson's supposed mentor Wordsworth.

This view of the essence of poetry, however limited it becomes, is precious to Jeffrey as a critic and indeed as a man. In 1831 he wrote to Jane Carlyle in semi-Wordsworthian vein:

> If it were not for my love of nature, I think I should die.... It is an especial mercy of Providence, I think, that our House of bondage [i.e., Commons] is placed among objects of grandeur and beauty.... I rush out, and walk on the bridge, or place myself at a window in our calm library, and look out on the white moonlight, and the shadows of the massive trees pencilled so sharp and dark on the turf below, and then muse and start, and back to that hot, glaring, tumultuous room again, where I pass for a gay, sarcastic, patient, acute sort of person - and so I am.[9]

Two years later Jeffrey wrote again, 'If it were not for my love of beautiful nature and poetry, my heart would have died within me long age.'[10] And towards the end of his life, in 1846, 'My affections and my enjoyment of beautiful nature [are] as fresh and lively, as in the first poetical days of my youth.'[11]

As a critic Jeffrey applies this enthusiasm to a reading of Shakespeare, but he does not bring himself to do so with Wordsworth. However, where among Jeffrey's contemporaries Wordsworth loses, Keats gains. The younger poet does not possess the artistic balance which Jeffrey had admired, but the imbalance in his work is in favour of imagination and pure poetry. In his

> rash and headlong career he has of course many lapses and failures. There is no work, accordingly, from which a malicious critic[12] could cull more matter for ridicule, or select more obscure, unnatural, or absurd passages. But we do not take that to be our office; - and just beg leave, on the contrary, to say, that any one who, on this account, would represent the whole poem as despicable, must either have no notion of poetry, or no regard to truth (XXXIV, August 1820, 205).

When Jeffrey enthuses over Keats, he writes of 'pure poetry,' a phrase which he probably derived from the Dedication to Joseph Warton's Essay on the Genius and Writings of Pope (1756).[13] What does Jeffrey mean by the phrase? For him, in line with the view expressed in the article on Alison, pure poetry occurs when 'a fine feeling [is] expressed of those mysterious relations by which visible external things are assimilated with inward thoughts and emotions, and become the images and exponents of all passions and affections' (XXXIV, August 1820, 206). Jeffrey holds to this view through the succeeding years. He repeats it in his last literary contribution to the Edinburgh Review, the article on Mrs. Hemans in October 1829, where he yields the palm of contemporary poetic fame to the taste and elegance of Rogers and Campbell. In this valedictory critical article Jeffrey nevertheless affirms:

> It has always been our opinion, that the very essence of poetry, apart from the pathos, the wit, or the brilliant description which may be embodied in it, but may exist equally in prose, consists in the fine perception and vivid expression of that subtle and mysterious analogy which exists between the physical and the moral world - which makes outward things and qualities the natural types and emblems of inward gifts and emotions, and leads us to ascribe life and sentiment to every thing that interests us in the aspects of external nature (L, October 1829, 35).

Thus Jeffrey refers the feelings of the poet to nature. However, he also refers them to the feelings of the public. This enables him to appeal to the public always as able to decide with the help of the critic's pleadings, but occasionally as having decided without such help. Even though 'the diligent readers of poetry, in this country, are by no means instructed. They consist chiefly of young, half-educated women, sickly tradesmen, and enamoured apprentices' (IX, January 1807, 348) - despite this sobering view, Jeffrey can affirm elsewhere, 'the fame of a poet is popular, or nothing' (XXXI, March 1819, 470). 'Present popularity...is...the only safe presage of future glory' (XXXI, March 1819, 466). In the case of Scott, as well as the Byron of Childe Harold's Pilgrimage (XXVII, December 1816, 292), 'A popularity so universal is a pretty sure proof of extraordinary merit' (XVI, August 1810, 263). Southey having failed popularly, may be assumed to have failed artistically (XVII, February 1811, 431). In reviewing Scott Jeffrey does discriminate between the multitude and cultivated judges, but only to look forward to their ultimate coalescence (XVI, August 1810, 266). He sums up his position concerning Scott himself with a characteristic image:

> He will always be a poet, we fear, to whom the fastidious will make great objections; but he may easily find, in his popularity, a compensation for their scruples. He has the jury hollow in his favour; and though the court may think that its directions have not been sufficiently attended to, it will not quarel with the verdict (XVI, August 1810, 293).

Jeffrey's appeal to the public leads him into difficulties in the treatment of poetic originality. The originality of Lyrical Ballads is admired (XI, October 1807, 214), but elsewhere Jeffrey objects to a 'poor ambition of originality' in Wordsworth because this sets him against 'ordinary minds' (XIX, February 1812, 374). This is where Crabbe, for example, has the advantage. He appeals to the 'common sympathies of our nature.... Mr Crabbe, in short, shows us something which we have all seen, or may see, in real life; and draws from it such feelings and such reflections as every human being must acknowledge that it is calculated to excite' (XII, April 1808, 133). His characters, unlike the eccentrics of Wordsworth, especially the protagonist of The Excursion, 'are drawn from

11

that eternal and universal standard of truth and nature, which every one is knowing enough to recognize' (XII, April 1808, 136). Byron comes to fail by the same standard as Wordsworth: 'He has too little sympathy with the ordinary feelings and frailties of humanity, to succeed well in their representation - "His soul is like a star, and dwells apart"' (XXXVI, February 1822, 420). Jeffrey generalises this view when he writes, 'the most powerful and enchanting poetry is that which depends for its effect upon the just representation of common feelings and common situations' (XIV, April 1809, 3).

Indeed, Jeffrey trusts the experience of the public in many ways: not only its judgment and feeling but also its way of life. Wordsworth has done wrong to seclude himself from society and to scorn the 'inhabitants of towns...and most of those who are engaged in the ordinary business or pleasures of society' (XIX, February 1812, 375). In personal terms, Jeffrey later feels that this is a danger for Carlyle, whom he adjures, 'you must begin by tolerating the ordinary specimens of our common nature a little more than you now do.'[14] What is needed is an 'habitual and general knowlwdge of the few settled and permanent maxims, which form the canon of general taste in all large and polished societies.... If Mr Wordsworth, instead of confining himself almost entirely to the society of the dalesmen and cottagers, and little children, who form the subjects of his book, had condescended to mingle a little more with the people that were to read and judge of it, we cannot help thinking, that its texture would have been considerably improved' (XXIV, November 1814, 3-4). As opposed to Byron Jeffrey believes that men 'of truly great powers of mind have generally been cheerful, social, and indulgent' (XXVII, December 1816, 299). By contrast, Southey is monastic (XXVI, June 1816, 482), and Coleridge's habits of thinking out of touch 'with the general mass of intelligence' (LXII, October 1835, 244). In a letter to Carlyle of 1831 Jeffrey even goes so far as to declare that 'the more I see of philosophers and men of genius the more I am inclined to hold that the ordinary run of sensible, kind people, who fill the world, are after all the best specimens of humanity, and that the others are, like our cultivated flowers, but splendid monsters, and cases of showy disease.'[15]

More attractively, Jeffrey sees writers as

fulfilling a necessary and health-giving political role. He considers those 'who seek to soften and improve our social affections, not only as aiming <u>directly</u> at the same great end which politicians more circuitously pursue, but as preparing those elements out of which alone a generous and enlightened love of political freedom can ever be formed' (XXXVII, November 1822, 342).

iii

In trying to uncover Jeffrey's principles from his brilliantly free-flowing critical discussions of poetry, I have identified amongst them a demand for cultured language with its appropriate subject-matter, and an insistence upon the primacy of feeling. This feeling is both refined and virile, and like the language has an appropriate subject-matter. This subject-matter embraces external nature and society. Society is furthermore important not only as poetic subject but also as the judge of poetry, in possession of the standards to which the poet should refer. Beyond these principles, Jeffrey adheres to a group of values which can, I hope not misleadingly, be clustered around the term 'decadence.' He believes not only that the principles of literature were laid down a long time ago, but also that the great writers came first: 'almost all the great poets of every country have appeared in an early stage of their history, and in a period comparatively rude and unletterd' (XIII, January 1809, 251). 'The age of original genius...seems to be over' (XXI, February 1813, 20).

Not only did the great writers come first, but education, highly developed with the advance of civilisation, and the sophistication of civilised society itself are unfavourable to genius. Hence Burns's relative lack of education and obscurity could be seen as a positive advantage to him. On the poetic disadvantages of education and refined society Jeffrey writes fully in a review of Franklin's <u>Works</u> (VIII, July 1806, 329). He elaborates upon the same point of view in discussing Burns two and a half years later:

> We ventured, on a former occasion, to say something of the effects of regular education, and of the general diffusion of literature, in repressing the vigour and

originality of all kinds of mental exertion. That speculation was perhaps carried somewhat too far; but if the paradox have proof any where, it is in its application to poetry. Among well educated people, the standard writers of this description are at once so venerated and so familiar, that it is thought equally impossible to rival them, and to write verses without attempting it. If there be one degree of fame which excites emulation, there is another which leads to despair; nor can we conceive any one less likely to add one to the short list of original poets, than a young man of fine fancy and delicate taste, who has acquired a high relish for poetry, by perusing the most celebrated writers, and conversing with the most intelligent judges. The head of such a person is filled, of course, with all the splendid passages of antient and modern authors, and with the fine and fastidious remarks which have been made even on these passages. When he turns his eyes, therefore, on his own conceptions, they can scarcely fail to appear rude and contemptible. He is perpetually haunted and depressed by the ideal presence of those great masters and their exacting critics. He is aware to what comparisons his productions will be subjected among his own friends and associates; and recollects the derision with which so many rash adventurers have been chased back to their obscurity. Thus, the merit of his great predecessors chills, instead of encouraging his ardour; and the illustrious names which have already reached to the summit of excellence, act like the tall and spreading trees of the forest, which overshadow and strangle the saplings which have struck root in the soil below, - and afford shelter to nothing but creepers and parasites (XIII, January 1809, 250).

Jeffrey admits in this eloquent passage that he has written extravagantly, yet one is struck by the tendency of these thoughts, which goes against the value elsewhere placed upon education and a sophisticated social order, and also against the tendency of his literary criticism at large. Jeffrey did not have these generally tolerant views in mind when attacking Wordsworth, though they may have underlain his comments on Keats.

Unfortunately, Jeffrey fears that modern writing as a whole is inevitably inferior to the old:

> Modern poetry has both been enriched with more exquisite pictures, and deeper and more sustained strains of pathetic, than were known to the less elaborate artists of antiquity; at the same time that it has been defaced with more affectation, and loaded with far more intricacy....the later poets, we conceive, must be admitted to have almost always written in a more constrained and narrow manner than their originals, and to have departed farther from what was obvious, easy and natural.... Whatever may be gained or lost, however, by this change of manner, it is obvious, that poetry must become less popular by means of it (XVI, August 1810, 268-269).

According to Jeffrey, the modern writer in his generally difficult situation faces particular problems of originality and style. The situation gravely handicaps the writer both in his unobjectionable desire to imitate and in his praiseworthy attempt to achieve originality. Thus 'All poets' are described as 'great imitators' (XXIX, Nov. 1817, 33), and Keats especially is praised for his imitation of 'our older dramatists' (XXXIV, August 1820, 203). On the other hand, Cowper is highly praised for the originality which makes him an initiator of the new era of poetry which Jeffrey comes to recognise (XLVIII, September 1828, 49). Perhaps for Jeffrey the best, because central, position is that occupied by Scott who 'took only what he would have given if he had been born in an earlier generation' (XVI, August 1810, 270).

On the difficulty of naturalness of writing in modern sophisticated and complex times Jeffrey comments:

> In an advanced state of society, the expression of simple emotion is so obstructed by ceremony, or so distorted by affectation, that though the sentiment itself be still familiar to the greater part of mankind, the verbal representation of it is a task of the utmost difficulty. One set of writers, accordingly, finding the whole language of men and women too sophisticated for this purpose,

have been obliged to go to the nursery for a phraseology; another has adopted the style of courtly Arcadians; and a third, that of mere Bedlamites (XIV, April 1809, 3).

Thus Jeffrey's view of English literary history as on the whole a process of decline leads him to take a gloomy view of the various attempts of his contemporaries.[16]

iv

Jeffrey's second, 'complex' view of English literary history, which finds expression after 1811, allows his view of his literary contemporaries to brighten to a certain extent. In his first, 'simple' view, as we have seen, Jeffrey sets the modern rebels, perniciously influenced from abroad, against the long tradition of great English writing. In his second view Jeffrey discovers an earlier break in the tradition at the time of the Restoration. The foreign influence is thrust back from the end of the eighteenth to the middle of the seventeenth century, and part of the modern achievement, which gains better recognition in this more complex view, is in throwing off foreign, particularly French, domination and regaining contact with the old English tradition. Jeffrey puts forward this historical perspective when he welcomes the revival of interest in Elizabethan and Jacobean drama in reviewing Weber's edition of Ford's Dramatic Works in August 1811: 'All true lovers of English poetry have been long in love with the dramatists of the time of Elizabeth and James; and must have been sensibly comforted by their late restoration to some degree of favour and notoriety' (XVIII, August 1811, 275). The critic goes on to eulogise the Elizabethan and Jacobean age and to declare that 'the Restoration brought in a French taste upon us, and what was called a classical and a polite taste; and the wings of our English Muses were clipped and trimmed, and their flights regulated, at the expense of all that was peculiar, and much of what was brightest in their beauty' (XVIII, August 1811, 278). This view is not merely echoed by Keats in 'Sleep and Poetry,' but by later Edinburgh Reviewers, for example, Procter (XLII, April 1825, 58), Macaulay (XLVII, January 1828, 19), and Aubrey De Vere (XC, October 1849, 415).

In August 1811 Jeffrey can set Shakespeare and Milton high above Dryden and Pope, though not yet with the assurance of Macaulay who asserts, 'The public voice has assigned to Dryden the first place in the second rank of our poets' (XLVII, January 1828, 1). Jeffrey himself, reviewing Scott's edition of Swift in September 1816, finds the 'sprightly...good sense' of 'the wits of Queen Anne's time' not enough. In Dryden 'the evil [French] principle prevailed.' Darkness fell, until the emergence of Gray who at least 'had the merit of not being in any degree French' and Cowper who 'for the first time, made it apparent to readers of all descriptions, that Pope and Addison were no longer to be the models of English poetry' (XXVII, September 1816, 1-7).

Again, in August 1811, Jeffrey can see the new writers as being on the side of Shakespeare and Milton against Dryden and his immediate successors:

> Southey, and Wordsworth, and Coleridge, and Miss Baillie, have all of them copied the manner of our older poets; and, along with this indication of good taste, have given great proofs of original genius. The misfortune is, that these copies of those great originals, are all liable to the charge of extreme affectation.... But we have said enough elsewhere of the faults of these authors; and shall only add, at present, that, notwithstanding all these faults, there is a fertility and a force, a warmth of feeling and an exaltation of imagination, about them, which classes them, in our estimation, with a much higher order of poets than the followers of Dryden and Addison; and justifies an anxiety for their fame, in all the admirers of Milton and Shakespeare (XVIII, August 1811, 283).

Macaulay again follows Jeffrey after the necessary time-lag (XLVII, January 1828, 13).

* * * *

In this discussion I have touched upon Jeffrey's views of English literary history, his principles and their relation to the problem of contemporary poetry. He believes that the greatest works of literary art were created and the basic critical principles were laid down in the past. In his first view of English literary history, he sees the critical principles and creativity interacting fruitfully until the appearance of the shocking poets of the present age. Jeffrey's principles concern language, feeling and society; and Wordsworth offends against them all. The language of poetry should be aesthetically appropriate and socially acceptable: here Jeffrey makes a distinction between Wordsworth and Crabbe to the advantage of the latter. Poetry, being unintellectual, expresses feeling, but the feeling is manly and strong, and relates to an appropriate subject-matter. This last is provided by the beauty of external nature and the common sympathies of mankind. On all counts, according to Jeffrey, Wordsworth fails. Furthermore, the poet to understand and to communicate the common sympathies of men does well to mingle with them.

After all, mankind provides not only much of his subject-matter but also his audience, by whose judgement - exercised as that of the critic, the exponent of 'the silent, practical judgment of the public' (XVII, February 1811, 429), or the educated few, or even the mass - he will succeed or fail. As the heir of the ages, a mere follower in the great creative and critical footsteps of the past, and a dweller in a changing, complex, artificial society, the modern writer considered in the abstract has Jeffrey's sympathy: but he does not extend this feeling to any extent to Wordsworth, Southey or Coleridge. However, Jeffrey's general sympathy is broadened as he comes to consider English literary history as a more complex development. Now the present is not merely set against the past, but the present is set beside the distant against the more recent past. That is, the English tradition is seen as having been interrupted at the Restoration and the interruption lasting until the appearance of Cowper. In this historical vein, Jeffrey sympathises, again in the abstract, with the new poets, in their efforts to revive the past tradition and to achieve originality at the same time. Though he cannot bring himself to apply this generality wholeheartedly to Wordsworth and his contemporaries, he does apply it in Keats's favour. After all, Keats, despite the views of <u>Blackwood's Magazine</u>, is not flagrantly radical, he shares Jeffrey's view of English literary history, and he falls in with the association dear to Jeffrey's heart, between poetic feeling and beautiful nature.

If this analysis of some tendencies in Jeffrey's thought is correct, he shows himself to be a lively, if at times slippery, critic, a lover of both argument and poetry, yet careless of the effect of his writing on the sensitive poet or the sensitive poet's livelihood and influence. As a critic he is a conservative intellectual, yet he shares in and leads the reaction against the neoclassical elements of the eighteenth century; positively, he shares in and leads the revival for his generation of the older writers, the admiration of the beauties of external nature, and the exaltation of feeling.

NOTES

1. This part was written before the appearance of two relevant books. Derek Roper discusses Reviewing before the 'Edinburgh' (Methuen, London, 1978). He argues for the quality of this reviewing but does not examine Jeffrey's criticism with equal closeness, nor does he consider Jeffrey's important role in initiating the review format. Philip Flynn's Francis Jeffrey (University of Delaware Press, Newark, 1978) is a valuable survey of its subject's contribution, but he does not examine the criticism or Jeffrey's relationships with the closeness that I do here.

2. Figures in parentheses in Chapter 1 indicate volume number of the Edinburgh Review, date of publication, and page number. For Jeffrey's generalising tone cf Hume, 'Enquiry concerning Human Understanding,' as quoted by Philip Flynn, Francis Jeffrey, p. 71.

3. Jeffrey is probably referring to the Advertisement to the first edition of Lyrical Ballads, 1798, where Wordsworth writes that his aim is 'to ascertain how far the language of conversation in the middle and lower classes of society is adapted to the purpose of poetic pleasure.' Prose Works, ed. Owen and Smyser (3 vols, Clarendon Press, Oxford, 1974), vol. 1, p. 116.

4. Compare F.R. Leavis, New Bearings in English Poetry (Chatto & Windus, London, new ed., 1950), p. 8f, on 'the nineteenth-century idea of the poetical....Poetry...must be the direct expression of simple emotions, and these of a limited class: the tender, the exalted, the poignant,

and, in general, the sympathetic.'
5. *Poetical Works*, ed. E. De Selincourt (5 vols, Clarendon Press, Oxford, 1940-49), vol.1, p. 359.
6. *Letters*, ed. E. De Selincourt, rev. A.G. Hill (Clarendon Press, Oxford, 2nd ed., 1967-), vol. 3, p. 641.
7. John Forster, *Walter Savage Landor* (2 vols, Chapman and Hall, London, 1869), vol. 2, p. 90, attributes to Jeffrey this phrase inserted into a review by Hazlitt.
8. The affinity which the poet finds between mind and external nature is expressed in a purer form by both Wordsworth and Coleridge. John Forster, *Eclectic Review*, vol. 7 (1811), p. 918, observed that both poets possessed minds 'constructed to bear a certain indescribable analogy to nature' (quoted by David V. Erdman, *Wordsworth Circle*, vol. 6 [1975] p. 22). Later, Lamb admired in *The Excursion* the 'scheme of harmonies...between the external universe & what within us answers to it,' *Letters*, ed. E.W. Marrs, jr (Cornell University Press, Ithaca, 1975-), vol. 3, p. 129. Emerson praised what he called Jeffrey's 'true theory' of the relationship between the inward and the outward, *Journals*, vol. 4, p. 11. The notion persists in T.S. Eliot with his 'objective correlative,' *Selected Prose*, ed. F. Kermode (Faber and Faber, London, 1975), p. 48; and in Northrop Frye, *The Educated Imagination* (Indiana University Press, Bloomington, 1964), p. 110, where myth, the precursor of literature, is described as an effort 'of the imagination to identify the human with the non human world.' Morse Peckham, ed. *Romanticism* (George Braziller, New York, 1965), p. 18, goes further when he writes of 'the fundamental assumption of the Enlightenment: the isomorphism, or structural identity, of mind and nature;' after this Peckham presents 'analogism' as 'the first stage of romanticism,' p. 25.
9. David Alec Wilson, *Carlyle to 'The French Revolution'* (Kegan Paul, London, 1924), p. 212.
10. Henry Cockburn, *Life of Lord Jeffrey* (2 vols, Adam and Charles Black, Edinburgh, 1852), vol.1, p. 350.
11. The same, p. 400.
12. Jeffrey is here responding to Croker's attack on Keats, *Quarterly Review*, vol. 19 (1808).
13. Jeffrey had referred to Warton and put forward a cruder view of 'pure poetry' in reviewing Hogg's *Queen's Wake* (XXIV, November 1814,

163-64). It is noteworthy that F.R. Leavis quotes Warton's phrase as the first romantic formulation: New Bearings in English Poetry, p. 7f. The significance of the phrase is commented on by W.J. Bate, The Burden of the Past and the English Poet (Harvard University Press, Cambridge, Mass, 1970), pp. 75, 113.

14. D.A. Wilson, Carlyle to 'The French Revolution', p. 131.

15. The same, p. 204.

16. Cf Bate, p. 46. Bate eloquently indicates the tradition to which Jeffrey belongs, as well as Jeffrey's significant place in it, p. 99. He also discusses the problem of originality, p. 106f, which I touch on in my next paragraph.

PART TWO. JEFFREY AND WORDSWORTH

'This will never do.' We are all familiar with Jeffrey's sentence dismissing The Excursion at the beginning of his review of Wordsworth's poem in 1814. The outburst has led several critics to explore the attitudes behind it, and provoking it, and I offer no apology for adding to their number. I hope to survey the relevant writings of Jeffrey on the one hand and of Wordsworth, with Coleridge, on the other, in order to achieve a clear understanding of the relationship between them. What I think I discover - without claiming originality - is not merely the thick texture of literary history, but also Wordsworth's extreme poetic individualism and the fact that it eroded to a certain degree under the influence of pressures, some of which were given verbal expression in Jeffrey's criticism. I have also gained the feeling that the challenge posed by Jeffrey as a periodical critic, that is, his conviction that poetry has a function in actual society, recognisable by critics and the reading public, is one that needs taking up even, or especially, in the second half of the twentieth century. It was a challenge vehemently rejected by Wordsworth, though tacitly acknowledged by him.

Jeffrey chiefly expressed his critical attitudes towards Wordsworth in four articles in the Edinburgh Review between 1807 and 1822. The motives behind these and Jeffrey's attitudes in general are complex. They involve not merely in his own words 'Mere indifference and love of sport',[1] what Lockhart called 'levity and sarcastic indifference',[2] what Coleridge more severely considered 'a habit of malignity in the form of mere wantonness',[3] not merely the commercial success of the Edinburgh Review, not merely political animosity, especially after 1813 when Wordsworth obtained the government post of stamp-distributor, - though these are all important factors, - but also critical principles, however limited and however severe and unfairly enforced.

Jeffrey wishes to point out the deplorable nonconformity of Wordsworth's poetic theory and practice, not primarily in order to warn readers, but also, especially at first, for the benefit of the poet himself. He believes that the poet belongs to society, or at least to that cultivated part of it which the critic is the spokesman, and that he will and must respond to the demands of this society. In this spirit Jeffrey appeals to Wordsworth to change his ways. In 1807 he writes at length:

> It was precisely because the perverseness and bad taste of this new school was combined with a great deal of genius and of laudable feeling, that we were afraid of their spreading and gaining ground among us, and that we entered into the discussion with a degree of zeal and animosity which some might think unreasonable towards authors, to whom so much merit had been conceded. There were times and moods indeed, in which we were led to suspect ourselves of unjustifiable severity, and to doubt, whether a sense of public duty had not carried us rather too far in reprobation of errors, that seemed to be atoned for, by excellences of no vulgar description. At other times, the magnitude of these errors - the disgusting absurdities into which they led their feebler admirers, and the derision and contempt which they drew from the more fastidious, even upon the merits with which they were associated, made us wonder more than ever at the perversity by which they were retained, and regret that we had not declared ourselves against them with still more formidable and decided hostility.
> In this temper of mind [Jeffrey continues], we read the <u>annonce</u> of Mr. Wordsworth's publication [<u>Poems in Two Volumes</u>] with a good deal of interest and expectation, and opened his volumes with greater anxiety, than he or his admirers will probably give us credit for. We have been greatly disappointed certainly as to the quality of the poetry, but we doubt whether the publication has afforded so much satisfaction to any other of his readers: - it has freed us from all doubt or hesitation as to the justice of our former censures, and has brought the matter to a test, which we cannot help hoping may be convincing to the author himself (XI, October 1807, 215).

When such elaborate reasoning fails to move the poet, Jeffrey tries ridicule, in accordance with the general associationist theory to which both he and Wordsworth adhered. As he wrote Archibald Alison, his aesthetic mentor, in 1811:

> we [that is, people in general] are apt to consider all persons who make known their peculiar relishes,[4] and especially all who create any objects for their gratification, as in some measure dictating to the public, and setting up an idol for general admiration, and hence this intolerant interference with almost all peculiar perceptions of beauty, and the unsparing derision that pursues all deviations from acknowledged standards. This intolerance, we admit, is often provoked by something of a spirit of proselytism, and arrogance in those who mistake their own casual associations for natural or universal relations; and the consequence is, that mortified vanity dries up the fountain of their peculiar enjoyment, and disenchants, by a new association of general contempt or ridicule, the scenes that had been consecrated by some innocent but accidental emotion (XVIII, May 1811, 45-46).

After reason and ridicule, according to this formula, have failed to stir the poet, Jeffrey tries abuse in order to discourage the readers. When abuse is exhausted, silence follows.

I would now like to relate this summary of Jeffrey's motives and methods in dealing with Wordsworth's published poetry to an account of the relationship between poet and critic as it developed through the first quarter of the nineteenth century. This will involve paying some attention to Coleridge's defence and judgment of Wordsworth's poetry in Biographia Literaria, 1817.

Lyrical Ballads of 1798 was relatively well received and popular.[5] Jeffrey acknowledges the success of the work in his review of Southey's Thalaba four years later, though he picks out for adverse comment three individual poems by Wordsworth.

Wordsworth's prefatory matter of 1800 and 1802 provided a basis for the discussion of his poetry which unfriendly critics, including Jeffrey, were not loath to employ and to trample upon. However, the degree of similarity in point of view between Wordsworth in the Preface and Jeffrey in his later criticisms is remarkable. For example, in the Appendix of 1802 Wordsworth puts forward a pocket history of poetic language which might be seen as fitting in with the surveys of English literary history which Jeffrey attempts in the Edinburgh Review after 1811.[6]

In the body of the Preface of 1800 Wordsworth appeals, like Jeffrey, to good sense. He shows the same interest in general psychology, that is, what he calls 'the primary laws of our nature'.[7] Like Jeffrey, he emphasizes the moral purpose of poetry, and he seeks to reconcile this with an emphasis on its emotionality.

Jeffrey differs from Wordsworth largely in rejecting his theory of poetic language, at least in its crudest form, but he also differs from him in regard to feeling. Jeffrey is himself an emotionalist, but as a critic he is primarily concerned with general emotion and its interaction with the critical intellect. Wordsworth, on the other hand, is primarily concerned as a poet with his own emotion. He admits the peculiarity of some of his work, but defends this as being the result of relying on the authority of his own feeling. In this he is not inclined to distrust himself. At the end of the Preface he appeals from his own feeling to that of the reader. It seems that in Wordsworth's view the critic, hence Jeffrey, is nowhere.

Wordsworth shows his distrust of the critic more openly in the Essay of 1815, soon to be discussed. As he declares much later, 'I am not a Critic - and set little value upon the art.'[8] 'I hold critical writings of very little use. They do rather harm.'[9] 'I never cared a straw about the "theory" and the "preface" was written at the request of Mr. Coleridge, out of sheer good nature.'[10]

According to William S. Ward, Jeffrey with his review of Thalaba in 1802 became the first 'competent spokesman' for the opposition to Wordsworth.[11] His first direct review of Wordsworth, that of Poems in Two Volumes, occurs in 1807 as part of a generally 'hostile reception', marking the beginning of the depression of Wordsworth's literary fame,[12] a depression which lasted for some twenty years.[13]

In his review, already quoted from, Jeffrey regrets that Wordsworth has not amended his defects, pointed out earlier. The critic gives the impression that he feels these defects sincerely, going so far as to suggest that they may arise not 'from affectation and conceit alone', but 'from

25

the self-illusion of a mind of extraordinary sensibility, habituated to solitary meditation' (XI, October 1807, 218)[14]

However, faced with the truly revolutionary character of Wordsworth's poetry, Jeffrey is unable to articulate a relation between the general comments with which the review begins and the particular, often merely abusive, remarks which follow. G.M. Harper well points out the unfairness of Jeffrey's omission from the admiring quotations from 'Song at the Feast of Brougham Castle' of the one stanza which epitomises Wordsworth's views:[15]

> Love had he found in huts where poor men lie;
> His daily teachers had been woods and rills,
> The silence that is in the starry sky,
> The sleep that is among the lonely hills.

Wordsworth is peppered by Jeffrey through succeeding issues of the Edinburgh Review, though in 1811 the critic shows anxiety for the fame of Wordsworth, Coleridge and Southey, as well as Joanna Baillie, whom he here considers to be the heirs of Shakespeare and Milton and thus far superior to the followers of Addison and Dryden (XVIII, August 1811, 283). However, following upon Wordsworth's appointment to the government post of stamp-distributor in 1813, Jeffrey's contributor Sir James Mackintosh sadly laments over the poet's failure. He writes:

> The failure of innumerable adventurers is inevitable, in literary, as well as in political Revolutions. The inventor seldom perfects his invention. The uncouthness of the novelty, the clumsiness with which it is managed by an unpractised hand, and the dogmatical contempt of the criticism natural to the pride and enthusiasm of the innovator, combine to expose him to ridicule, and generally terminate in his being admired, though warmly, by few of his contemporaries - remembered only occasionally in after times - and supplanted in general estimation by more cautious and skilful imitators. With the very reverse of unfriendly feelings, we observe that erroneous theories respecting poetical diction - exclusive and proscriptive notions in criticism, which in adding new provinces to poetry would deprive her of ancient dominions and lawful instruments of rule - and

> a neglect of that extreme regard to general sympathy, and even accidental prejudice, which is necessary to guard novelties against their natural enemy the satirist - have powerfully counteracted an attempt, equally moral and philosophical, made by a writer of undisputed poetical genius, to enlarge the territories of art, by unfolding the poetical interest which lies latent in the common acts of the humblest men, and in the most ordinary modes of feeling, as well as in the most familiar scenes of nature. (XXII, October 1813, 38)

This orotund comment was followed in the following year, 1814, by Jeffrey's review of <u>The Excursion</u>. This article shows the difficulty of finding perfect consistency in literary trends. One rightly remembers the hostility epitomised in Jeffrey's first sentence, but one should also remember that his strictures bear some similarity to those of Coleridge who, in letters of early 1815 and in <u>Biographia Literaria</u>, also objects to the prolixity of the poem, the commonplace character of its thought, and the peculiarity of the protagonist. Coleridge also accepts the charge of sectarianism which Jeffrey levelled against Wordsworth. At the same time, both Coleridge and Jeffrey admire the tale of the ruined cottage.[16] Furthermore, Jeffrey's strictures themselves constituted a minority opinion in the contemporary periodical reaction to Wordsworth's poem.[17] Again, Jeffrey's review is thirty pages long: of the nineteen pages largely comprising extracts from the poem, seven are devoted to specimens objected to and twelve, the majority, to specimens admired. As Coleridge notes, Jeffrey cites 'a large number of single lines and even of large paragraphs, which he himself acknowledges to possess eminent and original beauty'.[18]

Thus Jeffrey still finds qualities to admire in Wordsworth, but he must set these against defects which the poet has failed to remedy. He writes:

> considering the peculiarities of his former writings merely as the result of certain wanton and capricious experiments on public taste and indulgence, [we] conceived it to be our duty to discourage their repetition by all the means in our power. We now see

clearly, however, how the case stands; and, making up our minds, though with the most sincere pain and reluctance, to consider his as finally lost to the good cause of poetry, shall endeavour to be thankful for the occasional gleams of tenderness and beauty which the natural force of his imagination and affections must still shed over all his productions, - and to which we shall ever turn with delight, in spite of the affectation and mysticism and prolixity, with which they are so abundantly contrasted (XXIV, November 1814, 2-3).

There is at least a structural balance to the review, as to this comment, even if it is unevenly and unfairly weighted and quite inadequate to the richness, variety and originality of the style and thought of the poem under discussion.

In the month following Jeffrey's review Wordsworth appears to have first spurned it and then, 'morbidly sensitive to criticism'[19] as he was, to have read it. He found it the work of 'a depraved Coxcomb; the greatest Dunce in this Island, and assuredly the Man who takes most pains to prove himself so.'[20] Through January 1815 Wordsworth composed the 'Essay, supplementary to the Preface' for the edition of his poems to be published in the spring. Though in the Essay Wordsworth says, like Jeffrey, that poetry is both sensory and passionate and at the same time moral, yet he further emphasises its subjective and 'transcendant' character.[21] Wordsworth surveys the history of English literature in order to show to his own satisfaction that the great poets were unacclaimed by and unpopular with their contemporaries. He memorably declares that the original poet must create the taste by which he is to be admired,[22] though he finds that taste alone, being passive, is not enough. The poet must lead, the reader must follow, but his response must be active - a _reaction_. We cannot rely, as Jeffrey would, on 'immediate and universal' associations, since language is

> subject to endless fluctuations and arbitrary associations. The genius of the poet melts these down for his purpose; but they retain their shape and quality to him who is not capable of exerting, within his own mind, a corresponding energy.[23]

The interaction between poet and reader, here as in the Preface to <u>Lyrical Ballads</u>, leaves small space for the mere critic. Wordsworth, like Coleridge later in <u>Biographia Literaria</u>, paints a portrait of the ideal critic, in order to show by implication how far such men as Jeffrey are removed from it, but he adds that even the ideal critic is untrustworthy. He turns away from such a figure towards the individual reader who, with his fellows, comes to make up, not the unreliable 'public', but the 'people' whose sanction is won only through the course of long centuries. Thus again Wordsworth rejects the critic - and the public - in favour of the inspired poet and sensitive reader.[24]

Wordsworth begins the Preface to the edition of 1815 with an analysis that would gratify Jeffrey. His account of the modifying imagination with its appeal to the affections links with Jeffrey's theory put forward in his review of Alison in 1811 and applied to Shakespeare in his essay on Hazlitt's <u>Characters of Shakespeare's Plays</u> in 1817 (XVIII, 23; XXVIII, 473; and above, p. 8). However, concerning the creative imagination which 'recoils from everything but...the indefinite', with its 'sublime consciousness of the soul in her own mighty and almost divine powers',[25] Wordsworth with an 'O altitudino' soars high above Jeffrey's reach.

If Jeffrey read this lofty counter-criticism in the Preface of 1815, one cannot be wholly surprised at his entirely negative opinion of <u>The White Doe of Rylstone</u>, reviewed this year, and, incidentally, defiantly published, like <u>The Excursion</u>, in an expensive quarto for the enjoyment of the wealthy and the cultivated few. Jeffrey's opinion, though influential, is still at this time a minority one amongst the periodicals.[26] However, Wordsworth deeply resents his hostility, for he flashes out against him in <u>A Letter to a Friend of Robert Burns</u> of 1816, going back for material to Jeffrey's article on Burns of seven years before, or rather to extracts quoted from it in a pamphlet of 1815.[27] In the <u>Letter</u> Jeffrey is termed an 'infatuated slanderer...this persevering Aristarch' - Aristarch being the Greek critic who presumed to revise the poems of Homer; Jeffrey is obtuse, superficial and inept, yet comparable even to the abominated Napoleon and Robespierre.[28]

Wordsworth's doughty defence of himself is

supported by the judicious arguments of Coleridge in Biographia Literaria, published in 1817, though much of the work seems to have been completed two years before, that is in the year following the publication of The Excursion.[29] In chapter XXI of Biographia Coleridge lucidly objects to the literary criticism of the Edinburgh Review and Jeffrey on five grounds: it is unphilosophical, personal, political, trivial, and uncritical. Under this last heading Coleridge points out Jeffrey's use of satirical devices as part of his critical method. This objection is valid if one thinks of Jeffrey as a pure critic rather than as a periodical satirist as well as critic. Jeffrey perhaps yielded a little to this comment, since in his collected Contributions to the Edinburgh Review, 1844, he omitted a devoutly religious quotation from The Excursion which Coleridge observes he had simply termed 'downright ravings'.[30] On the other hand, Coleridge objects to Jeffrey ridiculing Wordsworth's use of the pedlar as protagonist of The Excursion, a technique which Coleridge himself objects to critically in the following chapter. The question with regard to Jeffrey is whether ridicule is a valid device in periodical or indeed any criticism. Of course, Coleridge himself is not writing as a cool philosopher when he compares the critics' 'intellectual claims to the guardianship of the muses...to the physical qualifications which adapt their oriental brethren for the superintendence of the Harem'.[31]

In spite of Coleridge's hostility to Jeffrey, one can yet discover general points of contact between their criticisms of Wordsworth. Indeed, David Masson wrote, 'if Jeffrey's criticisms on Wordsworth's poetry be now compared with the criticisms of...Coleridge, as published in the Biographia Literaria, it will be found that, immeasurably as the two critics differ in spirit... there is still an almost perfect coincidence in their special objections to his style.'[32] Jeffrey's balanced narrow view tilts heavily against Wordsworth, whereas Coleridge's balanced large view tilts heavily in his favour. Of course Jeffrey's argument lacks Coleridge's profundity, subtlety and judicial sympathy. His view of poetic unity is feebly conventional beside that of Coleridge, and he cannot appreciate the vital contribution of idealism towards creating the poetic whole. Nevertheless, for both Coleridge and Jeffrey poetry is general in concern. For both the poet gives pleasure, partly through the unity of his work. Both criticise Wordsworth's theory of poetic language and subject matter on social and aesthetic grounds. Both oppose Wordsworthian prolixity and what Coleridge terms his 'mental bombast.'[33] Furthermore, in making a distinction between poetry and poem Coleridge is moving in the same current of thought as Jeffrey when the latter points to 'pure poetry' as the quintessential mark of the genius of Keats (XXXIV, August 1820, 205). Similarly, Coleridge's view of Shakespearian imagery is parallel with that set forth by Jeffrey in his articles on Alison and on Hazlitt.[34] And when Coleridge appeals to good sense and taste, when appeals rhetorically to 'TRUTH, NATURE, LOGIC and the LAWS of UNIVERSAL GRAMMAR', to 'grammar, logic and the truth and nature of things, confirmed by the authority of works, whose fame is not of ONE country nor of ONE age',[35] he is employing language which Jeffrey would understand and sympathise with.

Nevertheless, Jeffrey as inferior critic, hostile editor and politician, published Hazlitt's bitter review of Biographia Literaria in 1817, as he had published the scurrilous piece on Christabel[36] and Hazlitt's attack on The Statesman's Manual in the previous year.

After Wordsworth's and Coleridge's defence, Jeffrey passes over Peter Bell and The Waggoner, both published in 1819, even though he considers that they perfectly represent the aspect of Wordsworth's poetry that he abhors.[37] Jeffrey does attack Memorials of a Tour on the Continent, 1822. Only after this does his criticism, expressed directly through four reviews in fifteen years, cease.

One aspect of Jeffrey's attitudes towards Wordsworth and nature has not been touched upon in this chronological survey. Since Jeffrey himself loved nature and renewed his emotional resources at its fountain, why did he criticise Wordsworth so vehemently? Partly because the poet's view of nature, superficially similar to his, is fundamentally different. Both men find spiritual sustenance in nature, but Jeffrey finds it merely through its picturesqueness and the healthful aspects of it which correspond to his own happier feelings.

This can be seen by examining a number of passages where Jeffrey expresses his enthusiasm. For example, as a weary Lord Advocate involved in

31

effecting the passage of the Reform Bill through the House of Commons in 1831 he writes in a spirit comparable to that of Wordsworth in composing the sonnet on Westminster Bridge twenty-nine years before:

> It was a beautiful, rosy, dead calm, morning when we broke up a little before five to-day; and I took three pensive turns along the solitude of Westminster Bridge; admiring the sharp clearness of St. Paul's, and all the city spires soaring up in a cloudless sky, the orange red light that was beginning to play on the trees of the Abbey, and the old windows of the speaker's house, and the flat, green mist of the river floating under a few lazy hulks on the tide, and moving low under the arches. It was a curious contrast with the long previous imprisonment in the stifling roaring House, amidst dying candles, and every sort of exhalation.[38]

This and similar passages[39] are comparable to passages in Wordsworth, but whereas Jeffrey stops to admire the various colourful beauties of the scene, Wordsworth goes through it so to speak with the courage of a lonely explorer in order to penetrate to the spirit which lies within and beyond. Jeffrey cannot follow him in his mystical quest, since he is hemmed in by his notions of the primacy of <u>common</u> feelings and of social relationships. He is humanistic and gregarious, fearful of solitude and of the unknown. As Lewis E. Gates writes, 'We cannot doubt that his whole mental life was perturbed by such of Wordsworth's poems as the great <u>Ode</u>, and that it was an act of self-preservation on his part to burst into indignant ridicule and violent protest.'[40]

With Jeffrey's underlying feelings laid bare - they were concealed by the severe, antithetical yet powerfully flowing style of the reviews - we can understand the complete lack of <u>rapport</u> between him and Wordsworth. At the same time we can understand why he made the attempt to persuade Wordsworth to change his ways. His standards being social and emotional, he could not imagine any others, and sought to have the poet conform to what he thought all men must feel.

Because of the great theoretical differences between Jeffrey and Wordsworth, Jeffrey's attempts to reform the poet were doomed to failure. He made matters worse by mingling the attempts to reform by reason with an attempt to reform by ridicule, and an attempt to promote the sales of the <u>Edinburgh Review</u> by the same and other critically suspect methods. Wordsworth's immediate reaction to an attack by the leading periodical critic of the age was to wish to kick Jeffrey in the backside;[41] as an intellectual alternative he published the comments in the <u>Letter</u> on Burns and a general defence in the 'Essay, supplementary to the Preface'. He always justifiably felt that Jeffrey retarded his fame. But at the same time one must notice that the early years of the nineteenth century saw the beginning of Wordsworth's shift to conformity in poetic style and to reaction in political views. One cannot help but suspect that insidiously Jeffrey's comments from the standpoint of convention must have provided some impetus to this movement.

This suspicion is supported by the comments of G.M. Harper and T.M. Raysor. Harper writes:

> It cannot be denied that Wordsworth was affected by the hostile criticism of Jeffrey and a number of less influential reviewers. Owing to several other causes, and yet also to this criticism, he drew inspiration henceforth [that is, after about 1808] far less directly from nature...than had been his wont. The episodes of his own everyday life and of the simpler lives of dalesmen and chance wayfarers ceased almost suddenly to give him material for poetic inspiration.... The [later] subjects bear no resemblance to those formerly chosen, and many startling examples of reversion to conventional poetic diction might be cited.... It really seems as if Jeffrey had succeeded in making him pay 'due honour and authority' to 'that ancient and venerable code', the 'established laws of poetry'.[42]

Raysor, writing nearly forty years later, expresses the same view in summary: Wordsworth 'reluctantly but surely yielded ground after 1807 to the hated Jeffrey and other critics'.[43]

Detailed concrete support for such contentions is gained if one examines the passages referred to critically by Jeffrey and the changes made in those passages by Wordsworth in subsequent editions. The changes, particularly noticeable in

the poems published in 1807, are many, and move in
the direction of Jeffrey: that is, Wordsworth
often seems to be striving for the Jeffreyan virtues of clarity and common sense, as well as
avoiding ridicule through the application of a
veneer of what he himself calls 'elegance and
dignity'.[44] Either Wordsworth is responding to the
urgings of Jeffrey and the despised 'small critics',[45] or he is unconsciously making changes of
which the editor would approve. Of course this
superficial tinkering cannot change the underlying
resistant character of his work.

I would like to follow this general survey
with an examination of particular passages of The
Excursion, book IV, which illustrate Wordsworth's
sturdy individualist position, his slightly moving
away from it, and the gulf which separates it from
the views of Jeffrey. In his 1814 review Jeffrey
briefly objected to book IV as an 'inconceivably
prolix...exposition of truisms' (XXIV, November
1814, 8). Indeed, book IV and book II share the
distinction of being the only books from which
Jeffrey does not admiringly quote long passages.

Some of Wordsworth's 'truisms' in book IV
express the thought that religion is essential to
human well-being. He summarises his discussion of
this view in the Argument of the poem: 'Apathy...
unknown in the infancy of society. - The various
modes of Religion prevented it. - Illustrated in
the Jewish...and Grecian modes of belief.' The
implication of the discussion here summarised is
that formerly religion was nation-wide; now,
Wordsworth, feeling with his Solitary a 'loss of
confidence in social man' (IV.261), finds that
religion, together with imagination, pervades only
that segment of society which is humble and rural.
The Argument continues: 'Wanderer points out the
influence of religious and imaginative feeling on
the mind in the humble ranks of Society, in rural
life especially.... Observation [on the part of
the sceptical Solitary] that these principles tend
to recall exploded superstions and Popery. -
Wanderer rebuts this charge, and contrasts the
dignities of the Imagination with the presumptuous
littleness of certain modern Philosophers.'

In the text of the poem itself Wordsworth
suggests that these philosophers,

> Viewing all objects unremittingly
> In disconnection dead and spiritless;
> And still dividing, and dividing still,

> Break down all grandeur, still unsatisfied
> With the perverse attempt, while littleness
> May yet become more little; urging thus
> An impious warfare with the very life
> Of [their] own souls! (IV, 961)

These philosophers dominate modern urban society, particularly Edinburgh, Wordsworth slyly notes, a city

> Now simply guarded by the sober powers
> Of science, and philosophy, and sense!
> (IV. 917)

Wordsworth's affirmation concerning the humble and rural life of modern times is summarised when he writes:

> Acknowledge, then, that whether by the side
> Of his poor hut, or on the mountain-top,
> Or in the cultured field, a Man so bred
> (Take from him what you will upon the score
> Of ignorance or illusion) lives and breathes
> For nobler purposes of mind: his heart
> Beats to the heroic song of ancient days;
> His eye distinguishes, his soul creates.
> (IV. 826)

Both Jeffrey implicitly and Coleridge explicitly refuse to make this acknowledgement.

The passages discussed here illuminate the controversy over the protagonist of the poem. It was indeed essential to Wordsworth's artistic and philosophic purpose that his hero should be a pedlar, though a retired one, and even though in the poem itself he is referred to euphemistically as the wanderer. It is essential for Wordsworth's purpose that there should be a disturbing contrast between the philosophic content of the poem and the medium through which it finds expression, that is, the words of a pedlar. It is part of Wordsworth's purpose to show the spiritual failure of modern society. The wisdom which can take this failure into account is to be found not in the philosophic mouthpieces of society, for its philosophy is bankrupt, but only in out-of-the-way places. This message is unacceptable to Jeffrey who occupies a place of literary, judicial and political authority in a modern society to whose values he must be committed.

Wordsworth's daring is shown not only in the

nature of the protagonist but also in the imagery of the poem. For example, he writes orthodoxly, and almost in the manner of Thomson and Akenside:

>   Ambition reigns
> In the waste wilderness: the Soul ascends
> Towards her native firmament of heaven,
> When the fresh eagle, in the month of May,
> Upborne, at evening, on replenished wing,
> This shady valley leaves. (IV. 394)

Here is a situation in which human feeling is made parallel with natural event perfectly in accordance with the associationist theory which Jeffrey admired in Alison. But Wordsworth is not content with the conformist image. He continues with the words of the pedlar:

>   'List! - I heard,
> From yon huge breast of rock of rock, a solemn bleat;
> Sent forth as if it were the Mountain's voice,
> As if the visible Mountain made the cry.
> Again!' - The effect upon the soul was such
> As he expressed; for, from the mountain's heart
> The solemn bleat appeared to come; there was
> No other - and the region all around
> Stood silent, empty of all shape of life.
> - It was a Lamb - left somewhere to itself,
> The plaintive Spirit of the Solitude!
> (IV. 402)

Here we have a further natural event, but only a suggestion of its human significance, to Wordsworth infinite. The orthodox set-up of the first passage quoted here Jeffrey cannot quit with Wordsworth only as guide, so he objects strenuously to the lamb's 'solemn bleat'. Sadly, Wordsworth accepts such a censure, and the 'solemn bleat' becomes a 'solemn voice', and only later the mere 'unanswer'd bleat/Of a poor lamb'.

It is noteworthy that Wordsworth's retreat appears to have begun even before the publication of the poem. In manuscript he declares emphatically, 'It is a Lamb.' In the printed versions from 1814 to 1843 the past tense is used; then in 1845 the simple statement is obliterated.

In conclusion, this discouraging statement of a partial Wordsworthian withdrawal might be set against the comment of Southey made in 1814:

> Jeffrey I hear has written what his admirers call a <u>crushing</u> review of the Excursion. He might as well seat himself upon Skiddaw and fancy that he crushed the mountain.[46]

The moral of all this may be that Wordsworth's poetry has an irreducible quality of spiritual greatness and originality which can be diminished and obscured neither by the afterthoughts and the revisions of the poet himself, nor by the appraisal and cavillings of the critic, nor yet by the scholar's search for historical fairness and truth. On the other hand, the scholar must sympathise with Jeffrey, the harassed man of affairs yearning, on behalf of himself and of the public, for spiritual refreshment.

NOTES

1. Francis Horner, <u>Memoirs</u>, ed. L. Horner (2 vols, Murray, London, 1853), vol. 1, p. 465.
2. John Gibson Lockhart, <u>Peter's Letters to his Kinsfolk</u>, 2nd edn (3 vols, Blackwood, Edinburgh, 1819), vol. 2, p. 204.
3. Samuel Taylor Coleridge, <u>Biographia Literaria</u>, ed. J. Shawcross (2 vols, Clarendon Press, Oxford, 1907), vol. 2, p. 86.
4. This phrase is modified to read 'communicate their tastes' in Jeffrey, <u>Contributions to the Edinburgh Review</u> (4 vols, Longman, London, 1844), vol. 1, p. 78. The later phrase 'even for them' is there omitted.
5. William S. Ward, 'Wordsworth, the "Lake" poets, and their Contemporary Magazine Critics, 1798-1820,'<u>Studies in Philology</u>, vol. 42 (1945), p. 88.
6. See for example <u>Edinburgh Review</u>, vol. 18 (1811), pp. 275, 278.
7. Wordsworth, <u>Poetical Works</u>, ed. E. De Selincourt, 2nd edn (Clarendon Press, Oxford, 1952), vol. 2, p. 386.
8. Wordsworth, <u>Letters</u>, 2nd edn, vol. 5, pt. 2, p. 352.
9. Henry Crabb Robinson, <u>On Books and their Writers</u>, ed. E. J. Morley (3 vols, Dent, London, 1938), vol. 2, p. 479.
10. <u>Letters of the Wordsworth Family</u>, ed. W. Knight (3 vols, Ginn, Boston, 1907), vol. 3, p.

121.
11. <u>Studies in Philology</u>, vol. 42 (1945), p. 88.
12. The same, p. 89.
13. See Thomas M. Raysor, 'The Establishment of Wordsworth's Reputation,' JEGP, vol. 54 (1955), pp. 68-69.
14. In the versions of the Preface which appeared before 1836 Wordsworth himself admitted to the possession of 'diseased impulses.' See <u>Poetical Works</u>, ed. E. De Selincourt, 2nd edn, vol. 2, p. 402.
15. George McLean Harper, <u>William Wordsworth</u> (two vols, John Murray, London, 1916), vol. 2, p. 141.
16. Earl Leslie Griggs, 'Wordsworth through Coleridge's Eyes,' particularly pp. 65, 80-81, in <u>Wordsworth Centenary Studies</u>, ed. G.T. Dunklin (Princeton University Press, Princeton, 1951).
17. <u>Studies in Philology</u>, vol. 42 (1945), p. 91.
18. <u>Biographia Literaria</u>, ed. Shawcross, vol. 2, p. 92.
19. George Whalley, 'The Integrity of <u>Biographia Literaria</u>,' <u>Essays and Studies</u>, n.s., vol. 6 (1953), p. 90.
20. William and Dorothy Wordsworth, <u>Letters</u>, 2nd edn, vol. 2, pt 2, p. 197.
21. <u>Poetical Works</u>, 2nd edn, vol. 2, p. 412.
22. This notion appeared earlier, attributed to Coleridge, in a letter of 1807, <u>Letters</u>, 2nd edn, vol. 2, p. 428.
23. <u>Poetical Works</u>, 2nd edn, vol. 2, p. 428.
24. The same, p. 430. See also a letter of 1808, <u>Letters</u>, 2nd edn, vol. 2, p. 194. The relation between Jeffrey's criticism and the Essay is discussed by W.J.B. Owen, 'Wordsworth and Jeffrey in Collaboration,' RES, n.s., vol. 15 (1964), pp. 161-67.
25. <u>Poetical Works</u>, 2nd edn, pp. 439, 441.
26. <u>Studies in Philology</u>, vol 42 (1945), p. 92.
27. Wordsworth, <u>Prose Works</u>, ed. Owen and Smyser, vol. 3, p. 126.
28. The same, p. 127.
29. Coleridge, <u>Biographia Literaria</u>, ed. Shawcross, vol. 1, pp. xc-xci.
30. See James A Grieg, <u>Francis Jeffrey and the Edinburgh Review</u> (Oliver and Boyd, Edinburgh, 1948), p. 224. n. 1.
31. <u>Biographia Literaria</u>, ed. Shawcross, vol.

2, p. 42.

32. David Masson, Essays Biographical and Critical (Macmillan, Cambridge, 1856), p. 364.

33. Biographia Literaria, ed. Shawcross, vol. 2, p. 109.

34. The same, vol. 2, pp. 16-18. Edinburgh Review, vol. 18 (1811), p. 24, and vol. 28 (1817), p. 473.

35. Biographia Literaria, ed. Shawcross, vol. 1, p. 14; vol. 2, p. 68.

36. The authorship of this review, which Jeffrey denied, remains unclear. See Wellesley Index to Victorian Periodicals, ed. W.E. Houghton (Routledge & Kegan Paul, London, 1966), vol. 1, p. 455.

37. Jeffrey, Contributions, vol. 3, p. 234.

38. Henry Cockburn, Life of Lord Jeffrey, vol. 1, p. 317.

39. For example, the same, vol. 1, p. 271; vol. 2, p. 219.

40. Lewis F. Gates, Three Studies in Literature (Macmillan, New York, 1899), p. 23.

41. Letters, 2nd edn, vol. 2, p. 192.

42. G. M. Harper, William Wordsworth, vol. 2, p. 142.

43. JEGP, vol. 54 (1955), p. 61. See also J. H. Alexander, Two Studies in Romantic Reviewing, vol. 1, p. 156f.

44. Letters, 2nd edn, vol. 3, p. 641.

45. Poetical Works, ed. E. De Selincourt (Clarendon Press, Oxford, 1952), vol. 1, p. 359.

46. Robert Southey, Life and Correspondence, ed. his son (6 vols, Longman, London, 1849-50), vol. 4, p. 97.

PART THREE. JEFFREY AND CARLYLE

As we have seen, as a relatively young man Jeffrey had been harsh to Wordsworth. On the other hand, as a man over fifty he lent an encouraging hand to his young compatriot Carlyle even though the latter's style and thought often seemed outrageous to him. Though he attacked Goethe's <u>Wilheim Meister</u>, translated by Carlyle (August 1825), yet he welcomed the translator himself to the pages of the <u>Edinburgh Review</u>. Carlyle seized the opportunity to contribute sizzling articles pleading the cause of German literature and castigating the times. With regard to Carlyle, Jeffrey's attempts at editorial control, what he called 'vamping and patching',[1] were relatively mild. The <u>Edinburgh</u> needed new blood, and he was glad of <u>Carlyle's</u>, even boiling.

Jeffrey chose a milder method than that which he had employed upon Wordsworth in order to win Carlyle to what might be called sociability. This word is used in preference to 'sociality', of which Carlyle himself was fond. 'Sociality' seems to mean good fellowship in the company of intimates. 'Sociability' in this essay means both more and less than this: living in the world, and at the same time adopting some of its standards for the sake of social harmony. Jeffrey's ideal was what a successor as editor of the <u>Edinburgh</u> called 'the easy-citizenship of good-breeding' (CXIII, April 1861, 442).

Jeffrey's method to win over Carlyle took the form of social intercourse, indirect pressure through Jane Welsh with whom he flirted, and a frequent correspondence. His persuasive technique also involved the offer of remarkable generosity: chiefly the annuity of one hundred pounds, and help for Carlyle's brother John. However, Carlyle remained adamant. Early in the relationship he stubbornly retreated from Edinburgh to Craigenputtock; and when Jeffrey finally became demanding and even rude, comparing Jane to Titania and Carlyle to Bottom (himself by inference Oberon), he terminated the intimacy.

To illustrate this view of the relationship between Carlyle and Jeffrey I would now like to examine its chronological development, and its literary fruition in Carlyle's contributions to the Edinburgh Review. His early attitude towards the review was significantly ambivalent. Although he regretted living in times 'when Plato would be dissected in the Edinb<u>r</u> review',[2] he considered its editor 'an extra-ordinary man',[3] and he urged Jane Welsh to read it along with Shakespeare and Milton.

When Carlyle returned to Edinburgh at the end of 1819, 'intending...darkly towards potential "Literature"',[4] his friend Edward Irving advised him:

> The 'Edinburgh Review' you are perfectly fit for....writers in the Review...obtain the very opinion you want, opinion among the intelligent and active men in every rank.[5]

Abandoning possible careers in the church, the schoolroom and the lawcourt, Carlyle read 'some fifty volumes [sic] of the Edinburgh Review' in preparation for a literary career.[6] He submitted a contribution, but nothing came of this. However, his estimation of Jeffrey remained high, though qualified.

Jeffrey reviewed Carlyle's translation of Goethe's Wilhelm Meister in the Edinburgh, August 1825, with feelings ranging from wonderment at its author's genius to contempt for Germanic vulgarity; however, he spared a few words of praise for the translator. Carlyle's immediate comment on the review was most acute and even grateful: he could afford gratitude, having already won the approbation of Goethe himself. He observed that Jeffrey was unable to penetrate the essence of the work, seeing it only 'as a heap of beautiful and ugly fragments'.[7]

In December 1826 Carlyle commented critically on Alison's work on taste:

> O Parson Alison, what an Essay on Taste is that of thine! O most intellectual Athenians, what accounts are those you give us of Morality and Faith, and all that really makes a man a man! Can you believe that the Beautiful and Good have no deeper root in us than 'Association,' 'Sympathy,' 'Calculation'?.... You strive...'to work from the outside inward,' and two inches below the suface you will never get....'

The philosophy of Voltaire and his tribe exhilarates and fills us with glorying for a season; - the comfort of the Indian who warmed himself at the flames of his - bed.[8]

This account of the work which Jeffrey admired and popularized, with the appendage on Voltaire and his followers, with whom Carlyle came to associate Jeffrey, makes an ironic introduction to the personal relation between the two men which commenced in February 1827.

When they met, Jeffrey felt at once that Carlyle was 'a Man of Genius - and of original character and right heart'.[9] Carlyle himself responded to the 'little Jewel of Advocates'.[10] The latter had been eager to obtain new blood for the Edinburgh Review which was indeed beginning to enjoy lavish infusions from Macaulay. Though Jeffrey, whilst protesting his ignorance, felt Carlyle's opinions of the great value and talent of his German idols to be erroneous, yet he declared himself not at all frightened at his 'Teutonic fire' and offered to receive a larger exposition of the faith that was in him 'with all respectful thankfulness'.[11] Carlyle in his turn understood Jeffrey as being 'to all appearance anxious that I would undertake the task of Germanising the public, and ready even to let me do it con amore, so I did not treat the whole Earth not yet Germanized as a 'parcel of blockheads'; which surely seemed a fair enough request'.[12]

Carlyle avidly seized this opportunity to communicate through such a powerful channel as the Edinburgh Review the revelation which German literature, particularly the work of Schiller and Goethe, had been to him. He began obliquely with a short paper on Jean Paul Richter (June 1827). This was followed in the next issue with an article on German literature as a whole. These articles were 'printed with scarcely any alteration'.[13]

Despite evidence of earlier interest in German and European literature in the Edinburgh Review, Carlyle himself rightly felt the importance and originality of his own contributions. He also appreciated their importance in his own literary career, an appreciation shared by his students, Froude and Carlisle Moore. Part of this latter importance lay in the articles' immediate effectiveness: they brought him into prominence in literary circles.

In the article on Jean Paul itself, Carlyle compliments his author on his humorous sensibility which does not degenerate into sentimentality, and lauds him for his originality which is yet not eccentricity. Carlyle pleads with enthusiasm, but Jeffrey surely admired this bounded admiration for sensibility and originality.

In discussing the general field of modern German literature, Carlyle stands up as its champion against such charges as had been casually laid by Jeffrey himself, that is, charges of bad taste and mysticism. In doing so, he appeals to universal rules, as Jeffrey did, but at the same time he rejects social criteria, which his editor found difficult to do. Unlike Jeffrey, Carlyle appears to be indifferent to modern English literature, including its criticism. On the other hand, he admires the modern criticism of Germany, because it is highly articulated and philosophically grounded; and he admires the transcendental and intuitive German philosophy, free as it is from the sensational defect of Hume and Locke. Following Schiller and Fichte, Carlyle considers the poet to be aloof and idealistic, yet, since he shows the ideal in the real, as making a vital contribution to modern life. In all this he is a long way from the nationalistic, empirical orthodoxy of Jeffrey.

After this auspicious Germanophile entry into the periodical world, as well into the purview of influential men like Jeffrey, Carlyle submitted applications for two academic posts, at London and St. Andrews, thus testifying to his dissatisfaction with the prospect of journalism and independent writing as a career. Jeffrey supported the application to London University, though he expressed his reservations with favourite religious imagery: Carlyle is 'a sectary in taste and literature', intent on magnifying the differences between his sect and the establishment.[14] Certainly Jeffrey's friend Brougham was 'rather alarmed at [his] German predilections'.[15]

In January of the following year, 1828, Jeffrey sent an eloquent testimonial on Carlyle's behalf to St. Andrews' University, though he knew that its Principal was 'very zealous for moderation' and against 'sectary enthusiasm'.[16] In connection with this application Carlyle termed Jeffrey his Palinurus, an unhappy allusion, since this person, though the pilot of Aeneas, was destroyed by Neptune.

Despite the help of Jeffrey's recommendations, both of Carlyle's academic applications failed, and he decided to carry out his plan of retiring to Craigenputtock. He made his move in spite of the objections of Jeffrey. These were based on grounds of sociability, like those which he was to put forward repeatedly in the following years to both Carlyle and his wife. Jeffrey assured him:

> you will very soon tire of planting fir trees among granite rocks...do not cast away the fair chances of happiness that lie before you - merely because they lie on what you think a vulgar & jostling road, in pursuit of an unsocial & contemplative felicity, not made for man...condescend to be social.[17]

In spite of this difference of view, Carlyle spent his last two nights in Edinburgh 'In the house of Francis Jeffrey; surely one of the kindest little men I have ever in my life met with', a 'wonderful little man' who 'half hates half loves me with utmost sincerity.'[18] One suspects that the mingling of feeling was mutual.

At Craigenputtock, Carlyle turned some of his attention from German literature to Scottish, in particular Burns. Defending Mrs. Hemans and Moore against his 'ungallant, unkind insensible prejudices', Jeffrey advised him to 'renounce paradox, & outlandish absurdity & stand on your own feet - a true British man'.[19] The advice was not taken, for, receiving the article, Jeffrey objected to Carlyle's Germanizing mysticism, dogmatism, 'unlucky ambition to appear more original than you are', exaggerated opinions, jargon and verbosity; these objections were those which he had made twenty-five years earlier to the Lake poets. He urged Carlyle, as he had urged them: 'be contented to write like your famous countrymen of all ages - as long at least as you write to your countrymen & for them'.[20] As Froude observes, 'this was not merely the protest of an editor, but the reproach of a sincere friend'.[21] However, Carlyle did not relish the comments. He wrote at indignant length concerning the mutilations inflicted by Jeffrey. For his part, the latter wrote bluntly: 'I do my duty - He who comes into a crowd must submit to be squeezed'; but he continued with growing mildness and winning persuasion:

> you mystics will not be contented with kindness of heart and reasonable notions in any body - but you must have gifts and tasks

and duties - and relations with the universe, and strugglings to utter forth the truth - God help you and your vainglorious jargon, which makes angels smile...and sensible men laugh outright....

You will understand that your article is actually printed, - and has the honour of standing in the van - and yet you think yourself shabbily used - o vanity of vanities! I enclose a draft on account of it....Write me soon, and tell me whether you have any good matter in your head for another review.[22]

Jeffrey concluded the correspondence on a note of patient capitulation, admitting only to 'very few, and temperate corrections'.[23]

The article on Burns appeared in the <u>Edinburgh Review</u>, December 1828, and no doubt provoked comparison with Jeffrey's own controversial paper of 1809. In that article he had praised Burns as a manly adherent of nature and the tradition as opposed to the wrong-headed poets of the Lake school. At the same time, he indicated that Burns's achievement was to a degree questionable from the standpoint of orthodox morality.

Carlyle, though he eloquently vindicates Burns's original genius, is less generous than Jeffrey towards their compatriot. His criticism, like that of Jeffrey, is moralistic - an approach, incidentally, which Wordsworth had deplored. However, he views Burns not from the standpoint of conventional morality, but from that of his nascent morality of the hero. Carlyle is interested in Burns 'as a man'. As such, he fails, because of his 'hapless attempt to mingle in friendly union the common spirit of the world with the spirit of poetry, which is of a far different and altogether irreconcilable nature' (XLVIII, 271, 306). This failure Carlyle himself, despite the pleas of Jeffrey, was determined to avoid.

According to F.W. Roe in his study of the essay, Carlyle overemphasises the effect on Burns of his visits to Edinburgh. This aspect of his discussion would naturally follow from the effects on Carlyle himself of his own stay in Edinburgh as well as London, and his resistance to the seductive wiles of Jeffrey. He writes of his subject as he might have written of himself: 'At the end of this strange season [in Edinburgh], Burns gloomily sums up his gains and losses, and meditates on the chaotic future' (XLVIII, 298).

Burns's decision to prefer self-help, however humble, to dependence, however promising, was in Carlyle's view the right one:
> after all, it was no failure of external means, but of internal, that overtook Burns. His was no bankruptcy of the purse, but of the soul; to his last day, he owed no man anything (XLVIII, 299).

In Carlyle's view Burns's failure in the last resort is due not to the temptation in his environment but to his own weakness. He fails, like Byron, because he is unable to recognize and thus respond to the challenge which life presents.

Here we see Carlyle turning from literature to the spiritual biography of the artist, indeed of man; we also see the Christian concern with moral freedom and failure developing into his own theory of the hero. He surely saw not only Burns and Byron and their worlds but also himself in relation to Edinburgh including Jeffrey in the light of this theory, and Jeffrey might have felt this. His epistolary criticism of Carlyle's article was strongly worded, and not confined to narrow aspects of style. In writing and more elaborately in conversation he assailed on larger aesthetic and philosophic grounds the views behind the article, which he blanketed under the term 'mysticism'.

After a later discussion of this chief bone of contention, Carlyle exclaimed: 'The Dean of Faculty seems slowly coming over to "Mysticism", were he not long age a "<u>vollendeter</u> Stümper"'.[24] Writing on the state of German literature, Carlyle had quoted Fichte on the 'bungler (Stümper)' (XLVI, October 1827, 330). He discusses the passage similarly, only more quotably, in 'The Hero as Man of Letters':

> Fichte discriminates with sharp zeal the <u>true</u> Literary Man, what we here call the <u>Hero</u> as Man of Letters, from multitudes of false unheroic. Whoever lives not wholly in this Divine Idea, or living partially in it, struggles not, as for the one good, to live wholly in it, - he is, let him live where else he like, in what pomps and prosperities he like, no Literary Man; he is, says Fichte, a 'Bungler, <u>Stümper</u>'.[25]

This elaboration upon the meaning of the word

'Stümper' shows Carlyle's low estimation of Jeffrey's pretentions as literary man as well as philosopher.

Having received rough editorial treatment over the 'Burns' and in the process of discovering just how profound his differences of opinion with Jeffrey were, Carlyle was probably relieved to continue in periodical work for the less demanding Foreign Review. Articles on Voltaire and Novalis appeared there in April and July 1829.

The essay on Novalis, published after that on Voltaire, was in fact written before it. In the Voltaire we will be able to see a shadowy portrait of Jeffrey; in the Novalis there is a clear antagonism to the values which he represents. This appears in full comments on reviewing, on Novalis as mystic, and on the state of modern British thought. Carlyle begins with self-wounding sarcasm by describing the reviewer as 'a sort of sieve and drainer for the use of more luxurious readers'. He continues, 'Coleridge's works were triumphantly condemned by the whole reviewing world',[26] - especially the Edinburgh Review, we may note. On the other hand, Carlyle's own attitude towards the man of genius is one of reverence. In the spirit of Wordsworth and Coleridge, he goes on to give an elaborate analysis of bad reviewing, an analysis which might have been based on a hostile view of Jeffrey's article on The Excursion, and which centres on the image of the little critic asserting his authority by perching on the shoulder of the man of genius.

With regard to Novalis himself, Carlyle rejects the legalistic appeal of Jeffrey, as well as his scorn of mysticism:

> Many of his opinions [Novalis] would despair of proving in the most patient Court of Law; and would remain well content that they should be disbelieved there....[He] had an affinity with Mysticism, in the primary and true meaning of that word...which at this day carries no opprobrium with it in Germany, or, except among certain more unimportant classes, in any other country.[27]

The sarcasm here does not conceal the absence of substance in Carlyle's own discussion of the term 'mysticism'. He concludes by referring again to his own serious style of reviewing and exulting in the decline of the sceptical philosophy for which

Jeffrey stands: 'It appears to us that, in England, there is a distinct spirit of tolerant and sober investigation abroad in regard to [mysticism]...; a persuasion, fast spreading wider and wider, that the plummet of French or Scotch Logic [represented by Voltaire and Hume], excellent, nay, indispensable as it is for surveying all coasts and harbours, will absolutely not sound the deep-seas of human Inquiry'.[28]

The significant reference to Voltaire here leads us to the article on him, finished in March 1829 for the Foreign Review. In this respect, it is suggestive that Carlyle concluded his sketch of Jeffrey some thirty-eight years later by terming him 'a potential Voltaire; say "Scotch Voltaire"'.[29] In the light of the article to be discussed, this comment is equivocal. Carlyle was not at all equivocal, however, when in the recent Foreign Review article on Goethe's Helena he linked Voltaire with Mephistopheles: 'The shrewd, all-informed intellect he has, is an attorney intellect; it can contradict, but it cannot affirm'.[30]

Carlyle begins the essay on Voltaire himself by defying the worldly values which Jeffrey represents, particularly the value of contemporary fame. He declares that we are all of us influential, known and unknown alike; in fact, the famous in one age are forgotten in the next. Further, the celebrated and the city go together. As in his own life Carlyle set Edinburgh against Craigenputtock, as in the account of Burns he set that city against Mossgiel, so in the account of Voltaire he sets the 'peace and roses...the benignant quietude of Ferney' against 'Parisian display', in yielding to which and the 'many-headed god, POPULARITY' Voltaire indeed died.[31]

Carlyle feels that, instead of supercilious critical scorn, Voltaire demands tolerance, sympathy and love. Extending these to him, he still finds his character confined by many limitations; certain of these he shared with Jeffrey. He is marked by levity rather than earnestness, bienséance rather than heroism. 'He sees but a little way into Nature....His view of the world is a cool, gently scornful, altogether prosaic one'. He regards life as a 'grand farce', yet his sincere sentiment is, 'J'ai fait un peu de bien; c'est mon meilleur ouvrage'.[32] His intellect is not great but expert, not strong but agile, not deep but superficially extensive. In short, he is a concionator, indeed a mere persifleur.

Perhaps Jeffrey appreciated more slowly than did Carlyle the fundamental difference thus fully indicated as separating them on the critical and philosophical levels. His early advice to Carlyle was not merely editorial, critical and philosophical, but also domestic and personal. He asked such questions as: are you doing right to seclude yourself at Craigenputtock? are you doing right to seclude Jane there? In August 1828 he urged:

> You have no mission upon earth - whatever you may fancy - half so important as to be innocently happy.... That is my creed - & right or wrong - it is both a simpler & a humbler one than yours.[33]

Over a year later, he adjured Carlyle:

> I do not care a farthing for your opinions - and never imagine that either your speculative errors or mine are much worth enquiring into - But the unsocial dispositions which yours lead you to indulge are a matter of regret to me, and I cannot but suspect a source of discomfort to yourself.[34]

Carlyle's next article, 'Signs of the Times', published in the Edinburgh Review, June 1829, is virtually untouched by the editor. He himself too strongly called it 'Jeffrey's last speech',[35] an allusion to Jeffrey's resignation from the editorship at this time. Here his view moves significantly from literature to society. The article is a trenchant criticism of the modern mechanical age in which men have lost faith in the invisible, their sense of wonder and their inspiration. The view is forthrightly expressed, the solution to the crisis is far-sought, yet the conclusion is optimistic. Since he believes that life in general consists in struggling forward, he is hopeful of social progress.

Apart from publishing such opinions, which to him seemed extravagant, Jeffrey in March 1830 generously offered Carlyle an annuity of one hundred pounds; this was rejected on the Burnsian principle referred to above. Soon after, he lent Carlyle a sum, later repaid, and helped set up his brother in a professional position. He also, later still, tried to obtain a publisher for Sartor Resartus. Thus Carlyle enjoyed Jeffrey's practical benevolence, along with Hazlitt, Leigh Hunt and others.

At Craigenputtock, as well as reviewing, Carlyle set to work on an original piece of writing, <u>Sartor Resartus</u>, begun in August or September 1830 and finished in July of the following year. He must have delighted not only in rural seclusion, but also in the opportunity to write as his own man, unfettered by editorial shackles. There is a trace of this feeling in the character of Teufelsdröckh's baffled English editor as well as at the beginning of the work, which otherwise transcends the discussion of the personal relations between Carlyle and Jeffrey. Teufelsdröckh is marked with 'rusticity...fatal to his success with our public'. His 'genial capability [is] marred too often by...rudeness, inequality, and apparent want of intercourse with the higher classes'. At the end of the book the cautious editor enquires with Jeffreyan bewilderment, 'How could a man occasionally of keen insight, not without keen sense of propriety, who had real Thoughts to communicate, resolve to emit them in a shape bordering so closely on the absurd?'[36]

When Jeffrey was succeeded by Macvey Napier as editor of the <u>Edinburgh Review</u>, he offered himself to Carlyle as an intermediary, warning him against further mysticism. Carlyle on his part was eager to contribute, but he warned Napier against editorial interference. He eventually contributed another article on German literature (March 1831). Here Carlyle provides a survey which would warm the speculative hearts of his fellow <u>Edinburgh Reviewers</u>, but his chief contribution is a characteristic affirmation of the present and future dynamic of the historical process. Perhaps in Germany 'that change from Negation to Affirmation, from Destruction to Re-construction, for which all thinkers in every country are now prepared, is... already in action'. Carlyle is evidently growing less and less interested in literature as such. He is concerned not only with 'written Poetry', but also 'the <u>inarticulate</u> Poetry' of 'popular Mythology' and the 'acted Poetry' of political life (LIII, March 1831, 159-161). After all, as he says in 'Characteristics', published in the <u>Edinburgh Review</u>, December 1831, 'Thought [is] but the... <u>Symbol</u> of Action' (LIV, 370). This tendency to interrelate categories and to break down the barriers between them would disturb both Jeffrey and Napier. However, Jeffrey assured Carlyle that the article was admired by him for its comparative indulgence, and by Macaulay for its 'force and originality'.[37]

In suggesting a further article, on various philosophical works, Carlyle amiably pictured himself as reviewer standing 'peaceably in the middle of them all'.[38] However, what he did contribute was 'Characteristics', which Napier found 'inscrutable'. Carlyle himself feared 'that it might be too <u>scrutable</u>; for it indicates decisively enough that Society...is utterly condemned to destruction, and even now beginning its long travail-throes of Newbirth'.[39] With disappointment Jeffrey confided to Napier:

> I fear Carlyle will not do.... The misfortune is, that he is very obstinate and... conceited - and unluckily in a place like [London, whither he had moved], he finds people enough to abet and applaud him, to intercept the operation of the otherwise infallible remedy of general avoidance and neglect - It is a great pity, for he is a man of genius and industry - and with the capacity of being an elegant and impressive writer.[40]

Jeffrey had suggested to Carlyle the choice between public approbation and isolation. He now regretted the possibility of his gaining the approbation of a metropolitan coterie.

Jeffrey might well be disappointed in 'Characteristics'. Carlyle argues from the text, 'The healthy know not of their health, but only the sick' (LIV, December 1831, 351), and on this basis he constructs a critical analysis of modern society more penetrating than that of 'Signs of the Times'. He sets conscious against unconscious, speculation against poetry, argument against prophecy, manufacture against creation, artificial against natural, mechanic against dynamic, and boisterously noise against silence. Only in the latter values are to be found the seeds of anticipated regeneration.

On the particular plane, Carlyle in this article rejects reviewing itself not only implicitly in his practise of virtually ignoring the works supposedly under review, but also explicitly when he declares it a mere symptom of the age:

> Nay, is not the diseased self-conscious

state of Literature disclosed in this one fact, which lies so near to us here, the prevalence of Reviewing!...your Reviewer is a mere taster.

Similarly, Carlyle rejects 'the Debater and Demonstrator' - such as Jeffrey. If this person 'whom we may rank as the lowest of true thinkers' - admittedly, he is a true thinker - 'knows what he has done, and how he did it, the Artist, whom we rank as the highest, knows not' (LIV, 369, 354). No wonder that Jeffrey turns away with a frown of impatient disapproval, an attitude shared by Brougham and Macaulay. The editor Napier's own undoubted disapproval he himself would perhaps justify on stylistic grounds. It was also philosophical and personal, Napier being, in Carlyle's view, 'a man of wooden structure; limited in all ways', that is, 'a solid old-established Edinburgh Whig'.[41]

Carlyle's last of seven contributions to the Edinburgh Review is a light-weight 'speculative-radical'[42] article on the poetry of Ebenezer Elliot, published in July 1832. He begins grotesquely:

> Smelfungus Redivivus, throwing down his critical assaying-balance, some years ago, and taking leave of the Belles-Lettres function, expressed himself in this abrupt way: 'The end having come, it is fit that we end. Poetry having ceased to be read, or published, or written, how can it continue to be reviewed?' (LV. 338).

Admittedly, Elliot's preoccupation in Corn-Law Rhymes is social, but for Carlyle poetry is now completely engulfed in the social concern. He finally advises Elliot to come to grips with the contemporary crisis by writing in prose. This advice he also gave to others.

Napier did not interfere with Carlyle's contributions. There was some difficulty over subject and length, but Carlyle's main complaint concerned slowness of payment. One cannot but suspect that the editorial delay was merely a symptom of disagreement not only concerning style but also outlook on society and life.

In the last few pages I have been following Carlyle's brief but impressive career as contributor to the Edinburgh Review. With the consent of

Jeffrey, but to his growing dismay, he has communicated to English readers something of the force and profundity of modern German literature; he has presented Burns as a failed hero; and he has expressed his sense of the crisis in modern English life. Thus he has used the journal to indicate a major source of his own inspiration, to show his view of the struggle of life, his own, the poet's and all men's, and to demonstrate how this struggle is working itself out on the contemporary social scene. He has shown the weakening of his interest in literary criticism, and his preference for the roles of moralist, social critic and even prophet. Thanks to the <u>Edinburgh Review</u> he has made his voice influentially heard at home and abroad. At the same time, on the personal level, Carlyle's article on Burns in the <u>Edinburgh Review</u> and his articles on Voltaire and Novalis in the <u>Foreign Review</u> can be seen as not only showing his philosophy, but also as betraying the tension in his significant relation with Jeffrey and what he felt that he stood for.

I would now like to go back two years in order to continue the account of Carlyle's personal relations with Jeffrey. The latter had paid a second visit to Craigenputtock in September 1830, influential on <u>Sartor Resartus</u>. After this Carlyle wrote to Mrs Basil Montagu, calling Jeffrey 'a more interesting and better man; a sadder and a wiser; than I had ever seen him'. The visit itself had been a splendid experience, but he went on to name Goethe as 'the <u>only</u> literary man, whom...I can view without a considerable admixture of contempt', and for poetry to consider the Scotch peasant hugely superior to the Scotch reviewer.[43] At this time Carlyle attempted a full, judicial and penetrating assessment of his friend, which reaches its apogee in two sentences:

> A true Newspaper Critic, on the great scale; no Priest but a Concionator! Yet on the whole, he is about the <u>best</u> <u>man</u> I ever saw.[44]

In London a year later Carlyle commented on their declining intimacy, using significant biblical phraseology: 'his path is not my path; nor are his thoughts my thoughts'.[45] However, in March 1832 Jeffrey consoled Carlyle in serious terms: 'I can see that you are improving, and have good hope that in time you may become almost as tolerant of your fellow sinners as the Sinless Being who made

53

them'.[46] Two months later Carlyle himself assured Leigh Hunt that Jeffrey 'affects...the philosophy of a man of the world, and has no settled <u>creed</u> of any higher sort: but there is a perpetual noble contradiction to it in that poetical heart of his. He loves all men, and especially loves the love of all men'.[47]

Just as Jeffrey lamented the lack of sociability in Carlyle, so he did that in Jane. Unfortunately, his advice and condescension to her, however playful and well-intentioned, became hard for Carlyle's loyal help-meet to bear. Because of his facetious comments on her 'pet fancies - or convictions as you call them',[48] he lost Jane as a correspondent.

Very soon afterwards, the intimate correspondence between Carlyle and Jeffrey also ceased.[49] In January 1834 the latter abruptly refused Carlyle help in obtaining the astronomy professorship at Edinburgh, strongly blaming him for his lack of sociability. He wrote splenetically of his 'deep regret' at Carlyle not having some regular profession,

> That of a <u>Teacher</u> is no doubt a most useful and noble one - But you cannot actually exercise it, unless you offer to teach what is thought worth learning, and in a way that is thought agreeable - and I am afraid you have not fulfilled either of these conditions.... You will never find (or make) the world friendly to your doctrines, while you insist upon dragooning it into them in so hyperbolical a manner....forgive me all this - I am sick - and scrawl, tired of my own compelled activity.[50]

Hardly forgiven, Jeffrey wrote three weeks later in a similar tone, adding,

> I have [word omitted] vivacities with my fair cousin too - for which - if they vex her, I ask her pardon - But who would not be provoked to see Titania in love with Bottom?[51]

It was probably the last provocative allusion which brought the intimate relationship between Jeffrey and Carlyle to its breaking-point.

Though their future meetings were occasional and unrewarding, Jeffrey continued to admire

Carlyle's work as much as he was able. He recommended <u>The French Revolution</u> to Brougham as 'strange, but most original', the work of a man 'half crazy, & intractable - but a man of Genius'. Six years later he took a similar view of <u>Past and Present</u>, the work of 'the most original man of our time - qualified to produce a greater & more beneficial effect by [his] writings, than any other man'.[52]

In September 1834 Jeffrey had urged Jane, 'My Very Dear Friend - For Mercy's sake let us be friends still'. He made this claim on the basis of his 'old creed - that to be happy, & to make happy, is the chief end of man'. However, it was only three years later that he was able to rejoice in the 'return to our first feeling towards each other', on the same philosophical basis.[53] In 1844 Jeffrey presented a copy of his <u>Contributions</u> to his 'indulgent and Beloved Friend...Jeanie Carlyle'.[54] This year she apologized for a display of feeling on Jeffrey's part on the grounds of his 'strong natural tendency for <u>cuddling</u> people' and a '<u>Paternal</u> affection' which he had shown towards her for over fifteen years.[55] Carlyle himself finally summed up Jeffrey in 1867:

> He was not deep enough, pious or reverent enough, to have been great in Literature; but he was a man intrinsically of veracity; said nothing without meaning it in some considerable degree; had the quickest perceptions, excellent practical discernment of what lay before him; was in earnest, too, though not 'dreadfully in earnest'; - in short was well fitted to set forth that <u>Edinburgh Review</u>...and become Corypheus of his generation.... A beautiful little man...and a bright island to me, and to mine in the sea of things; of whom it is now again mournful and painful to take farewell.[56]

Jeffrey offered Carlyle a good deal, in fact more than he was willing to accept. What he offered and the younger man accepted was a vantage point, a temporary platform in contemporary letters gained through contributing to the <u>Edinburgh Review</u>, and the interest and friendship of an important man of letters and affairs. Jeffrey's friendship must have been gratifying to Carlyle as he struggled out of social obscurity. What he offered to a degree and what Carlyle wanted on his own terms was a position in the world. Jeffrey helped him towards publication and employment, but failed him with regards to the latter at the end of their intimacy. He helped Carlyle with money, a little of which he borrowed, but some of which he was too independent and proud to accept.

What Jeffrey offered and Carlyle did not want to accept on any terms was advice. He felt that he did not need the advice which Jeffrey proffered concerning how to manage his wife, where to live, how to get on with other people, what to write and how to think. Similarly with Jane. The advice which Jeffrey offered her, playfully and condescendingly, she rejected. The break came, never to be entirely healed. The respectful friendship between Jeffrey and Carlyle was never resumed. The flirtation between Jeffrey and Jane was, though doubtless within very narrow bounds of which they were both keenly aware.

Jeffrey's critical theorising and political and philosophical speculations were no doubt easily swallowed up in the maw of Carlyle's philosophy. On the other hand, Carlyle in retrospect and in a few moments of social intercourse delighted in and was fascinated by Jeffrey's vivacity, even though he recognised the shallowness of its intellectual base and the way in which it was hemmed in by the narrowing limits of mortality. For Carlyle life was a struggle, but because of the breadth of his sympathy he knew Jeffrey as a 'bright island' in the midst of the stormy ocean of experience. Memories of him rose, with others more poignant, 'benignantly luminous from the bosom of the grim dead night!'[57]

NOTES

1. Henry Cockburn, <u>Life of Lord Jeffrey</u>, vol. 2, p. 148.

2. Thomas and Jane Welsh Carlyle, <u>Collected Letters</u>, ed. C.R. Sanders (Duke University Press, Durham, N.C., 1970-), vol. 1, p. 142.

3. <u>Collected Letters</u>, vol. 1, p. 23.

4. Carlyle, <u>Reminiscences</u>, ed. C.E. Norton (2 vols, Macmillan, London, 1887), vol. 2, p. 232.

5. James Anthony Froude, <u>Thomas Carlyle A History of the First Forty Years of His Life</u> (2 vols, Longmans, London, 1882), vol. 1, p. 76.

6. Francis Espinasse, <u>Literary Recollections</u> (Hodder and Stoughton, London, 1893), p. 208. Hill

Shine, <u>Carlyle's Early Reading</u> (University of Kentucky, Lexington, 1953), p. 67, considers that this 'is obviously a mistake for fifty <u>issues</u>. Fifty issues would constitute the file of the periodical from the beginning to approximately the time when Carlyle first mentioned reading the current issues (August 1814)'.

7. <u>Collected Letters</u>, vol. 3, p. 400.
8. Carlyle, <u>Two Note Books</u>, ed. C.E. Norton (1898, reprint ed., Appel, Marmaroneck, N.Y., 1972), p. 84f.
9. National Library of Scotland MS 787 f. 1. Paraphrased by Froude, vol. 1, p. 393.
10. <u>Collected Letters</u>, vol. 4, p. 228.
11. <u>NLS MS 787 f. 1. David A. Wilson, Carlyle to 'The French Revolution'</u>, p. 28.
12. <u>Collected Letters</u>, vol. 4, p. 228. In later years Carlyle recalled Jeffrey's kindness, courtesy, and tolerance towards him at this stage, <u>Scotsman</u>, 12 August 1967, p. 3.
13. <u>Collected Letters</u>, p. 270.
14. <u>NLS MS 787, f. 7. Wilson</u>, p. 30.
15. NLS MS 787, f. 9.
16. NLS MS 787, f. 14. Wilson, p. 42.
17. NLS MS 787, ff. 10, 15.
18. <u>Collected Letters</u>, vol. 4, pp. 382, 399.
19. <u>NLS MS 787</u>, f. 26. Wilson, p. 61.
20. NLS MS 787, f. 29. Wilson, p. 66.
21. Froude, vol. 2, p. 40.
22. NLS MS 787, ff. 34, 35. Wilson, pp. 73-74.
23. NLS MS 787, f. 36. Wilson, p. 75.
24. <u>Collected Letters</u>, vol. 5, p. 20.
25. Carlyle, <u>On Heroes, Hero-Worship and the Heroic in History</u> (Chapman and Hall, London, 1872), p. 146.
26. Carlyle, <u>Critical and Miscellaneous Essays</u> (7 vols, Chapman and Hall, London, 1872), vol. 2, p. 184.
27. The same, p. 200f.
28. The same, p. 229.
29. <u>Reminiscences</u>, vol. 2, p. 273.
30. <u>Critical and Miscellaneous Essays</u>, vol. 1, p. 135.
31. The same, vol. 2, pp. 148, 155.
32. The same, pp. 135, 146f, 154.
33. NLS MS 787 f. 32. Wilson, p. 62. Cf Jeffrey's letter to Charles Bell of 1804 in which he asserts that 'true happiness is to be found' only in the 'good affections,' NLS MS Acc. 7555.
34. NLS MS 787 ff. 46-47. Wilson, p. 117.

35. Two Note Books, p. 140.
36. Carlyle, Sartor Resartus, bk 1, ch. 4; bk 3, ch. 12.
37. Wilson, p. 203.
38. Macvey Napier, Selections from the Correspondence, ed. his son (Macmillan, London, 1879), p. 116.
39. Collected Letters, vol.6, p. 85.
40. British Museum Add. MS 34615 f. 268. Napier, p. 126.
41. Collected Letters, vol. 6, pp. 319, 301.
42. Two Note Books, p. 267.
43. Collected Letters, vol. 5, p. 185.
44. Two Note Books, p. 175f.
45. Collected Letters, vol. 5, p. 417.
46. Wilson, p. 318.
47. Collected Letters, vol. 6, p. 375.
48. Wilson, p. 348.
49. Carlyle's article on Diderot in the Foreign Quarterly Review (1833), may have played a part in the slackening of intimacy between the two men, as Jane suspected: Letters, vol. 7, p. 42. In the article Carlyle eloquently puts Diderot in his place - in a sceptical company which would include Jeffrey.
50. NLS MS 787 ff. 67-68. Wilson, p. 353. Jeffrey's follower Macaulay in 1851 considered 'that ass Carlyle...quite out of his element in general society,' R.C. Beatty, 'Macaulay and Carlyle,' PQ, vol. 18, (1939), p. 32.
51. NLS 787 f. 71. Wilson, p. 355. John Clubbe provides a less satisfactory explanation of the break in his abridgment of Froude's Life of Carlyle (Murray, London, 1979), p. 669.
52. NLS MS 1809 f. 102; 1766, f. 117.
53. NLS MS 787 ff. 80, 81, 84.
54. Volume in the possession of Dr H.W.E. Walther of New Orleans, referred to by Maxwell H. Goldberg, Thomas Carlyle's Relation with the Edinburgh Review (unpublished Ph.D. thesis, Yale University, 1933), p. 270. I wish here to express my indebtedness to this study.
55. Jane Welsh Carlyle, Letters to Her Family, ed. L. Huxley (Murray, London, 1924), p. 198.
56. Reminiscences, vol. 2, pp. 272-73. The phrase quoted is Jeffrey's concerning Carlyle, NLS MS 787 f. 41.
57. Reminiscences, vol. 2, p. 273; vol. 1, p. 163.

PART FOUR. CARLYLE AND MACAULAY

Here I would like to examine the critical writings in the Edinburgh Review of its two most distinguished literary contributors in the second major phase of its existence, that is, in the late eighteen-twenties and thirties. These contributors are Carlyle and Macaulay. The former wrote seven articles between 1827 and 1832, before relations were broken off between this non-conformist and the Whig review of Jeffrey and Napier. These articles, though few in number, constitute his main early literary statement before Sartor Resartus, and I will summarise what I consider to be their trend, before turning to the major topic of this section, Macaulay. More orthodox, and so entirely acceptable and welcome, he contributed some thirty-six articles to the Edinburgh Review between 1825 and 1844. These essays constitute his main corpus of literary work, apart from the History of England. I would like to outline the literary views of Carlyle as indicated in his articles, then to examine Macaulay's views, and finally to indicate some similarities and divergences between them.

i

Carlyle as reviewer, like Macaulay and other of his fellow contributors, often shows himself but little interested in the work supposedly under discussion. Edinburgh Reviewers often move very easily from the particular work to the general topic. This is indicative of the review's speculative tendency, but with Carlyle it is symptomatic of a special impatience with the restrictive particular. The significance of this impatience for his critical views will be discussed later.

Also important is Carlyle's predominating interest in the character of the literary genius. He is not primarily interested in the work of art or in its impact on a body of critics or readers, so much as in the character of the man who produces it. The interest itself, I hope to show, is not a final one.

Carlyle applies to the character of the literary genius two slippery terms, which yet were of great importance to his contemporaries and to their successors throughout the nineteenth century. These terms are 'genuine' and 'sincere.' In his view both Jean Paul Richter and Burns stand high because they are marked by these characteristics. Ebenezer Elliot's uncouthness is compensated for because he possesses them. Byron's cardinal defect is that he lacks them. Carlyle and his contemporaries admire a writer whom they feel they know, and especially whose feelings - whose strong feelings - they feel they know. Since Byron is evasive, especially as a satirist, he is not revered by Carlyle. It is significant that both Carlyle and Macaulay play down the value of the satirical kind, and that the former declares, in his essay on Jean Paul, that the essence of humour springs from the heart: it is love. Love indeed is the essence not merely of humour, but of genius itself. The 'loving heart' of genius 'flows out in sympathy over universal Nature' with 'all-comprehending fellow-feeling' (XLVI, Oct. 1827, 336; XLVIII, Dec. 1828, 272). An equivalent to such feeling is needed in the reader as well as in the critic who must transpose himself 'into the author's point of vision' (XLVI, Oct. 1827, 314).

The literary genius is strong not only in feeling but also in thought. The genius, like the best critic, is indifferent to questions of superficial form, since he is concerned with achieving an insight into a deeper unity, with discovering what is essential. Carlyle himself as critic seeking what is essential in literature by-passes the contemporary English writers, who in his limited view have achieved no more than a negative frame of mind. He looks instead to Germany and the insight there gained.

The preeminent unity which the genius discovers and expresses, in Carlyle's view, is that between the spiritual and the material, the metaphysical and the physical: the poet for his own age discovers the first in the second. Carlyle believes that this discovery has been made even by Ebenezer Elliot; it has been made by Burns at his best; it is above all the achievement of Goethe.

Carlyle is intent on observing the character of the literary genius. Whilst he does so, we can observe him as critic observing. As such, he is hopeful of the continuing appearance of the poet and of the continuing significance through history of the poetic message. This hope blends into his faith in the progress of humanity, such progress being both necessary and desirable. An affirmation

of progress constitutes an important part of the
perorations of the articles on German literature,
as well as that on 'Signs of the Times.' For
Carlyle here, life is progressive, annihilating
merely temporal barriers. But so is Carlyle's own
experience. As critic, he moves rapidly from the
work of literature to the character and the life
of its author: this emphasis is particularly evident in the study of Burns. By seeing the author's
life as significant of the national or the general
life, he advances still further. What is important
becomes not literature but life working itself out
in history. We move from words to thought to
action, and our attention is finally concentrated
on decisive, heroic action. A little light is
thrown on this movement by phrases in the essay on
German poetry where Carlyle declares that he is
concerned not only with 'written Poetry' but also
with the 'inarticulate Poetry' of 'popular Mythology' and the 'acted Poetry' of political life
(LIII, March 1831, 159f).

ii

I would like to deal with Macaulay more fully. In
part this is warranted by the bulk of his contributions to the Edinburgh Review; in part, because
this aspect of his work has been neglected.
Macaulay like Carlyle is often little interested
in the work to be examined. In a review of October
1841 he begins with characteristic assurance and
with implicit scorn for the Tory editor whose work
is supposedly under consideration: 'We are inclined to think that we shall best meet the wishes
of our readers, if, instead of dwelling on the
faults of this book, we attempt to give...our own
view of the life and character of Mr Hastings'
(LXXIV, 160).
    This cavalier treatment of the business of
reviewing yet goes together with an acute awareness of the stylistic demands of the periodical
medium.[1] Macaulay shows an equally fresh awareness
of his own gift and critical limitation, when in a
letter to Napier he expresses his unwillingness to
review Lockhart's Life of Scott. Here he declares
bluntly: 'I am not successful in analyzing the
effects of works of genius'. He is anything but
critical; he enjoys but does not dissect.[2] To the
'accuracy' of a literary 'judge' Macaulay (like
Wordsworth) prefers the pleasure of a sympathetic

reader, or, where the literature of Greece is concerned, 'the veneration of a worshipper, and the gratitude of a child' (I. 140).[3] He thinks of himself less as a critic than as an expert in literary biography, after the manner of Plutarch or Tacitus, or as a portrait-painter, no doubt his favourite Van Dyke.

Though Macaulay makes no claims as an analytical critic, he possesses the critical virtue of reading and writing with pleasure. He wants a book which gives pleasure. For example, Campbell's Frederic the Great is 'more than a compilation... it is an exceedingly amusing compilation, and we shall be glad to have more of it' (LXXV, April 1842, 218). The narratives of Johnson's Lives of the Poets are 'as entertaining as any novel' (II. 298). Macaulay himself likes to write not under pressure, as so often for the Review, but with pleasure. He wants his own writing, especially the History of England, to give pleasure. As he observes when commencing it, 'The materials for an amusing narrative are immense'; he wants 'for a few days [to] supersede the last fashionable novel on the tables of young ladies'.[4] How different from the rugged aspirations of Carlyle! One might only question whether the pleasure here invoked might not inhibit philosophical depth and critical acumen, and note that Macaulay's own enjoyment is not always of a highly sophisticated kind. He shies away from the mysticism of Wordsworth and Coleridge, as from the theology of Newman.

As a critic Macaulay shows only a degree of interest in critical terminology. As Carlyle writing on Jean Paul redefines 'humour', so Macaulay on Byron redefines 'correct'. He reaches the opposite extreme of verbal laxity when he writes of poetry that 'The domain of this imperial art is commensurate with the imaginative faculty' (LIII, June 1831, 559).

However, Macaulay as critic is mainly interested in literature not in its linguistic but in its social and human context. He says that it is important to the historian as revealing the character of the times when it was composed. Thus the Elizabethan drama shows the religious toleration of that era, and the comedy of Congreve and his fellows shows the moral turpitude of the Restoration. Literature is in this way significant for Macaulay, but not historically symbolic as it tends to be for Carlyle. It illumunates both the broad canvas and the small detail of the historical scene. Macaulay delightfully and without jarring brings together history and literature when in a footnote to the History he refers to the 'memorable wound' of Captain Shandy at the battle of Namur.[5] In the essays, for example, he compares the romantic courtliness of Warren Hastings with that of Sir Charles Grandison, and less appositely the childhood of Frederic the Great with that of Oliver Twist.

Macaulay is indeed so impressed by the connection between literature and history that at times he suggests that the character of the former is determined by the epoch in which it appears. The early statement that 'Shakespeare was in a great measure produced by the Reformation, and Wordsworth by the French Revolution' (I. 58) is amplified into a generalisation in the essay on Dryden: 'it is the age that forms the man, not the man that forms the age' (XLVII, Jany 1828, 2). The determinism is less strident when Macaulay attributes the singularities of Johnson not to the man but to his class, and similarly when, outside the field of English literature, he explains away Machiavelli's inconsistency as that of his place and time. Macaulay discusses recent English political history in similar terms, when he affirms that men are to a large extent 'the creatures of circumstances'. He depicts Pitt and Canning as 'merely going passively down the stream of events' (LV, July 1832, 557).

More freedom of movement may be allowed to Macaulay if we consider his historical distinction between 'the men who produce revolutions' and 'the men whom revolutions produce' (LXVIII, Oct. 1838, 118), and extend this to the field of literature. The writers of the second rank, Dryden and Byron, certainly Congreve and Wycherley, are the products of their age. On the other hand, a primary genius, like Milton, triumphs despite the spirit of his age.

Thus Macaulay sees literature as illustrative of history, as to a degree determined by history, and as to a degree transcendent of it. He also sees a conflict between literature and its social context. In a sparkling antithetical passage at the beginning of the essay on Milton, paralleled by one in the succeeding essay on Dryden, he sets poetry with the infantile, the primitive, the abnormal, the insane and the illusory, against the mature, the civilized, the sane, the normal and the real. In the essay on Dryden he adds to these terms unconscious against conscious, and creative against critical. Since society is indubitably becoming more civilised, the task of the poet grows greater with the passage of the centuries.[6] In such a task Wordsworth perhaps has failed, but Milton gloriously succeeded.

Since the various relations between literature and history are of such importance to Macaulay, it is natural that he should see a close connection between literature and historical writing. After all, when he made his choice between politics and literature, by the latter he meant writing the <u>History of England</u>. In the essays, Macaulay suggests that the glamorous life of Warren Hastings has aspects which can be 'scarcely paralleled in romance', and which are 'distinguished by incidents which might furnish matter for a novel' (LXXIV, Oct. 1841, 161, 168). Pondering the essay before writing it, Macaulay thinks of it not in terms of fictional prose narrative but of the drama, and in the work itself he presents Hastings dramatically as a hero with extraordinary powers and fame who is 'compelled to make a choice between innocence and greatness, between crime and ruin' (The same, 163). Dumont and Barère are also seen in literary, or rather as transcending literary, terms. Dumont, unconsciously portraying himself in his memoirs, approaches 'nearer to perfection than any of the Grandisons and Allworthys of fiction' (LV, July 1832, 576); and Macaulay compares 'the Barère of history' with 'the filthiest and most spiteful Yahoo of the fiction', to the Yahoo's advantage (LXXIX, April 1844, 351).

In his important essay on history in general Macaulay asserts that history needs the appeal and even the form of literature. For example, he declares strikingly that 'history begins in Novel and ends in Essay' (XLVII, May 1828, 331f). He considers Herodotus and Tacitus as dramatists. He sets the historian as advocate - Hume and Mitford - against the historian as biographer - Voltaire, Marmontel, Southey and Boswell - and the historian as novelist - Scott. In Macaulay's view the historian must by no means neglect 'the art of narration, the art of interesting the affections, and presenting pictures to the imagination' (The same, 361). In other words, 'The perfect historian... gives to truth those attractions which have been usurped by fiction' (The same, 364). Thus he appeals both to the imagination and to reason.

At the same time as he insists that history needs to possess literary qualities, Macaulay insists on the distinction between history and literature. He asserts that the procedures of fiction and history are opposed, since the former characteristically moves from the general to the particular, whilst the latter moves from the particular to the general. A similar basic division separates the drama from history, since 'The dramatist creates; the historian only disposes' (XLVII, May 1828, 364). Through such aphoristic phrases Macaulay suggests his awareness of real distinctions.

Macaulay's social, if not historical, preoccupation as a critic continues to appear if we examine what he considers literature in itself to be. His views are akin to those of Jeffrey. Literature is moral in character. It imitates nature, especially human nature, in the manner of the painter. It is concerned with the individual and the material. It is preeminently concerned with the emotions, especially sincere emotions.

For Macaulay literature is moral in character. This appears in his admiration not only of the universally admired Puritans Milton and Bunyan, but also of Jeremy Collier, 'one of the greatest public benefactors in our history', as against 'Wycherley, and the other good-for-nothing fellows', with whom Macaulay is nevertheless fascinated.[7] It is perhaps significant that although he condemns the period of the Restoration on moral grounds he is yet most interested in it, as the essay on the dramatists and the History show. Carlyle, on the other hand, abominates the 'stinking doggery' of the Stuarts and cannot understand anyone writing about 'that scandalous period'.[8]

On moral grounds Macaulay not only admires Jeremy Collier, but also Addison as a more widely influential reformer of English morals, and Fanny Burney, whom he considers to be in her field of the novel as beneficially influential a figure as Collier in the field of the drama.

Macaulay also admires literature as true to nature. He praises the Elizabethan drama, 'the highest form of composition he can conceive', because its object is 'to represent life as it is'.[9] On the other hand, since he considers literature to be imitative of the particular and the human, he condemns the drama of Dryden, as well as that of Congreve and Sheridan. On this ground, he admires the fiction of Fanny Burney and Boswell's life of Johnson rather than Johnson's writings themselves:

> Boswell's book has done for him more than the best of his own books could do. The memory of other authors is kept alive by their works. But the memory of Johnson keeps many of his works alive.

Macaulay is quite satisfied with this relationship between Johnson and his works, because it leads him to the contemplation of 'a great and a good man' (II. 303).

In an early essay Macaulay sets the poet of man, Shakespeare, against the poet of nature, Wordsworth, and there is no doubt where his preference lies. For possessing the supreme gift of human imitation Macaulay puts Addison on a level with Shakespeare and Cervantes. This must be a chief reason for his admiration of Jane Austen, whose 'dishwashings' Carlyle rejects.[10] On the other hand, Johnson and the gloomily egotistical Byron lack in Macaulay's eyes the desired power of 'personation' (LIV, Sep. 1831, 37).

Some of Macaulay's own gift as an historical artist is due to the power of individuation which he admires in others. The gift is exemplified in the literary essays, for example, when he brilliantly describes the lot of the mid-eighteenth century author (LIV, Sep. 1831, 23-24).

Finally, for Macaulay the predominant literary tone is emotional. What takes away from this tone detracts from literary value. Thus Fanny Burney's work, fine as it is, loses because she insists on viewing human nature in terms of artificial 'humours' (LXXVI, Jany 1843, 563). Bunyan, like Spenser, succeeds not through but in spite of his allegory, allegory which Macaulay elsewhere dismisses as 'tame and cold' (I. 68). The intellectual dubiousness of Milton's theology is indeed a poetic virtue, since his poetry is a 'gorgeous haze' (I. 63), a poetry of 'dim intimations' which demands only 'quasi-belief' (XLII, Aug. 1825, 316, 320). Macaulay similarly suggests in his essay on Addison that poetry requires but a degree of truth. However, earlier he had declared that truth was the object of both history and fiction, the latter bearing 'the same relation to history which algebra bears to arithmetic. The merit of poetry...consists in its truth, - truth conveyed to the understanding...circuitously by means of imaginative associations' (I. 134, 135).[11]

Despite the last discussion of truth, Macaulay generally puts intellect in a secondary position in his evaluation of literature, emotion first. For example, he admires Collier's didactic prose because it is the vehicle of an eloquence which comes from and goes to the heart. He judges Dumont's *Mirabeau* in terms of emotion. The work is admired because Dumont's unconscious self-portrait springs from the heart of the author. Outside literature, in the realm of morality Macaulay must admire Mirabeau because he came close to virtue through 'a sensibility...which sometimes amounted to sincere enthusiasm' (LV, July 1832, 575).

Elevating unalloyed emotion, Macaulay depresses satire. Just as Carlyle looks beyond humour for its essence, so does Macaulay with satire, believing that Addison's greatness as a satirist is due to his moral purity. This raises him above the level of Voltaire and Swift. Below their level Macaulay puts Horace Walpole, because he lacks passion and sincerity. For Macaulay, the very charm of Walpole's writing consists in 'the art of amusing without exciting'. Paradoxically, 'affectation is the essence of the man.... We are never sure that we see him as he was' (LVIII, Oct. 1833, 238-240). His wit is of the esoteric, fatiguing school of Cowley and Donne, which may be traced back to the 'coldness of sentiment' of the overingenious Petrarch (I. 81). Out of literature, in the world of politics Sir William Temple disappoints because of his lack of enthusiasm, his coldness and languor: at an important juncture he becomes 'merely a neutral' (LXVIII, Oct. 1838, 177).

Outside the *Edinburgh Review*, in the earlier review articles, the same condemnation of coldness and weakness, the same admiration of strength can be traced in both extra-literary and literary comments. Macaulay criticises the mercenary soldiers of renaissance Italy and the Greek orators alike on the same page for their lack of emotional involvement. He regrets that Quintilian and Cicero are more concerned with 'the grace of the attitude' than with 'the direction and vigour of the thrust' (I. 127). Finally, Dante is great because of 'the great powers of his imagination and the incomparable force of his style'. In the course of a few later lines Macaulay refers to Dante's 'energetic' expression, his 'strong' pictures, the

67

'force' of his diction (I. 54, 71). Thus strength, passion, genuineness and 'earnest' (I. 62, 65) sincerity are seen as characteristics of the literary genius by Macaulay as well as by Carlyle.

iii

For Macaulay, as for Carlyle, criticism and literature itself are but two human activities amongst many. Like his contemporary, he moves away from literature even in the essays of which it is the ostensible topic; only this movement does not have the fierily energetic character that it has with Carlyle. It is perhaps significant that in an early essay Macaulay finds Petrarch's genius of more importance than his works. In writing on Milton and Addison he moves from the mere literary works to the biography and character of the man of letters. He stresses the central importance of this character. Addison is admirable on account of his integrity, the blend in him of the gentlemanly virtues; in this he is unlike Johnson who unfortunately, indeed ludicrously, combines 'great powers with low prejudices' (LIV, Sep. 1831, 27), and also Walpole who is essentially unbalanced, his epicurean writings being the product of 'an unhealthy and disorganized mind' (LVIII, Oct. 1833, 227). On the same side as Addison, but greater than him, Milton admirably combines the roles of poet and man of affairs, as well as the virtues of both Puritan and Royalist sides. Here in 1825, in an article admired by Carlyle, we have the hero as poet and man of action sixteen years before the delivery of Carlyle's lectures on this topic.

Macaulay admires integrity not only in men of letters such as Addison and Milton. He writes of Machiavelli as author: 'The qualities of the active mind and the contemplative statesman appear to have been blended, in the mind of the writer, into a rare and exquisite harmony' (XLV, March 1827, 289). He writes similarly of Cromwell, bending the eulogy quite away from literature and in a patriotic direction: 'He possessed...that equally diffused intellectual health, which...has peculiarly characterised the great men of England' (XLVIII, Sep. 1828, 144f). In these men Macaulay admires the combination of moral virtues. The abominable character of Barère is yet aesthetically pleasing to him: 'In him the qualities which are the proper objects of hatred, and the qualities which are the proper objects of contempt, preserve an exquisite and absolute harmony' (LXXIX, April 1844, 276). The virtue of harmony is extended from the real to the ideal sphere when Macaulay pictures the historian in whose mind 'Powers, scarcely compatible with each other, must be tempered into an exquisite harmony' (XLVII, May 1828, 376). We finally move back into the literary field when he praises the portrayal of harmony as an achievement of the historian. All Mirabeau's 'opposite and seemingly inconsistent qualities are in [Dumont's] representation so blended together as to make up a harmonious and natural whole' (LV, July 1832, 574).

In the category of great men admired by Macaulay must be included Warren Hastings, though his crowning virtue is less integrity than a 'noble equanimity, tried by both extremes of fortune, and never disturbed by either' (LXXIV, Oct. 1841, 255). A similar stoical quality is almost the redeeming feature in Frederic the Great. Despite Frederic's perfidy and sadism, his unbalanced character, Macaulay admires him as soldier and administrator. Above all, he admires Frederic because the temper of his 'strong mind' is 'tried by both extremes of fortune' and endures the trial (LXXV, April 1842, 273).

Thus for Macaulay the outstanding characteristics of great men, including great writers, are harmony and equanimity. Below this class stand those who are defective in such virtues. For example, unlike that of Hampden and Somers, Pitt's is 'not a complete and well-proportioned greatness' (LVIII, Jany 1834, 509). Macaulay's judicious view of Hastings' opponent Burke is interestingly dynamic in this respect. He deeply admires Burke's sympathy for the people of India, and expresses this admiration through praise of his balanced mental qualities:

> In every part of those huge bales of Indian information which repelled almost all other readers, his mind, at once philosophical and poetical, found something to instruct or to delight. His reason analysed and digested those vast and shapeless masses; his imagination animated and coloured them.

However, in seeking to punish Hastings for his maltreatment of India Burke allowed the balance here observed to be upset:

> His imagination and his passions, once excited, hurried him beyond the bound of justice and good sense. His reason, powerful as it was, became the slave of feelings which it should have controlled.

Thus he is 'a great and good man, led into extravagance by a sensibility which domineered over all his faculties' (LXXIV, Oct. 1841, 232-234). As Macaulay writes in a later essay, 'through his whole life, his judgment was biassed by his passions' (LXXX, Oct. 1844, 575). This is the error not only of Burke but also of Pitt: 'As soon as he was brought face to face with royalty, his imagination and sensibility were too strong for his principles'. With regard to America, 'his passions overpowered his judgment' (The same, 580, 592). Macaulay also associates Pitt with theatricality, a special defect in the eyes of an observer (like Carlyle) whose criterion is sincerity, the seamless unity between the inner and the outer man.

The defect of Voltaire, like that of Burke and Pitt, is excessive sensibility, but his character is more radically unbalanced than theirs, for his 'wisdom and fortitude' are gravely out of proportion with 'the fertility of his intellect, and...the brilliancy of his wit', so much so that he achieves the unworthy distinction of being wittily named 'the very Vitruvius of ruin' (LXXV, April 1842, 248, 254). The defect of imbalance, perhaps a mere inclination in Burke and Pitt, is radical in the foreigners, both Voltaire and his patron Frederic the Great. Frederic's character is 'strangely compounded'; his 'ill regulated' mind Macaulay deplores at the same time as he is amused and amazed by it (The same, 275, 220). He hardly knows 'any instance of the strength and weakness of human nature so striking, and so grotesque, as the character of this haughty, vigilant, resolute, sagacious blue-stocking, half Mithridates and half Trissotin, bearing up against a world in arms, with an ounce of poison in one pocket and a quire of bad verses in the other!' (The same, 266).

Thus Macaulay appears to be essentially concerned less with writings than with authors, and perhaps less even with the events of history than with the characters of great men which they reveal and mould. The mental qualities which he admires in great writers as in great men of action are harmony, integrity and equinamity. A defect in these qualities is a defect in greatness.

iv

In their early review essays both Carlyle and Macaulay see history in general as progressive, though the smoothness of its movement is more evident to Macaulay than to Carlyle. At the same time, both writers sense a modern crisis, though the sensation is a stronger one in Carlyle. Macaulay declares in June 1829, 'What society wants is a new motive - not a new cant' (XLIX, 295). Like Carlyle he prefers to the cant of democracy and utilitarianism 'the energy of truly great rulers; of Elizabeth, for example, of Oliver, or of Frederick' (LXXIX, April 1844, 311). He contrasts the feeble French Chamber of Representatives babbling about 'the rights of man and the sovereignty of the people' with the brave and triumphant 'soldiers of Wellington and Blucher' (The same, 345).

Against the movement of history Carlyle is more confident than Macaulay that literature has a vital function to perform, both permanent and contemporary. He insists strongly, even directly in opposition to Macaulay, on the poet's independence of historical conditions. Macaulay declares in the essay on Dryden of January 1828 that not merely this poet, not merely the poet, but 'the man' is formed by his age (XLVII, 2). Carlyle believed that this essay showed that Macaulay$_2$ had 'no glimpse or forecast...of <u>true</u> Poetry'.[12] He refuted Macaulay's view in his own essay on Burns published at the end of the year, asking defiantly, 'Is not every genius an impossibility till he appears' (XLVIII, Dec. 1828, 279). For both critics, their contemporary Byron fails this vital test of poetic independence. They both take a view similarly grounded but more strongly negative of Scott, though Macaulay politely chose not to publish his.

For both critics, the true poet triumphs over circumstances because of the creative, indeed unconscious power within him. It is significant that these potent terms, creative and unconscious, are to be found not only in Carlyle, where we expect them, but also in Macaulay, who, for example, finds Dante unconscious of his own proper greatness. However, the power which he admires is of the surface, political, whereas that of Carlyle is penetrative, metaphysical, reaching beyond Macaulay's range. In Carlyle's words of 1832, Macaulay 'without divine idea...rests satisfied with being a Critic'.[13] In this he is akin to Jeffrey. Macaulay's range is shown incidentally in his private comments on his fellow contributor. After the appearance of 'Characteristics' in 1832, he writes scornfully: 'as to Carlyle, or Carlisle, or whatever his name may be, he might as well write in Irving's unknown tongue at once'.[14] He can write more tolerantly later, hoping to learn German on the way home from India, so as to be able to write 'reviews of German books more readable than Carlyle's used to be, if not so profound'.[15] The later observations of both men concerning one another are remarkable largely for their obtuseness.

Since both Carlyle and Macaulay as critics stress the sheer emotional power of literature, they share a disinclination to rank satire highly, and a similar disinclination with regard to critical laws. In this last they are moving away from the firm authoritarian position of Jeffrey. One cannot but feel that this undermining of their own position provides one reason for their abandoning it. However, neither of them sees the literary man in isolation. The critic is discarded, as he had been by Wordsworth, but his place is taken by the sympathetic, cooperative reader; and the man of letters writes for the public, in a society where the press is of great importance. The modern situation is a tempting but also a challenging one. The public is looking for moral leadership, and the man of letters is an important kind of leader; but what both Carlyle and Macaulay discover that they are interested in is not the literary qualities of leadership but leadership itself. Hence Macaulay's study of Milton is that of a many-faceted patriot, and Carlyle's essay on Burns is reshaped to become part of his series of lectures On Heroes and Hero-Worship. Both men admire Cromwell and use their literary skills to show with other more important things that literary skill is not essential to greatness. As men of letters they admire the man of action. This admiration appears eloquently in Milton's words in Macaulay's early dialogue between that poet and Cowley:

> I suspect that you are not free from the

> error common to studious and speculative men. Because Oliver was an ungraceful orator, and never said, either in public or private, any thing memorable, you will have it that he was of a mean capacity. Surely, this is unjust. Many men have been ignorant of letters, without wit, without eloquence, who yet had the wisdom to devise, and the courage to perform, that which they lacked language to explain. Such men often, in troubled times, have worked out the deliverance of nations and their own greatness, not by logic, not by rhetoric, but by wariness in success, by calmness in danger, by fierce and stubborn resolution in all adversity. The hearts of men are their books; events are their tutors; great actions are their eloquence; and such an one, in my judgment, was his late Highness, who, if none were to treat his name scornfully now, who shook not at the sound of it while he lived, would, by very few, be mentioned otherwise than with reverence. His own deeds shall avouch him for a great statesman, a great soldier, a true lover of his country, a merciful and generous conqueror (I. 117-118).

These lines, like passages in the early Carlyle, possess an eloquence of which Jeffrey was not capable. They show Macaulay, like Carlyle, not sharing in the compartmentalisation between literary and political activity which generally characterised Jeffrey's approach. However, it is remarkable that the developing literary concern with life and heroic action was accompanied by a certain lack of confidence in the man of letters and his writings themselves. Thus Macaulay and Carlyle led the readers of the _Edinburgh Review_ forward into the turbulence of the mid-Victorian cultural climate. Their bold manner belies an uneasiness of spirit.

NOTES

1. I discuss this in _Victorian Periodicals Newsletter_, no. 1 (January 1968), pp. 26-27.
2. _Letters_, ed. T. Pinney (6 vols, Cambridge University Press, Cambridge, 1974-81), vol. 1, p. 245.
3. In this part references beginning with

Roman numerals I and II are to Macaulay, *Miscellaneous Writings* (2 vols, Longman, London, 1860).

4. *Letters*, vol.4, p. 15.

5. *History of England*, ed. C.H. Firth (6 vols, Macmillan, London, 1913-15), vol. 5, p. 2525.

6. Macaulay's relation to this widespread view, and especially its articulation by Jeffrey, is discussed by Terry Otten, 'Macaulay's Secondhand Theory of Poetry,' SAQ, vol. 62 (1973), pp. 280-94. L.J. Starzyk, *Imprisoned Spendor* (Kennikat Press, London, 1977), p. 27, calls it 'Macaulay's law of inversion'.

7. *Letters*, vol. 3, pp. 342, 344.

8. David Alec Wilson, *Carlyle at his Zenith* (Kegan Paul, London, 1927), p. 83. 'Carlyle and Neuberg,' *Macmillan's Magazine*, vol. 50 (1884), p. 283.

9. G.O. Trevelyan, *Life and Letters of Lord Macaulay* (2 vols in one, Oxford University Press, Oxford, 1978), vol. 2, p. 139.

10. Francis Espinasse, *Literary Recollections*, p. 216.

11. Here on the indirectness of poetry's workings Macaulay belongs to a distinguished line, from Shelley through Mill to Frye.

12. *Collected Letters*, vol. 4, p. 362.

13. *Two Note Books*, pp. 236, 276.

14. *Letters*, vol. 2, p. 113.

15. The same, vol. 3, p. 196.

Chapter Two

QUARTERLY REVIEWERS

PART ONE. SCOTT

Scott's critical views are expressed in comments scattered throughout his voluminous work: in his editions of Dryden and Swift, his lives of the novelists, his reviews (many in the Quarterly), the introductions to his novels and poems, and casually and frequently throughout his letters and journals. Having gathered a number of these comments together, it is a difficult problem to analyse them. However, they can be separated according to primary relevance to author, style, subject and audience.

i

Scott views the author in three ways: as man of feeling, as conscious artist, and as responsive and responsible citizen. He agrees with Wordsworth that poetry is 'the spontaneous overflow of powerful feelings.' He declares, 'the only pleasure in writing is to write whatever comes readiest to the pen' (L. VIII, 190).[1] And he observes: 'He wrote from impulse never from effort and therefore I have always reckond Burns and Byron the most genuine poetical geniuses of my time' (J, 82).

On this basis Scott makes the Wordsworthian assertion that 'There is something about all the fine arts of soul and spirit which like the vital principle in Man defies the research of the most critical anatomist' (J, 4f). So he depicts as standing against the artist with his warm, spontaneously flowing feelings the cold, calculating, thoughtful critic, like Jeffrey in his 'theatre of Anatomy' (L. IV, 156), with such authors as Swift and Smollett in their anatomical moods. The distinction between emotional artist and reflective critic is elaborated upon and given personal form in Scott's comparison between David Hume the philosopher and John Home the dramatist:

> David Hume was no good judge of poetry; had little feeling for it; and examined it by the hackneyed rules of criticism; which, having crushed a hundred poets, will never...create...a single one. John Home's disposition was excursive and romantic - that of David, both from nature and habit, was subtle, sceptical; and he, far from being inclined to concede a temporary degree of faith to <u>la douce chimère</u>, was disposed to reason away even the realities which were subjected to his examination. The poet's imagination tends to throw a halo on the distant objects - the sophistry of the metaphysician shrouded them with a mist which...not only obscured but dwarfed their real dimensions. The one saw more, the other saw less, than was actually visible (MPW. XIX, 328).

Scott in general considers metaphysics to be a nut not worth the cracking, and moral philosophy a millstone. In his view literary criticism tends to betray their baneful influence.

The kind of literary critic Scott prefers would be untheoretic, sincere, careless, modest, generous, good-tempered, judicious, gentlemanly like himself in his own articles. As he writes of Lockhart, recommending him for the editorship of the <u>Quarterly Review</u>: 'He has a great stock both of c[l]assical and miscellaneous information a turn of composition as fluent as it is forcible and elegant, perfect good temper and the feelings of a gentleman which go far in my idea of a critic' (L. IX, 336).

Scott refers often to the lack of premeditation, the carelessness and the rapidity of his own creative writing. He describes his poems as 'the hasty production of [fortunate] impulses' (L. III, 344-345). He acknowledges that 'no man that wrote so much ever knew so little what he intended to do when he began to write' (L. IV, 292). He pens his novels in the '<u>hab nab at a venture</u> stile of compositions' (J. 433).

Thus Scott stresses his thoughtlessness as an author. Though in the area of emotion he allows for the softer feelings, he emphasises the buoyant militancy of the tone of his own poetry. He calls himself 'a soldier's lover' (L. V, 99). He looks forward to contributing to the <u>Minstrelsy</u> 'a kind of Romance of Border Chivalry in a Light Horseman sort of stanza' (L. XII, 231). Scott describes himself as writing poetry variously in a 'Cossack...blustering...dashing...swingeing...thumping' manner (L. III, 157, 176; IV, 388; VII, 438; XII, 349). He belongs to 'the Death-head Hussars of literature who neither <u>take</u> nor <u>give</u> criticism' (L. IV, 276). Finally, he declares robustly that 'if there be any thing good about my poetry, or prose either, it is a hurried frankness of composition which pleases soldiers sailors and young people of bold and active disposition' (J. 159).

Such enthusiasm takes a toll, and helps to colour Scott's picture of the writer in general. Involved in the 'feverish trade of poetry' (L. IV, 380), the writer pays for his 'ecstatic visions by the sad reality of a disordered pulse' (L. XI, 105). His 'variation of spirits' (L. XI, 117-118) brings him close to madness: Scott illustrates this in Ben Jonson, Boswell and Ritson. In Scott's view the writer is not only prone to ill health both physical and mental, but he is also marked by immaturity. Burns and Byron are the children 'of impulse and feeling' (MPW. XVII, 250), and 'Monk' Lewis is 'a child of high imagination' (Lockhart, <u>Memoirs of the Life of Sir Walter Scott</u> [Edinburgh, 1837-38], I, 293). It may be added that at one moment Scott reveals that his own life has been 'a phantasmogeria [sic] of grotesque imaginations' (L. V, 232). These views of the volatile character of the artist are like that put forward by Wordsworth in 'Resolution and Independence.' Their social implications will be discussed later.

In Scott's eyes the artist's fluctuating feelings and powerful imagination are restrained by other gifts which link him closely to the world around him. He possesses sympathetic insight into human psychology, situation and history, and the power of acute observation of external nature.

Scott shares the Jeffreyan position when he acknowledges that, as a social being, the artist's enthusiasm is tempered by his possessing the qualities of a gentleman: 'good sense, good taste, and good morals' (PW. XI, 13). The moral censor is constantly on guard as he writes; moreover, he writes prudently, in order to achieve a healthy and happy relationship with his public. Scott observes generally that 'every judicious author will use liberty with prudence' (MPW. VI. 312).[2]

Equally powerfully operative is the conscious artistic faculty of judgment, involving selection and discrimination among material and technique. Scott assures Maturin, of all people, that 'the redundancies of a powerful fancy can be brought within the rules of a more chastened taste' (L. XII, 338).

Thus Scott presents the writer as man of feeling - spontaneous, careless, buoyant, feverish, childlike - as against the critic. At the same time, the writer is a conscious artist and citizen, observant of the world and gentlemanly in his attitudes towards it. Here Scott seems to balance one with the other the views of Wordsworth his fellow poet and Jeffrey his fellow writer for the reviews.

ii

Scott's critical vocabulary as applied to style may be divided according to its closeness to his views of the writer as man of feeling and as conscious artist. From feelings springs the highly admired simplicity, ranging from 'true Ballad simplicity' (L. I, 161) to 'the simplicity of the true sublime' (Dryden. V, 92) in Milton and in Homer. With feeling also are associated freedom, wildness, originality, richness, intensity, warmth and softness (as against 'the French epopee, which of all styles of poetry is the most uniformly stiff and freezing' [Dryden. XIV, 141n]), sweetness and nervous strength (Campbell unites 'the sweetness of Goldsmith with the strength of Johnson' [MPW. XVII, 268]), and variety, like that of Burns and the 'terrific mixture' in Webster's Duchess of Malfi (L. II, 541).

Some of these values are of course capable of being artificially contrived. For example, Scott seeks variety in adapting Coleridge's 'mescolanza of measures' in 'Christabel' to 'The Lay of the Last Minstrel' (PW. VI, 24). Also, the originality of genius becomes Scott's own more and more painfully conscious quest after novelty in order to satisfy the insatiable fiction-reading public.

There is certainly an easy transition from emotional states to the artistic categories of the sublime and the pathetic which Scott uses and which he elevates at the expense of the satiric.

Satire itself is critical, and cannot be the product of the artist as man of feeling. However, Scott recognises the greatness of the kind as the product of the conscious artistry of Swift, Molière and Dryden. Thus it presents him with a major critical problem.

Scott points out at eloquent length that satire is potentially dangerously destructive.

> ...unless angels were to write satires, ridicule cannot be considered as the test of truth. The temptation to be witty is just so much the more resistless, that the author knows he will get no thanks for suppressing the jest which rises to his pen. As the public becomes used to this new and piquant fare, fresh characters must be sacrificed for its gratification. Recrimination adds commonly to the contest, and those who were at first ridiculed out of mere wantonness of wit, are soon persecuted for resenting the ill usage; until literature resembles an actual personal conflict, where the victory is borne away by the strongest and most savage, who deals the most desperate wounds with the least sympathy for the feeling of his adversary (MPW. VI, 250).

In the light of this view Scott objects strongly to personal satire, the 'mauvaise plaisanterie' of Boswell (L. XI, 117) and Blackwood's Magazine, though with Lockhart's Peter's Letters he looks forward to 'a volume of more respo[n]sible cast of which the characters ought to be manliness justice & generosity qualities which make praise worth having and censure dreaded' (L. VI, 89). In the same gentlemanly spirit he urges Lockhart to 'drill Hunt as he deserves [over his Byron] without descending to his own stile of Billingsgate' (L. X, 392).

Though Scott thus objects to the personality and the nihilistic tendency of satire, yet he is obliged to justify it as an essential part of the work of Swift, Molière and Dryden, which he greatly admires. He overcomes the major satirical problems presented by Gulliver's Travels by classifying it with Mary Shelley's Frankenstein as a romance, whose success follows from the author grounding on 'extraordinary postulates' (MPW. XVIII, 254) a logically coherent and psychologically convincing superstructure. Further, these works, unlike the German fantastic species of composition, extract from their 'extravagant fictions' 'philosophical reasoning and moral truth' (MPW. XVIII, 292). Scott also takes up the problem of <u>Gulliver's Travels</u> in his life of Swift. He admires the work greatly on account of its 'bold and irregular fictions...hardy and satirical morality...natural and minute narrative' (Swift. I, 342n). Thus satire is only one of its 'general attractions' (327); the fourth voyage is forcefully set on one side as being not only misanthropic but also improbable.

For Scott Molière's satire is legitimate because moral. He fights against vice and folly 'by means of wit and satire, without any assistance derived either from sublimity or pathos' (MPW. XVII, 206). He writes to the understanding, and belongs to a class of genius, not eccentric or enthusiastic, but possessing only more remarkably qualities which other men possess. This view is like that of Wordsworth put forward in the Preface to the <u>Lyrical Ballads</u>.

In discussing Dryden, Scott escapes from his critical dilemma over satire by appealing to 'honourable and just feeling' (Dryden. IX, 202), and to nature:

> In [the] skilful mixture of applause and blame lies the nicest art of satire. There must be an appearance of candour on the part of the poet, and just so much merit allowed, even to the object of his censure, as to make his picture natural (Dryden. I, 245).

Scott recognizes that Dryden, with Molière, satisfies the understanding and the fancy but not the heart. In spite of his own predilection towards the view of the artist as man of feeling, nevertheless for these qualities he places Dryden next to Shakespeare and Milton.

In this survey of Scott's views of satire we are moving from the man of feeling to the conscious artist. The same movement can be traced when he asserts such values as those of clarity, conciseness (of his own octosyllabics as against the heroic measure of Pope), polish, refinement (as against coarseness), and restraint. Moreover, the artist has to make a deliberate effort to achieve unity of effect, on which Scott especially insists in his comments on the drama and the novel. For example, in <u>Tom Jones</u> he admires 'The felicitous contrivance, and happy extrication of the story, where every incident tells upon and advances the catastrophe, while, at the same time, it illustrates the characters of those interested in its approach' (MPW. III, 104).

The writer needs a consciousness of more than one kind of art to achieve a musical harmony and a pictorial 'keeping' (MPW. III, 332) and chiaroscuro. The last is important: 'lights and shadows' are 'necessary to give effect to a fictitious narrative' (WN. VII, 6). Fielding 'painted life as it was, with all its shades, and more than all the lights which it occasionally exhibits, to relieve them' (MPW. III, 108). Contemplating Old Mortality Scott writes that 'there are noble subjects for narrative during that period full of the strongest light & shadow' (L. IV, 293), and he observes of Bulwer's Pelham, 'the light is easy and gentlemanlike the dark very grand & sombrous' (L. XI, 45). Still using the pictorial analogy, to the highly finished work of Richardson Scott prefers the sketches of Fielding, imaginatively suggestive as they are.

Scott is still in this area of conscious artistry when he refers to writing as ornament, sometimes as mere ornament. He admits that 'the majesty of history is...injured...by the ornaments of poetical fiction' (L. III, 234); in particular, 'the fate of [Nelson] is almost too grand in its native simplicity to be heightened by poetical imagery' (L. XII, 384).

A portion of Scott's critical vocabulary follows from his insistence on the importance of feeling. This insistence leads to a tension in his view of satire which he sees as potentially destructive of feeling and proceeding from the understanding rather than from the heart. Nevertheless, the satirical achievement in the work of Swift, Molière and Dryden is unassailable. From satire feeling is excluded, but in less debateable literary areas feeling accommodates itself to conscious artistic manipulation.

iii

Turning from author and style, Scott believes, with Jeffrey and Macaulay, that the subject of art is nature and human nature. The artist penetrates to the essence and grasps the distinctive in what he views. It is the hold on 'the minute and distinguishing features of truth' (WN. IV, 224) which Scott admires in Defoe and Richardson. This quality is discussed theoretically in relation to poetry: 'In order to produce a picturesque effect...a very intimate knowledge of the subject described is an essential requisite.' 'Circumstances' should be selected 'which, though individual and so trivial as to escape general observation, are precisely those which in poetry give life, spirit, and, above all, truth to the description.' Such circumstances are 'those natural touches of reality which ought to enliven and authenticate the poem' (L. XII, 383).

In line with this view of the artistic hold on reality, in history Scott admires 'old Pitscottie' because in his pages 'events are told with so much naiveté and even humour and such individuality as it were that it places the actors and scenes before the reader' (L. VIII, 48). Scott also admires Wenlocke's Restoration narrative because 'it lets you at once into all the minute and domestic concerns of a period so interesting' (L. VII, 68). The distinctiveness which Scott admires is not only one of history, but also of '<u>locality</u>' (L. I, 146) and nationality. This last is a basis for his praise of Maria Edgeworth and Fielding. The interests indicated in this paragraph place Scott in his view of history as a precursor of Carlyle and Macaulay.

In Scott's view artistic veracity implies morality: 'an accurate picture of human nature... can never be truly presented, without conveying a lesson of instruction' (Dryden. XIV, 134n). Scott is equally opposed to overt didacticism, though deviating from subject to style, when he insists 'that the direct and obvious moral to be deduced from a fictitious narrative, is of much less consequence to the public, than the mode in which the story is treated in the course of its details' (MPW. III, 35). Here he anticipates Shelley's and Macaulay's view that poetry teaches indirectly.

iv

Naturally turning in the direction of his audience, as Jeffrey would, Scott sees a basic community of interest between the literary genius and the society to which he belongs, both actual and ideal. As he publicly urges upon Byron:

> Nature, when she created man a social being, gave him the capacity of drawing that happiness from his relations with the rest of his race, which he is doomed to seek in vain in his own bosom. These relations cannot be the source of happiness to us if we despise or hate the kind with whom it is their office to unite us more closely. If the earth be a den of fools and knaves, from whom the man of genius differs by the more mercurial and exalted character of his intellect, it is natural that he should look down with pitiless scorn on creatures so inferior. But if, as we believe, each man, in his own degree possesses a portion of the etherial flame, however smothered by unfavourable circumstances, it is or should be enough to secure the most mean from the scorn of genius, as well as from the oppression of power, and such being the case, the relations which we hold with society, through all their gradations, are channels through which the better affections of the loftiest may, without degradation, extend themselves to the lowest (MPW. XVII, 359-360).

In Scott's eyes the present system of relationship works so perfectly that he can only think of two distinguished men of letters in difficult circumstances: these are Coleridge and Maturin. In arguing (unsuccessfully) against the establishment of a Royal Society of Literature Scott aligns men of letter such as himself with the polite world as against mere academic pedants:

> few men who have acquired some reputation in literature would chuse to enroll themselves with the obscure pedants of universities... most respectable doubtless and useful in their own way - excellent judges of an obscure passage in a Greek author - understanding perhaps the value of a bottle of old port -connoisseurs in tobacco and not wholly ignorant of the mystery of punch making but certainly a sort of persons whom I for one would never wish to sit with as assessors of the fine arts....to one who has lived all his life with gentlemen and men of the world to mingle his voice with men who have lived entirely out of the world and whose opinions must be founded on principles so different

from our own would be no very pleasing situation (L. VI, 400).

As this passage suggests, Scott himself prefers 'the conversation of men of the work-day world to the allspice society that is made up of authors critics and admirers' (L. VIII, 26). He writes facetiously of 'playing at ladies and gentlemen a game to which I have been partial all my life' (L. IX, 500). And he believes that Johnson showed bad taste in leaping 'over the little differences and courtesies which form the turnpike gates in society, and which fly open on payment of a trifling tribute' (L. XI, 115). Moreover, knowledge of the world was an advantage from the merely literary point of view which Fielding and Smollett possessed over the secluded Clara Reeve, learned in books alone. Here Scott is firmly on the sociable side with Jeffrey as against the eccentric Carlyle. He also piquantly reveals himself as the denizen of a world anterior to that of the university and authors' organisations as the strongholds of culture, later looked forward to with some enthusiasm by both Carlyle and Mill.

With such a comfortable, old-fashioned view of the place of the man of letters in society Scott can easily scorn the judgment of the hostile critic and the exclusive clique: 'Nothing is more valueless than the opinion of literary people of London coteries although it is unnecessary to tell them so' (L. IX, 290). The rider here is indicative of Scott's social caution. He also relies on the sympathetic interest of the individual reader and on the approbation of the judicious few. Scott's reader plays an active role, in the willing suspension of disbelief, to use Coleridge's phrase, and in imaginative involvement with what the artist presents: 'It is often in the slight and almost imperceptible touches that the hand of the master is shewn, and that a single spark, struck from his fancy, lightens with a long train of illumination that of the reader' (<u>Quarterly Review</u>, XVI, Oct. 1816, 183). Scott says that he would be content to please one such responsive reader. Like Wordsworth, he 'would rather please one man of feeling and genius than all the great critics in the kingdom' (L. IV, 28). He gives this view classical authority when he asserts, 'Lauderi per virum laudatum is indeed a greater treat than the applause of numbers can afford' (L. XII, 217). Finally, turning away from self, 'it is impossible that a man of Lord Byrons genius should not often feel the want of that which he has forfeited the fair esteem of those by whom genius most naturally desires to be admired and cherished' (L. IV, 203).

In spite of the exclusive movement of these last few quotations, Scott, in accordance with his view of the basic harmony between the man of letters and his society, himself generously wants to please all its members. He writes for Jeffrey's 'general class of readers' (WN. IV, 386). With Croker in his <u>Battle of Talavera</u> as well as with Pope he appeals to 'the general feelings of mankind' (L.XII, 404), as against 'the high-flying critics' (L. XII, 319).

In this catholic spirit Scott appreciates qualities in all the segments which make up society, particularly as they comprise the audience of the theatre. 'The better ranks' make an important contribution because of the refining influence which they bring (L. XII, 317). The 'middle classes' unquestionably provide 'the most valuable part of an audience; because, with a certain degree of cultivation, they unite an unhackneyed energy of feeling' (Dryden. IV, 230). Though Scott does not seem to admire the contemporary plebs, he looks back regretfully to the popular audiences of the past which came to the theatre not to criticise, but to admire. He looks back to the unique good taste of the Greek audience, mingled with its enthusiasm and religious awe. And he looks back to the 'rough and manly spirits' of 'the good old time,' the audience of the Elizabethan popular theatre, which 'came prepared with a tribute of tears and laughter, to bursts of pathos, or effusions of humour' (Dryden. IV, 229-230).

The aim of the modern writer is to please not only himself, as Scott does, but also the public, as Scott hopes to do. It is often <u>merely</u> to please, to satisfy the public's imperious demand for novelty. After all, the novel itself is 'a mere elegance, a luxury contrived for the...gratification of that half love of literature, which pervades all ranks in an advanced stage of society' (MPW. III, 108). Scott avers that 'it is better to be slatternly than tedious' (L. III, 205), and he quotes approvingly, 'tout genre est permis hors le genre ennuyant' (L. V, 61).

This view of the artist as entertainer has an important corollary in the view of the artist's own occupation. His work should be an entertainment to himself as well as to the public. Scott frequently recommends literature as an agreable diversion from the real business of life, as a 'respectable amusement' (L. IV, 491). Literature 'can only be gracefully executed as an occasional avocation' (L. IV, 204-205). For example, 'in a clergyman literary talent is always graceful' (L. IV, 467). With such an opinion Scott elaborately cautions a distant correspondent

> against an enthusiasm which, while it argues an excellent disposition and a feeling heart, requires to be watched and restrained, tho' not repressed. It is apt, if too much indulged, to engender a fastidious contempt for the ordinary business of the world, and gradually to unfit us for the exercise of the useful and domestic virtues, which depend greatly on our not exalting our feelings above the temper of well-ordered and well-educated society. No good man can ever be happy when he is unfit for the career of simple and commonplace duty, and I need not add how many melancholy instances there are of extravagance and profligacy being resorted to, under pretence of contempt for the common rules of life (L. II, 278).

In Byron especially 'It is a cruel pity that such high talents should have been joined to a mind so wayward and incapable of seeking content where alone it is to be found in the quiet discharge of domestic duties and filling up in peace and affection his station in society' (L. IV, 203).

Among Scott's poetic contemporaries, the acknowledged eccentricity of Wordsworth is reconcileable with his being 'a fine manly high principled man' (L. III, 468), that is, a gentleman. On the other hand, the eccentricity of Byron led him away from the possiblity of achieving historical distinction as a man of action, in the direction of the pathological extravagance of Hoffman, the insanity of a Rousseau or a Shelley.

Thus for the modern author literature is ideally a pastime rather than a maddening preoccupation. He entertains both himself and the public. Yet as well as entertaining he provides solacement and a momentary escape from the ills of human existence. His object is to 'alleviate for a time the more unquiet feelings of the mind' (J.

87). In this spirit Scott writes of the 'delightful dreams' of the theatregoer (MPW. VI, 306), 'the magic illusions of romance' (MPW. III, 322) and 'the seducing mazes of fictitious narrative' (MPW. III, 2). Late in life he himself wishes that he could 'wander back through the mazes of Mrs. Radcliffes romances' (L. XI, 406), and he enjoys 'the sleeping-waking kind of thing,' that is, The Tempest and A Midsummer Night's Dream (L. IX, 403).

The aim of the author is thus to please and soothe. At the same time, he has a moral responsibility and power. Though sceptical of 'the omnipotence of literary talent' (MPW. III, 453), Scott sees with Wordsworth that 'the vulgar must be taught what they are to admire' (L. III, 177).

Scott pays a good deal of attention to Dryden as a great author in the social context. He sees him not as the creature of his age, nor as an aloof genius like Milton, but, with Shakespeare, as involved in a process of interaction: 'he alternately influenced and stooped to the national taste of the day' (Dryden. I, 4). Like Scott himself, he 'professedly lived to please his own age' (190); from a hostile point of view, he 'sacrificed to the Belial or Asmodeus of the age' (499). The improvement of general manners which took place with the Revolution of 1688 coincided with an improvement in Dryden's own taste. Nevertheless, Scott suggests that the inferior elements in Dryden's work, for example, his coarseness, like that of Swift, can be attributed to the age, whereas his outstanding contribution was through his 'regenerating taste' (41). In this way he was - almost religiously - 'a light to his people' (526).

Scott felt that specific cultural benefits flowed not only from the work of Dryden but also from Swift who, like all great writers, brought forward the improvement of the language. Benefits in society at large resulted from the general reaction to the social criticism of Johnson in Scotland. Scott felt that Basil Hall might make a similar contribution in what he wrote concerning America, and that Maria Edgeworth had given humanity and dignity to the image of the Irish. He emulated her in behalf of his own countrymen in Waverley. Scott's first novel is thus an epitome of his critical attitudes, being intended as expressive of feeling, historically descriptive, entertaining, and socially corrective.

Like Jeffrey, Scott sees an essential harmony between author and society. Like Wordsworth, he dismisses the hostile critic and the unfriendly coterie in favour of the involved reader and the judicious friend. But, on the theoretical ground of the essential harmony, Scott wishes to please them all; and in the wake of this desire he constructs an imaginary audience to which all classes make a valuable contribution. The author pleases himself and his audience: he soothes their cares. At the same time, he exerts a genial moral influence, so that in a sense the unpretentious Scott anticipates Shelley's proud claim that 'Poets are the unacknowledged legislators of the world.' Scott's own assertion, however, is a diffuse one, expressed obliquely not only through his novels and poetry, but also through his miscellaneous criticism, including articles in the reviews.

NOTES

1. The following abbreviations are used in the parenthetical references throughout the part: Dryden, for Dryden, Works, ed. Scott (8 vols, Miller, London, 1808); J, for Scott, Journal, ed. W.E.K. Anderson (Clarendon Press, Oxford, 1972); L, for Scott, Letters, ed. H.J.C. Grierson (12 vols, Constable, London, 1932-37); MPW, for Scott, Miscellaneous Prose Works (30 vols, Cadell, Edinburgh, 1834-71); PW, for Scott, Poetical Works (12 vols, Cadell, Edinburgh, 1833-34); Swift, for Swift, ed. Scott, 2nd edn (19 vols, Constable, Edinburgh, 1824); WN, for Scott, Waverley Novels (12 vols, Cadell, Edinburgh, 1842-47).

2. This is a quotation from a contribution to the Encyclopdia Britannica. It is noteworthy that James Mill, Jeffrey, Hazlitt and Macaulay also at different times contributed to the Encyclopedia.

PART TWO. SOUTHEY AND POETRY

Both George Saintsbury and René Wellek have noticed a failure on the part of scholars to come to terms with the criticism of Robert Southey.[1] It is the opinion of the writer that this gap has only been partially filled by Jean Raimond in his comprehensive study of the poet (1968). Raimond is sympathetic to Southey on the whole, but he surveys his criticism without enthusiasm.[2] In his view, Southey is at fault for insisting on the primacy of moral values, and he lacks the genial insights which constitute the true critic.

The present discussion is based on a survey of Southey's published writings and directs its attention to his notions of poetry in general and modern English literary history in particular. A comprehensive view emerges which shows a stress not only on poetic morality but also on poetic feeling and purity of expression. In this, as Raimond has indicated, Southey aligns himself with the movement of his time dominated by Wordsworth. Like Wordsworth and Coleridge, Southey rejects the Augustan heroic couplet in favour of blank verse, belonging to an older English tradition, and in favour of his own experimental forms. When he looks at the history of modern English poetry, Southey again sees it with eyes like those of Wordsworth and Coleridge, a view which came to be shared even by their opponent Jeffrey. For Southey, the cultural greatness embodied poetically in Chaucer, Spenser, Shakespeare, and Milton was dealt a severe blow by the Puritan revolution and the Cavalier reaction. Dryden and Pope are poets of the second rank, as Macaulay was to agree later, their work badly marred. However, an upward movement in national morality, culture, and poetry took place, rising through Cowper to Wordsworth, whom Southey admires, without Coleridge's qualifications, as standing on an eminence beside the great poets of the past. As he looks around him and to the future, Southey sees this order threatened by the immorality, excess of feeling, and technical elaboration in the poetry of Byron and his followers.

I would now like to elaborate on these views of poetry in general and of English literary history in particular, with quotations which show Southey's characteristic lucidity, vigor and

89

vividness of expression. These qualities have been admired by critics from Southey's contemporary Hazlitt to Herbert Read in the modern age. Here Southey can be seen to be setting up a defence for the Wordsworthian view of poetry, to a large extent through his prolific contributions to the Quarterly Review.

i

For Southey poetry is 'the highest effort of the human mind' (QR, XII, Oct. 1814, 60).[3] He believes that the poet needs to possess a combination of powers, like Coleridge, who unites 'the strongest genius, the clearest judgment, the best heart' (Life, I, 210). Looking back to the great figures of the past, he sees that Shakespeare and Milton unite 'moral dignity and...intellectual strength,' and Spenser comprehensively manifests 'perpetual harmony, pure thoughts, delightful imagery, and tender feeling' (QR, I, May 1809, 283; XII, Oct. 1814, 73).

For Southey emotional enthusiasm is important in the poet. His own poem on Robert Emmet published in the Norwich Isis was 'written quite to disburthen my heart, & with an agitation that shook me like an ague fit.'[4] On the other hand, on the evidence of Gebir he regrets in Landor 'always an ambition to be philosophising, always the effort of thought, never the flow of feeling or the flush of passion' (AR, I, [1802], 665).

Emotion is a quality especially marked as a hopeful fault in the young poet. Southey himself looks back to 'those days when I thought of nothing but poetry, and lived, as it were, in an atmosphere of nitrous oxyd - in a state of perpetual excitement, which yet produced no exhaustion' (NL, I, 534). More soberly, he remembers that

> in boyhood and in youth I dreamt of poetry alone; and I suppose it is the course of nature, that the ardour which this pursuit requires should diminish as we advance in life. In youth we delight in strong emotions, to be agitated and inflamed with hope, and we weep at tragedy. In maturer life we have no tears to spare; it is more delightful to have our judgment exercised than our feelings. (Life, IV, 192)

In the light of this development it is unfortunate that 'thought and labour will not produce poetry' (Life, III, 219). However, a negative consolation emerges in the consideration of the poet as a being too sensitive. Southey makes this point in a letter to Landor: 'There is an evil, too, in seeing all things like a poet; circumstances which would glide over a healthier mind sink into mine; every thing comes to me with its whole force, - the full meaning of a look, a gesture, a child's imperfect speech, I can perceive, and cannot help perceiving; and thus am I made to remember what I would give the world to forget' (Life, III, 229). The same observation receives a remarkably stronger emotional and moral colouring a decade later, when Southey writes to C.H. Townshend:

> If there be any evil connected with poetry, it is that it tends to make us too little masters of ourselves, and counteracts that stoicism, or necessary habit of self-control, of which all of us must sometimes stand in need. I do not mean as to our actions, for there is no danger that a man of good principles should ever feel his inclination and his duty altogether at variance. But as to our feelings....We stand in need of all that fortitude can do for us in this changeful world; and the tears are running down my cheeks when I tell you so. (Life, IV, 242-243)

Thus one has to beware of the excess into which enthusiasm might lead. Indeed, Southey believes that in some contemporary poets, Landor and Coleridge, Blake, Byron, and Shelley, it has led to madness, metaphorical and literal. He has even felt a dangerous tendency of this kind in himself. As he explains to Landor:

> You wonder that I can think of two poems at once; it proceeds from weakness, not from strength. I could not stand the continuous excitement which you have gone through in your tragedy: in me it would not work itself off in tears; the tears would flow while in the act of composition, and would leave behind a throbbing head and a whole system in the highest state of nervous excitability, which would soon induce disease in one of its

most fearful forms. (Life, III, 300)

Southey argues thus to Caroline Bowles in insisting on the need for 'happier themes.'[5] Such themes are needed for the sake of the author as well as for that of the aging reader: 'I am arrived at that age when men like to be spared from as many painful feelings as possible; - in our youth we love to shed tears over fictitious sorrows, - as we grow older we have none to spare for them, and find too much cause for melancholy thoughts ever to have them willingly excited.'[6] In his insistence on the painless emotionality of poetry Southey is at one with many of his contemporaries, from Wordsworth on the one side, to Jeffrey and Macaulay on the other.

There is another side of poetry, from the author's own point of view, which he can set against its psychological and moral dangers. The poet writes for self-expression and ideally for the elevation of his own character. Late in life, Southey advises a young aspirant that poetry 'may be made the surest means, next to religion, of soothing the mind, and elevating it. You may embody in it your best thoughts and your wisest feelings, and in so doing discipline and strengthen them' (Life, VI, 329). He agrees with Henry Mackenzie that writing poetry is, 'at least, one of the noblest amusements. Our philanthropy is almost always increased by it' (QR, XLVII, March 1832, 92).

With regard to a source of inspiration outside the heart of the poet himself, Southey agrees with Wordsworth, 'Nature is a much better guide than antiquity' (Life, I, 176). However, much is to be gained by studying and emulating the great masters in one's own language, Shakespeare, Spenser, and Milton, for the good poet passionately admires the great.

Moving from poetry in relation to the poet and its sources in other poets and in nature, one can next consider it as it is in itself. Southey's ideal in this respect is summarized in the triads which he appropriately introduces at the beginning of Madoc:

> Three things must be avoided in Poetry; the frivolous, the obscure, and the superfluous. The three excellencies of Poetry; simplicity of language, simplicity of subject, and simplicity of invention.

> The three indispensable purities of Poetry;
> pure truth, pure language, and pure manners.
> Three things should all Poetry be; thoroughly
> erudite, thoroughly animated, and thoroughly
> natural. (PW. V [xxii])

Writing personally, Southey declares for the same ideals of simplicity and purity, as opposed to the poetic practice of Landor: 'I will swear, and I can prove out of my Homer and my Bible and my old ballads and Romances, that the finest passages in poetry are always and uniformly so plain and perspicuous that you catch their full force and meaning immediately.'[7]

For Southey poetry is primarily emotional in character. This is again a typical attitude of his generation. One must still move from the emotional to the moral, or rather the emotional must itself be of a moral character. Southey agrees with Scott, Shelley and Keats that 'there is no species of poetry so absurd as the didactic,'[8] and he asserts that 'It is by the habit of mind which it induces, that poetry of any kind is morally beneficial; not by inculcating any ethic aphorism' (AR, IV [1805], 631). His own purpose has been 'to diffuse through my poems a sense of the beautiful and good...rather than to aim at the exemplification of any particular moral precept' (Life, III, 351).

Turning directly to the effect of poetry on the reader, Southey agrees with Dennis that poetry is an art 'by which a poet excites passion in order to satisfy and improve, to delight and reform the mind, and so to make mankind happier and better' (QR, XII, Oct. 1814, 89). He believes that 'the best purposes of poetry' are 'soothing the heart and elevating and purifying its desires' (QR, XXXV, Jany 1827, 194). Indeed, 'The most gratifying reward that an author can receive, is to know that his writings have strengthened the weak, established the wavering, given comfort to the afflicted, and obtained the approbation of the wise and the good' (QR, XLI, Nov. 1829, 295).

Southey ponderously elaborates on the beneficence of poetry to both poet and reader in his Colloquies with Sir Thomas More. He ends this discussion on a striking note:

> it is in verse that the most consummate skill
> in composition is to be looked for, and all
> the artifice of language displayed, yet it is

in verse only that we throw off the yoke of the world, and are as it were privileged to utter our deepest and holiest feelings....we express in it, and receive in it sentiments for which, were it not for this permitted medium, the usages of the world would neither allow utterance nor acceptance. And who can tell in our heart-chilling and heart-hardening society, how much more selfish, how much more debased, how much worse we should have been, in all moral and intellectual respects, had it not been for the unnoticed and unsuspected influence of this preservative?[9]

The tone here is both ponderous and restrained, but the same important and individual view is expressed more colloquially in a private letter: 'nothing is so wholesome for the heart as to express its feelings in verse (the only way in which we <u>dare</u> express its best feelings), if this be done from its own free and pure impulse, but when the desire of applause becomes the prime motive, few things tend more surely to injure the moral character.'[10] The allusions to freedom here offer both the poet and the reader, the critic and his reviewer, a possibility of advance beyond narrow and severe moral and didactic considerations.

Thus for Southey poetry is expressive of feelings, largely moralized. His main stylistic criteria therefore are those of Wordsworth in the Preface to <u>Lyrical Ballads</u>, perspicuity and plainness, the degree to which the feelings freely flow through the style. This does not mean that Southey is unable or unwilling to make an effort to achieve an understanding of the poet's meaning despite his rugged style, for he makes this effort for the sake of Landor.

Southey is also able to consider style not merely as instrumental in conveying meaning, but also as ornamental. Moreover, ease of communication is the result partly of careful craftsmanship, correctness, and polish. In particular, Southey considers versification to be an art to be acquired; and in accordance with this view he pays special attention to the contrasting values of different verse forms, especially blank verse, rhyme, the heroic couplet, and the hexameter.

Southey asserts the purity of his own style in a letter of 1814:

> My mature style aims at nothing but to express in pure English what I have to say: and I profess nothing but to avoid the barbarisms and nonsense which have so long past current in verse. Briefly the subject being such as seems good to me, and the manner of treating it my own, I endeavour to write in such English as would bear the assay of Q. Elizabeths mint, and it is in this, and in this only, that the resemblance between my poetry and Wordsworths exists. Whether we write well or ill in other respects, all that we write is English, and this cannot be said of Scott, Ld Byron, Campbell, etc. etc. It may be good for nothing, but it is not <u>bad</u> in itself; the sense may be worthless, but it is not <u>nonsense</u>. (NL, II, 105)

Urging young John Heraud to read Dante, he writes, 'It is a chaste and severe style which you should study.'[11] Southey regrets the lack of perspicuity in the language of Landor which puts him below the level of Milton and Shakespeare; however, he himself is able to persevere in the rereading of <u>Gebir</u> 'till the meaning flashed upon' him (NL, I, 546).

Southey makes a transition between the consideration of style as instrumental in conveying meaning and as ornamental in a discussion of <u>The Curse of Kehama</u>: 'Where there is either passion or power, the plainer and more straightforward the language can be made the better.' On the other hand, a poem cannot be all passion and power, and in the unimpassioned parts, 'It gains by rhyme, which is to passages of no inherent merit what rouge and candle-light are to ordinary faces. Merely ornamental parts, also, are aided by it, as foil sets off paste' (<u>Life</u>, III, 44). This is an exaggerated application to rhyme of a point of view from which Wordsworth had considered metre. Southey is concerned with ornamenting his own poetry in other ways than with rhyme. For example, he describes himself as sprinkling <u>Madoc</u> with similes, but he warns Ebenezer Elliot against the dangers in this, reminding him of the more general painterly virtues of 'breadth and keeping...lights and shades' (<u>Life</u>, IV, 335, 336).

Southey often stresses that poetry is partly a craft to be learned, especially its versification: 'though the capability of becoming a poet is the gift of nature, the art of poetry requires no ordinary pains.'[12] With regard to versification, 'though the knack...is a gift, the art is an acquirement' (Life, III, 277).

Examining specific verse forms, Southey objects on both patriotic and aesthetic grounds to 'the detestable French heroic couplet, which epigrammatizes every thing' (PW, IV, 71), and to 'French blank verse' with its 'tame and slavish rhymes' (CR, IX [1806], 204, 205). He turns with a similar revulsion from 'the old tragic rhyme...rejected since the days of Dryden' (CR, 203-204). Indeed he considers

> of all measures the heroic couplet...the most unsuitable for narration [since] it continually seduces the writer to commit sins against good sense and good English. He aims at pointing his meaning instead of bringing it distinctly out, gets into all the tricks of antithesis and when he should be thinking and feeling, passes off a sort of way-jolt[13] of words both upon himself and his readers. Our poetry owes half its barbarisms to this metre. (NL, II, 13)

Against 'the regular Jew's-harp twing-twang, of what has been foolishly called heroic measure' (PW, IV, xvi) Southey sets his own experimental, ornamental, even wild style in Thalaba and The Curse of Kehama, and the 'richness, variety, and strength' of the hexameter of The Vision of Judgement (PW, X, 195). However, the traditional and the stoutest opposition to the heroic couplet comes from 'the regular blank verse; the noblest measure, in my judgement, of which our admirable language is capable' (PW, IV, xv). 'What is excellent in itself is best in blank verse, but everything below the excellence borrows something from rhyme.'[14]

Thus Southey has shown himself to possess an elevated and comprehensive view of the poet and his work, stressing its emotionality and moral value. He has insisted on purity of style. In the particular field of versification, he has rejected the heroic couplet in favour of his own experimental forms and the traditional blank verse. In all this he is an efficient spokesman of the critical and creative movement of his era which was led by Wordsworth. As a poet himself, he is more explicit about the challenges of versification than most reviewers.

Like Wordsworth and Coleridge, Southey views the modern English literary tradition largely in terms of a poetic development. In his survey of English literary history he goes back to Chaucer; then he moves forward to the 'golden age' of the Elizabethans (CR, XXV [1799], 41) with its great stars Spenser and Shakespeare, and then through the early years of the seventeenth century in which Milton shone. He deplores the influence of the Puritan rebellion followed by the Restoration, and feels that from that low point an advance has only been slowly made, coming up through Cowper to Wordsworth in the modern age. Concerning his own period Southey is in two minds. He admires the civility achieved in the era since Cowper, but he senses a failing away again both in manners and in the poetic style which so closely reflects them. This degenerative tendency is most striking and offensive in the writings of the new generation of Byron and what Southey calls the 'Satanic school' (PW, X, 206).

Southey considers Chaucer to be the founder of English poetry. He possesses the 'life strength and vivacity of original genius,'[15] having 'stampt for immortality...the English tongue.'[16] These views are elaborated on in <u>Specimens of the Later English Poets</u> (1807):

> he had an eye and an ear, for all the sights and sounds of nature; humour to display human follies, and feeling to understand, and to delineate human passions. As a painter of manners, he is accurate as Richardson; as a painter of character, true to the life and spirit, as Hogarth. (I, xvii)

In versification Chaucer became 'the model of succeeding Poets' because he found and trod a middle path: 'Avoiding the harshness and obscurity of alliterative rhythm on the one hand, and on the other the frequent recurrence and intricate intertexture of rhymes which are found in some of the romances; he preferred forms less rude than the one, less artificial than the other; less difficult, and therefore more favourable to perspicuity than either.'[17] Southey further extends his view of Chaucer in <u>Select Works of the British Poets</u> (1831): 'Shakespeare alone has equalled him in variety and versatility of genius - retaining what was popular, and rejecting what was barbarous, he at once refined and enriched [the language];...his ear led him to that cadence and those forms of verse, which...have been found most agreeable to the general taste, and may, therefore, be deemed best adapted to the character of our speech' (p.1).

Southey admires in general the 'elder simplicity and beauty and strength' to be found in English literature,[18] and he looks back in greatest admiration to the Elizabethan age. In particular, it was a great age for the drama, with its unsurpassable blank verse.

Southey's advice to poetic aspirants is always to read the great works of that age. For example, he tells Heraud to read 'our best old poets, above all others Shakespeare, Milton, Spenser,' adding that Wordsworth is the only contemporary to be reckoned with these.[19] He advises C.H. Townshend to 'Study our early poets.... You cannot read the best writers of Elizabeth's age too often. Do you love Spenser? I have him in my heart of hearts!' (Life, IV, 152). In particular, Southey admires the 'delightful' Spenser's fine ear and 'pure mind' (AR, IV, [1805], 545, 555). He is 'the great master of English versification,' and 'our great English master of narrative' (QR, XII, Oct. 1814, 72; Life, III, 266). Among poets less generally admired today, Southey praises the language of Daniel 'as easy and natural as it is pure' and, moving further into the seventeenth century, Cotton as 'one of the last poets, whose vein of language runs pure'.[20]

Though Milton's Paradise Lost is the only great poem in English, as Southey tells Landor, he believes that this does not reflect credit on Milton's age, since the great work of that time was written by men out of tune with it. According to Southey, putting forward a view which becomes general later, the decline of English poetry set in with the Puritan rebellion and spread deeply with the introduction of the superficial French culture at the Restoration. He declares: 'During the civil wars intolerance has produced cant and hypocrisy; a total depravity succeeded the Restoration; and poetry shared in the degradation of thought, feeling, manners, and principle' (QR, XII, Oct. 1814, 81-82). And figuratively,

> The period between Milton and Pope may be called the dark age of English poetry....

> Under Elizabeth our poetry was like a mountain brook, rough indeed and broken, but delighting the traveller with whatever is great, magnificent and sublime. After the Restoration it was the stream that passes by a city and receives its filth. (CR, XXV [1799], 41)

The villains of the piece were Dryden and Pope. The former prostituted his admitted powers in the service of self and the gratification of the public taste. Southey expresses this view sternly in the 'Life of Cowper': Dryden 'seems to have been the first eminent author in this country who practised literature as a profession, and regarding it exclusively as such, gave up his mind to temporary subjects, and contented himself with obtaining immediate profit by the easiest means.'[21] This was in a way close to Southey's own practice, but it was the opposite of the ideal which he shared with Wordsworth: the pursuit of literature for the sake of the values which it incorporates, and for the sake of inward gratification and the applause of a select few now and in the future. Writing to William Taylor, Southey anticipates Macaulay in listing Dryden 'at the head of our second-rate writers,' gravely flawed as he was by 'moral imbecility,' being 'the pimp and pander' of his age.[22]

Southey feels that a purification of English poetry took place with Pope, but this was only partial. Unfortunately, the taste which that poet introduced, 'was calculated rather to make mediocrity tolerable than to produce excellence' (CR, XXV [1799], 41). In particular, Southey agrees with Coleridge that Pope's translation of Homer had a bad effect, because of its constant inclination to unnatural ornament and exaggeration. Through the eighteenth century Pope's bad influence extended down to 'the brocade fashion' of the 'meretricious' Darwin (PW, V, xviii; AR, III [1804], 492).

Fortunately, a moral and hence necessarily cultural and poetic revival took place, developing in the second half of the eighteenth century. In fact, until the emergence of such reprobates as Byron, 'For more than half a century English literature has been distinguished by its moral purity, - the effect, and, in its turn, the cause of an improvement in national manners' (<u>Life</u>, V, 343). Thus Southey manages to believe in both progress and the tradition, and to associate poetry with both: a comprehensive conservative view hardly available to the Whigs of the Edinburgh Review. However, as a conservative he is more confident about the past than the future. The poetic aspect of improvement Southey traces from Thomson, through Akenside, Gray, Mason, the Wartons, Young, and Glover, through Percy to Cowper. As he writes in the Critical Review:

> We were sinking to the tame and tiresome regularity of French poetry; the stream began to stagnate like a Dutch canal. Young, Thomson, and Akenside, rose to excellence.... The Wartons led us back to a better school. The pupils of that school are now the candidates for fame....the school of Pope has had its day; a taste has been introduced for the rude but more vigorous effusions of our ancestors. (XXV [1799], 42, 40)

In particular, Thomson 'recalled the nation to the study of nature.'[23] In an interesting Hellenic revival,

> Glover imitated the Greeks; Gilbert West began a school half Greek, half Gothick, which was followed by Mason, Gray, and Warton, and is to be traced in Akenside and Collins.
> Meantime the growing taste for Shakespeare gradually brought our old writers into notice. Warton aided in this good work, which was forwarded more effectually by the publication of the Reliques of Ancient Poetry, the great literary epocha of the present reign.[24]

When he looks at the contemporary poetic scene Southey can see an improvement which puts it only below the age of Shakespeare. To support this view he names Cowper, Burns, Bowles, Montgomery, Joanna Baillie, Scott, Wordsworth, and himself. Above all Southey praises Wordsworth as the equal of Milton; he is 'the great moral and philosophical poet of the age' (QR, XXIII, July 1820, 584), 'the greatest of our living poets.'[25] In particular, Southey identifies himself with Wordsworth's protest in the Preface to the Lyrical Ballads against the barbarization of the language since the days of Pope.

100

However, when he looks out over the contemporary scene in general, the older Southey is not sanguine. Grateful himself to be able to enjoy the company of Wordsworth, he observes in 1819 that 'Morbid feelings, atrocious principles, exaggerated characters, and instances of monstrous and disgusting horror, make up the fashionable compound...slavered over with a froth of philosophy.'[26] In poetry Southey is most offended by the tendency which he comes to identify with Byron and what in his indignation he calls the 'Satanic school.' These men have 'rebelled against the holiest ordinances of human society' (PW, X, 205). Their aim is to disturb the 'moral perceptions,' to present 'wickedness in an attractive form,' to excite 'sympathy with guilt, and admiration for villainy.'[27] There is a moral fervour in Southey's protests against the Byronic school which had been lacking in Jeffrey's sneers at the Lakists.

Looking at the style of poetry in particular, Southey can trace a decline from the time of Milton: 'We have had froth and flummery imposed upon us, - contortions of language that passed for poetry because they were not prose, and phrases that have been admired by faith, never being designed to be understood.'[28] Southey not only sees impurity of morality, taste, and style in the present, which he can trace back in the past, but he also foresees a stylistic decline in the future: 'as our poetry in Cowley's day was overrun with conceits of thought, it is likely in the next generation to be overflown with...exuberance of feeling' (Life, IV, 302). 'Our successors,' he advises Scott,

> are falling into the same faults as the Roman poets after the Augustan age, and the Italians after the golden season of their poetry. They are overlabouring their productions, and overloading them with ornament, so that all parts are equally prominent, everywhere glare and glitter, and no keeping and no repose. (Life, IV, 338)

For example, Southey criticizes Keats for 'the exuberance of his ornaments.'[29]

Southey's admiration in his own English literary tradition of Chaucer, Spenser, Shakespeare, Milton, and Wordsworth is classical, but it is a pity that the rhythm of which he feels that they are exponents debars him from the appreciation of Donne, Dryden, and Pope. Significantly, he sees literary history not only in terms of these great individual figures, but also in relation to social movements. There is a vital connection between poetry on the one hand, and, on the othe, the upheaval of the Puritan revolution and the Restoration of a Frenchified court. The revival of manners and poetry proceeds together through the eighteenth century, leading in poetry to Cowper and Wordsworth. However, Southey sees a threat to the precariously achieved moral and poetic order through the dangerous aberrations of the genius of Byron and Shelley. Thus his complex schematic view of English social and poetic history leaves him as a spectator of a rich culture poised for radical developments through the later nineteenth century. Jeffrey, less moralistic, has seen the threat as posed by Wordsworth and Southey himself, but perhaps with Southey one senses a unique concern for the ongoing movement of English poetry, however inaccurate his judgment might have been.

In his comments on the general nature of the poet Southey has shown his appreciation of the need for comprehensive genius. However, his own demands concentrate on the need for feeling and morality combined. It is significant that he stresses the combination of the two, and also that he recognizes the dangers, both psychological and aesthetic, of too great a stress on feeling alone. Southey is sensitive to the psychology of the poet, but he has none of the intense philosophic interest in it of his greater contemporaries, Wordsworth, Coleridge, and Shelley. Poetry itself Southey regards as a transparent medium for the expression of the elevated and moralized emotion of the writer. On this ground he strongly criticizes the diction and technique of poetry since Dryden, but he also recognizes the need for poetic craftsmanship, and he makes a notable contribution to metrical debate. Thus for his insights into poetic technique, for his high estimation of the poetic calling, and for his lively appreciation of the development of his own literary culture, Southey's claims as a critic deserve to be recognized. It takes digging among the dusty pages of his collected works and of the magazines to discover their profile.

NOTES

1. Saintsbury, History of Criticism (3 vols, Blackwood, Edinburgh, 1900-04), vol. 3, p. 234n; Wellek, History of Modern Criticism...The Romantic Age (Yale University Press, New Haven, 1955), p. 381.
2. Jean Raimond, Robert Southey (Didier, Paris, 1968), pp. 387-401.
3. The following abbreviations are used in parentheses in the text: AR for Annual Review; CR for Critical Review; QR for Quarterly Review; PW for Southey, Poetical Works (10 vols, Longman, London, 1838); Life for Southey, Life and Correspondence, ed. C.C. Southey, 2nd edn (6 vols, Longman, London, 1849-50); NL for Southey, New Letters (2 vols, Columbia University Press, New York, 1965), ed. K. Curry.
4. Southey, Letters to John May, ed. C. Ramos (Pemberton Press, Austin, Texas, 1976), p. 84.
5. Southey, Correspondence with Caroline Bowles, ed. E. Dowden (Longman, London, 1881), p. 25.
6. A Wiltshire Parson and His Friends, ed. G. Greever (Constable, London, 1926), p. 152.
7. H.S. Scott, "Some Southey Letters," Atlantic Monthly, vol. 89 (1902), pp. 39-40.
8. Southey, Omniana (2 vols, Longman, London, 1812), vol. 2, p. 155.
9. Southey, Sir Thomas More, 2nd edn (2 vols, Murray, London, 1831), vol. 2, p. 306.
10. Southey, Selections from the Letters, ed. J. W. Warter (4 vols, Longman, London, 1856), vol. 4, p. 229.
11. Edith Heraud, Memoirs of John A. Heraud (Redway, London, 1898), p. 24.
12. William Cowper, Works, ed. Southey (15 vols, Baldwin and Craddock, London, 1835-37), vol. 1, p. 92.
13. Thomas Wright, Dictionary of Obsolete and Provincial English (2 vols, Bohn, London, 1857), gives "See-saw, Berks."
14. Southey, Selections, vol. 2, p. 166.
15. Select Works of the British Poets, ed. Southey (Longman, London, 1831), p. 1.
16. Byrth, Life and Actes of Kyng Arthur, ed. Southey (2 vols, Longman, London, 1817), vol. 1, p. i.
17. Specimens of the Later English Poets (3 vols, Longman, London, 1807), vol. 1, p. xv.
18. Southey, Selections, vol. 4, p. 362.

19. *Memoirs of John A. Heraud*, p. 22.
20. *Select Works of the British Poets*, p. 572; *Selections*, vol. 3, p. 486.
21. Cowper, *Works*, vol. 2, p. 133.
22. *Memoir of the Life and Writings of the Late Wm Taylor*. ed. J.W. Robberds (2 vols, Murray, London, 1843), vol. 1, pp. 513, 518.
23. *Specimens*, vol. 1, pp. xxxi-xxxii.
24. The same, vol. i, p. xxxii.
25. "Two Unpublished Letters by Robert Southey," *English Studies*, vol. 26, (1944), p. 8.
26. *Selections*, vol. 3, p. 135.
27. *Sir Thomas More*, vol. 2, p. 309.
28. *Memoir of Wm Taylor*, vol. 1, p. 461.
29. *Memoirs of John A. Heraud*, p. 26.

PART THREE. SOUTHEY AND PROSE

I have above presented Southey's position as critic of poetry. Now I would like to present in a similar way his views of prose, particularly historical writing and literary criticism, two areas in which he himself was very active. His comments on philosophy and satire are glanced at in passing. The comments show an interest in literature as extensive as those of his contemporaries already discussed.

Southey was highly ambitious not only as a poet, but also as a historian. He intended to present the historical truth about certain important nations, truth of quotidian fact as well as of spirit. At the same time, he does not aspire to a philosophy of history, since speculation and theory are a matter of indifference, and even of hostility, to him. The hostility occurs in his views of the adjacent intellectual spheres of satire and literary criticism. Southey deplores the spoiling tactics of the satirist, as he is troubled by the presumptuous intervention of the critic between poet and reader. Thus he himself plays the roles of historian and poet, but he excludes the speculative intellect in the shape of philosopher, satirist and critic. However, he thinks about history and literature himself, though not in an elaborately sustained way. In particular, he has to acknowledge the humbler, contributory role that a critic may play.

In these attitudes, as we have seen, Southey is not alone among his contemporaries. The spirit of systematic philosophy is alien to many of them. With Wordsworth especially Southey shares a distrust of the 'meddling intellect,' particularly that of the critic of the periodicals. In the age of Pope, satire and poetry had been synonymous; to Southey and to many of his fellow poets they are antithetical. Finally, with his positive stress on the importance of history, understood both morally and in vivid concrete detail, Southey stands beside Scott, Carlyle and Macaulay.

In his comments on historical writing Southey considers first himself as historian, then the subject and style of history, and its aims. As he grows older, Southey like Lamb comes to love the past in preference to the distracted present. He prefers the quiet dignified conversation of the dead to the irritating squabbles of the passing day. Moreover, for him the passion of historical writing itself is vindicated as a passion for truth, and this naturally brings with it moral and spiritual qualities. For example, the History of Brazil is 'an honest [book], with that pervading life and soul which nothing but free opinions and the love of God and man can give.'[1]

Southey may be somewhat egoistic in considering his historical work as a 'great Pyramid,'[2] but he sees with Carlyle and Macaulay that there is a real gap to be filled in British historiography. Ambitiously he aligns himself with such older writers as Froissart, Geoffrey of Monmouth, Holinshed and Milton, as against the eighteenth-century Hume who does not show the men of the past as they actually were. Southey's attack on recent historical writing is most fully developed when he asserts that the modern historian has overlooked 'everything that enlivens and distinguishes,' together with 'the accidents which give the varieties of colour and beauty' (AR, III, 1804, 190).

Southey moves from the easily accepted assertion that history is based on truth of fact to the claim that history presents moral truth. He declares that the study of history teaches more successfully than poetry: its great lesson is forbearance of judgment. Further, he keenly hopes that his own historical work possesses prophetic power: 'No man has ever taken more interest than I have done in looking back into the history of the human race, or in looking forward to their amelioration, and collecting the light of the past as in the focus of a mirror, to fling it before me that I may see into the future.' (NL, II. 53).

Moral and factual truth can best be communicated in history by a simple style. For this subject Southey puts forward a stylistic triad like that which he elsewhere proposes for writing in general: 'Say what you have to say as perspicuously as possible, as briefly as possible, and as rememberably as possible, and take no other thought about it.' However, he continues, 'Omit none of those little circumstances which give life to narration, and bring old manners, old feelings, and old times before your eyes.'[3] Here there is a glimpse of the demand for a particular revelation of humanity which Carlyle made and satisfied so strikingly himself. Southey glancingly anticipates Carlyle when he writes of the old chronicles: 'A good monk illuminates his own convent only for the honour and glory of the order; but we see what is passing by, by the light. There is a sort of sportsman pleasure in this startling information.'[4] Thus, as well as insisting on the communication of truth through a perspicuous style, Southey welcomes the observation of historical detail and allows for some idiosyncrasy of manner.

Southey's concern with historical values plainly stated unfortunately accompanies a more than insular prejudice against philosophy, ranging from teasing metaphysics, 'a foul weed that poisons whatever it clings to,' to 'experimental philosophy' which 'always deadens the feelings' (NL, I, 261; Life, II, 156). In particular, political economy is for Southey as for Carlyle 'the worst kind of Metaphysics;' it dives 'like an eel, into the mud of metaphysical metapolitics.'[5] Historically, Southey's objection ranges down from Plato and the 'frigid maxims' of Aristotle (Life, I. 166), through Locke and Bentham, to Coleridge and Shelley. The last 'fell in metaphysics, and as is usual for metaphysicians his next step was to fall in atheism' (NL, II, 20).

Southey's anti-intellectual bias, more pronounced than that of Scott, turned him not only against philosophy in general, but also against satire and literary criticism, particularly in the form of contemporary reviews whose authors had what he called 'the malice of a satirist, and the enmity of a critic' (QR, XII, Oct. 1814, 65). However, it is worth noting that a dubiousness about the nature of satire and a hostility to criticism were feelings shared by many of Southey's contemporaries. Satire might have its value, but it was a dangerous medium both for the reader and for the writer himself. This was the warning which Scott gave his son-in-law Lockhart. Southey wrote later in life that satire based on principles might make a valuable contribution at the present time, but that it was hardly worth the cost to the mental ease of the writer himself. He rejoiced that he had overcome his own leaning towards satire, but he felt that he was justified in unleashing a bolt against the delinquent Byron.

Southey thus provides next to no room for the philosopher or the satirist. He also excludes, like Wordsworth, the practising literary critic. He believes, for instance, that Bowles's poems 'won their way' through being 'treasured up in the memory of young readers, repeated in company by lovers of poetry, and imitated by young poets.' Neglected by the reviewers, the 'beautiful imagery, the natural feeling, with which they abound, had found their way to the heart of those for whom poetry is written' (AR, IV, 1805, 568). As a young poet himself, Southey assured Humphry Davy that he wished to be judged by 'an equal reader... one whose knowledge and taste is commensurate with mine...or else one who pretends not to criticise, but will surrender his feelings to me.'[6]

With such Wordsworthian views of a romantic intimacy between writer and reader, excluding the critic, it is understandable that Southey should consider criticism in general as an 'epidemic disease.'[7] He prefers the healthy response of pure feeling. In this spirit he communicates a cautionary anecdote to Anna Seward: 'Surely nothing was ever more calculated to deaden & dwarf the mind than that fashion of breeding up all persons to be critics! Did you ever see Dr. Aikin's letters to a young lady upon a <u>course of poetry</u>, as if it were a course of physic....in these letters the Doctor says to his daughter, "Make yourself mistress of the <u>Paradise Lost</u>." This book fell into Thomas Erskine's hands - when he came to this passage he repeated the words "Make yourself mistress of the <u>Paradise Lost</u>," & with a wholesome malediction upon the author,...he whisked the unhappy volume behind the fire.'[8] This passage shows Southey like Scott in his response to the professionalism of the study of literature as clearly living in a pre-modern age.

Southey heartily disapproves of 'the prevailing fashion of criticism, the direct tendency of which is to call bad passions into...play' (<u>Life</u>, V, 15). This situation has its ironical aspect, since he himself was a life-long reviewer. However, like Wordsworth and Coleridge, he writes strongly on this topic: 'I look upon the invention of reviews to be the worst injury which literature has received since its revival. People formerly took up a book to learn from it, and with a feeling of respectful thankfulness to the man who had spent years in acquiring that knowledge, which he communicates to them in a few hours; now they only look for faults. Every body is a critic, that is, every reader imagines himself superior to the author, and reads his book that he may censure it, not that he may improve by it' (<u>Life</u>, II, 276f). Southey makes a striking application of this general view in discussing contemporary books of travel. He believes that modern criticism has deterred 'plain men from relating a plain tale. Since the influence of reviews has been so considerable, we have no longer such writers as Atkyns, Wafer, and Dampier....instead of the straightforward language of our excellent navigators, descriptions taken on the spot, and feelings fresh from the circumstance, we have a tale at second hand, rounded off in the smooth periods of a fashionable essayist' (AR, III, 1804, 659).

In spite of these statements, Southey's attitude toward reviewing is not entirely negative, for as a committed periodical writer himself he is aware of an ideal alternative to the prevailing mode, and he feels that his own work approaches it. He declares: 'I myself object to the whole tendency of Reviews, - the only way of lessening the evil which they do is to write for them with scrupulous conscientiousness, with a disposition to befriend the author in question rather than to injure him, and to recognise that he is likely to know more about his subject than the casual reviewer.'[9] He writes later that the Quarterly especially needs 'a humaner tone than it has been wont to observe.' He believes that 'a great deal of good may be done by conciliating young writers who are going wrong,' and he claims that 'Keats might have been won' in this way.[10] In brief, reviewing in general ought to be 'merely analytical, or according to any fair and written canons of criticism.'[11]

Though himself a full-time reviewer, Southey prefers not to handle contemporary literature. In the spirit of Lamb and Hazlitt, he would 'much rather be industriously and thankfully reading old books, than detecting the defects the vices of new ones' (Life, V, 208). He does not review modern literature, he explains, 'because I would never criticize a living writer so as to wound his feelings or injure his fortunes, unless there was a strong moral motive.'[12] When he does review, Southey claims to be not only morally upright, but also earnest and sincere, as well as warm and generous.

Southey's prose ideal is truth of subject matter and the plain style in presenting it. He applies this ideal in his view of history, and he strives to achieve it in his own historical writing, though he does allow for various dimensions of truth, for the need to bring to life the details which constitute historical fact, and for the idiosyncracy of a great style. Southey's prose ideal is akin to that of Wordsworth for poetry. His historical ideal anticipates the theory and practice of Carlyle. Unfortunately, his values are less philosophical than those of Wordsworth and Carlyle. No philosopher, he denigrates the systematic intellect and its particular literary weapons of satire and criticism.

Like Wordsworth and Coleridge, Southey significantly prefers a direct relation between writer and reader, without the arrogant self-interpolation of the fault-finding periodical critic. Thus he opposes the tendency of much contemporary reviewing, but as a reviewer himself he sets against it an ideal of sympathy and fairness and his own generally genial practice. As a critic, Southey occupied a middle ground, even more modestly than Scott. They helped create the catholic and balanced tradition on which the later men of letters of the nineteenth century could fruitfully draw.

NOTES

1. Memoirs of the Life and Writings of the late Wm Taylor, vol. 2, p. 232.
2. Journals of a Residence in Portugal, ed. Cabral (Clarendon Press, Oxford, 1960), p. 87.
3. Selections, vol. 2, p. 157.
4. The same, vol. 1, pp. 198-199.
5. Letter to C.W. Williams-Wynn, 5 June 1836, National Library of Wales. Selections, vol. 4, p. 101.
6. Humphry Davy, Fragmentary Remains, ed. J. Davy (Churchill, London, 1858), p. 35.
7. John Jones, Attempts in Verse, ed. Southey (Murray, London, 1831), p. 35.
8. Alfred Morrison, Catalogue of the Collection of Autograph Letters, 1st series (13 vols. Strangeways, London, 1883-97). vol. 6, p. 162.
9. 'Some Early Nineteenth-Century Letters hitherto Unpublished,' ed. L.N. Broughton, in Nineteenth-Century Studies, ed. H. Davis (Cornell University Press, Ithaca, 1940), p. 76.
10. W. Braekman, 'Letters by Robert Southey to Sir John Taylor Coleridge,' Studia Germanica Gandensia, vol. 6 (1964), pp. 149-150.
11. Memoirs of Wm Taylor, vol. 1, p. 384.
12. Memoirs of John A. Heraud, p. 39.

PART FOUR. CROKER

John Wilson Croker lived from 1780 to 1857. Born in Ireland, he was educated at Trinity College, Dublin. He was Member of Parliament from 1806 until the passing of the Reform Bill in 1832 when he gave up an active political career. He held the post of Secretary of the Admiralty from 1809 until 1830. In his second career as a journalist, Croker was a mainstay of the Tory <u>Quarterly Review</u> from 1809 until his death, particularly as an exponent of governmental politics. He also contributed as an historian, attracted to the courtly life of the last century-and-a-half in England and the memoirs which it produced, as well as the similar aristocratic phenomenon in France which came to an abrupt end with the Revolution. He edited volumes of eighteenth-century memoirs and letters, and his own papers constitute an important historical document. He also accumulated a significant body of materials on the French Revolution. He possessed an austere ideal of historiography, yet like Mill he lacked the creative verve, such as Carlyle possessed, to mold these materials into a full-scale account.[1]

Croker was also interested in the arts and their social value.[2] As far as the main currents of literature were concerned, he looked abroad to the contemporary French drama and novel with fascination and abhorrence. In English literature, he looked back with admiration to the master-work of Shakespeare. Scott, a fellow contributor to the <u>Quarterly</u>, admired and edited the work of Dryden and Swift. Croker had a similar ambition with regard to Pope and Boswell. He admired greatly the classicism and the polished satire of Pope, and he prepared materials for an edition which were subsequently used by Elwin. Croker also admired Johnson, and he produced the edition of Boswell which, though mauled by Macaulay in the <u>Edinburgh</u>, included much additional scholarly material. His work provided the foundation for the modern edition of G.B. Hill. Looking at the literature of his own day, Croker admired Crabbe, Scott and Byron. However, he is remembered for the stridency of his negative critical judgments of other contemporaries in the pages of the <u>Quarterly Review</u>. His conservatism was shocked by the radicalism of Lady Morgan and of Leigh Hunt, and

111

the incipiency of such a philosophy in the poetry of Keats and Tennyson. He made a futile attempt to demolish them in a frantic endeavor to serve the interests of the <u>Quarterly</u> and of the Establishment.

In the pages that follow I hope to indicate the broad nature of Croker's attitudes towards poetry, the novel, history and memoir-writing, as well as their moral and political underpinnings and the techniques which he adopted in putting them across. The criticism of poetry gets the least attention, as being the best known and the least well-founded.

Croker's Toryism and puritanism have an old-fashioned quality, but at the same time they are aroused most strongly in his critical articles in defence of contemporary manners and institutions and against subversive contemporary developments. The moral severity which he expresses has a long tradition behind it, but he invokes it particularly in defence of two values very characteristic of the nineteenth century, the innocence of woman and the sanctity of private life. Moreover, in dealing with these subjects Croker betrays an ambivalence characteristic of the period, or which indeed we tend to associate rather with the Victorians. He is actually more of a Victorian than the reviewers so far discussed, since, though born in 1780, he lived until 1857 and continued contributing to the <u>Quarterly Review</u> until the end of his life.

At a more elemental level, Croker defends what he values in literature against Pope's foe, stupidity, as it manifests itself in the incomprehensible, the incoherent, the ignorant, the dull, and the insipid. He also attacks the presumptuous and the egotistic, like John Galt foolishly setting himself up against Shakespeare (XI, April 1814, 37), Leigh Hunt laying down new canons of poetry and criticism (XIV, January 1816, 474), and Mme. D'Arblay showing 'the most horse-leech egotism that literature or Bedlam has yet exhibited' (LXX, June 1842, 251). Croker, like Pope, also attacks the mannered, the pompous, the inflated, and the false.

Croker is afraid that the virtue of the reader, especially that of the feminine and the young reader, is in peril. In 1836 he declares emphatically: 'she who <u>dares to read a single page</u> of the hundred thousand <u>licentious</u> pages with which the last five years have inundated society, is <u>lost for ever</u>' (LVI, April, 108). The danger is <u>even</u>

greater and more grotesque in the confrontation of two people in real life, for the presentation of the Socialist Robert Owen at Court poses a threat 'to the unsuspecting purity of a Virgin Queen' (LXV, December 1839, 305).

Croker is equally fearful that the 'security of private life' is threatened (LXXV, March 1845, 464), in particular by a tradition of intimate writing that goes back to Boswell's 'Journey with Dr. Johnson to the Hebrides.' On this ground he regrets the publication of the prayers of Johnson, as well as of the life of Benjamin Robert Haydon (XCIII, September 1853, 583n., 559). The threat to privacy must be diminished, as far as the severity of the written word can achieve this. Thus Croker, like Southey, his fellow Tory and Quarterly Reviewer, advocates censorship, either direct or indirect. He deplores the obscenity of Pope, Swift, and 'even Addison'; and he regrets the unbowdlerized publication of the works of Charles Hanbury Williams (XXVIII, October 1822, 49).

Croker feels that he must defend the citadel of Tory England against demoralised Frenchmen abroad and subversive Whigs and Liberals at home. Thus his critical posture is a defensive one. He delivers heavy blows in order to protect the values which he holds dear. He also feels the need to justify such severity, particularly in later years. For example, he writes concerning Walpole's Memoirs: 'If any reader should be inclined to think that we assign too much importance to this detection and exposure, we beg leave to remind him that...Walpole is likely at first sight to obtain a confidence which he in no degree merits, and that his pertinacious efforts to poison history require that at each successive attempt the antidote should be administered' (LXXVII, March 1846, 274).

Croker's Tory bias can be observed in most of his reviews. His animosity is aroused not only by the ultra-Liberal man of letters such as Hunt and Shelley, and, by association, Keats and later Tennyson, but also by his Parliamentary opponent, the Whig Macaulay. The threat posed by such men as Hunt is, of course, magnified in the light of contemporary events in France, but it is a political threat in only one of its aspects. It is even more dangerous morally and religiously. Such men, in Croker's view, are followers not of Christ, but of Lucretius and Epicurus (XVIII, January 1818,

327).

It is noteworthy that Croker's attack on Keats (XIX, April 1818) is preceded by onslaughts on Leigh Hunt, with a note directed against Shelley (XVIII, January 1818, 327), though this last is probably not by the author of the article himself. The attack on Keats is only incidental to a whole barrage directed about this time not merely by Croker, but also by other <u>Quarterly Reviewers</u>, against the body of what he calls 'ignorant scribblers and...exasperated jacobins' (XVIII, October 1817, 229). Besides the writers already named, these include Hazlitt. Croker considers Keats merely as a 'neophyte' in the faith of which Hunt is 'hierophant' (XIX, April 1818, 208, 204). Similarly, fifteen years later, Tennyson is presented as merely a follower of Keats (XLIX, April 1833, 81).

In Croker's criticism moralism, jingoism and Toryism go together with literary values which are asserted less explosively. Thus, he is grateful that English good taste and sense have discovered the golden mean between the extremes of classical and romantic which so perplex the French (LI, March 1834, 179). This literary evaluation parallels Croker's idealistic view of England politically, at least until the Reform Bill of 1832. Negatively, he attacks Keats and Hunt not merely for their supposed religious and political views, but also, more tolerably, for their innovations in versification and poetic diction.

Croker's literary values can be seen most pleasantly in his early treatments of fiction, particularly the work of Maria Edgeworth and Scott. He admires Edgeworth's novels because they combine the general with the individual, and 'the varieties of human character into one action' (VII, June 1812, 331). He praises such a combination of values later in George Croly, the author of <u>Paris: A Poem</u>, since he exhibits 'a union of piety and poetry, of what is right in politics, respectable in morals, correct in taste, and splendid in imagination' (XVII, April 1817, 229). Edgeworth's work is, moreover, probable, as well as moving and elevating. With his contemporaries Croker stresses the importance of feeling, and with him as with them it is feeling delimited by considerations of religion and morality. He emphasises the importance of feeling even in wit, and he deplores its absence from the heartless, misanthropic writings of Voltaire, Swift, and

Walpole (LXXII, September 1843, 539). The acceptable didactic element Croker admires in the fiction of Edgeworth, as he deplores its absence from Fielding and Smollett, not to mention Sterne with his 'obscure and filthy sensualities' (LIII, February 1835, 53). On the other hand, Croker later is unable to tolerate the didacticism of Charles Kingsley and 'the Socialist school' (LXXXIX, September 1851, 527).

Croker tackles the novel again in July 1814, inspired by the appearance of Waverley. The speculative slant of these early reviews is perhaps less innate than an attempt to emulate a similar feature in Jeffrey's contributions to the Edinburgh Review. In 1814 Croker presents a pocket history of the novel which he sees as progressing from the level of the ideal to that of the general, represented by the admired LeSage and Fielding, and to that of the individual, represented by Edgeworth and Scott. In these last down-to-earth writers there is less evidence of moral elevation, but the didactic element is happily still strong.

Croker admires realism in the novel, as in pictorial art, but this is realism tempered by the important considerations already noted. Unadulterated fidelity to the fact is to be deplored as morally dangerous. Only a short step separates the 'disgusting' accuracy of Godwin's Mandeville (XVIII, October 1817, 177) from the fantastic insanity of his daughter's Frankenstein (XVIII, January 1818, 382). This is comparable to the later attitude of Abraham Hayward in the Quarterly, where he objects to the excessive realism of Dickens's prison scenes in Pickwick as being out of place in 'books of this sort.' Hayward generalizes: 'When the object is merely to soften or agitate, the ideal should greatly preponderate over the actual' (LIX, October 1837, 512-13).

On anti-realistic grounds Croker regrets Scott's attempt to combine history with romance in Waverley. In reviewing The Antiquary in April 1816, he declares the attempt to have been a failure. Moreover, the combination is undesirable, not only for the sake of achieving the appropriate fictional aura, but also from the standpoint of general morality. Further, the combination takes away from the dignity and truthfulness of history itself. Croker thinks of history very austerely, carefully distinguishing, for example, between the quality of Walpole's letters and that of his memoirs: 'the gossip and scandal, which in a familiar letter are not merely tolerated, but, as it were, expected and welcomed, are grievous offences against good taste as well as good faith when it is attempted to array them in the grave and responsible character of history' (LXXVII, December 1845, 253). Thus, in dealing with memoirs the historian must work as carefully as a judge in a court of law: 'Walpole is like any other prejudiced witness: though there may be a predominance of falsehood and a general discolouration, there will yet be, in a long and varied narration, a considerable portion of voluntary or involuntary truth. The art of using such a witness to advantage is a minute study of the admitted facts - a general balancing of the antagonist testimonies, and a conscientious sifting of the evidence in each minute portion of the case, so as finally to discriminate between the real colour of the transaction and the partial colour of the narrative.' Croker's image of himself here as a judge is characteristic of the quarterly reviewer, but he develops the image in an attractive and unusual aesthetic direction, as he continues: 'It ought to be something like restoring an old picture which has been painted over: you must wash off the whole varnish, and then proceed with great care and caution to remove the suppositious touches from the original ground' (LXXVII, December 1845, 275). Similarly, Croker would examine such a work as Macaulay's in order 'to discover, to analyze, to decompose the anecdotal colouring...and to separate the general course of events from the exceptive instances which the anecdotical historians build so much upon.'[3] From such an austere, craftsmanlike point of view Croker criticises other historians as well.

All these comments can be read as subordinate to his grand attack on Macaulay on account of his <u>literary</u> approach, following in the footsteps of Scott (LXXXIV, March 1849, 551), relying too heavily on flashy rhetoric and insubstantial anecdote. The critic's attitude, which possesses the aesthetic quality already remarked, is vividly summarized in a letter written before reading and reviewing Macaulay's work:

> I should like to distinguish History properly so called, from history moralized or dramatized as by Shakespeare and Scott, or made anecdotical like, as I presume from the

extracts, Macaulay's. History should be a
statue, cold, colourless, if you will, but
giving the limbs and features, the forms and
the dimensions with unalterable, severe mechanical exactness; and not a picture to be
coloured to the artist's eye, to be seen in a
particular light, and to be helped out with
accessories of detail selected not for truth
but for effect. I admit that such pictorial
history is more amusing; but does it really
give you a truer view of the state of things?
I doubt - and I can quite understand your eye
being relieved in turning from the gaudy
gaslight of Macaulay to the soberer taper of
Mr. Grote. (Brightfield, pp. 370-71)[4]

Though he aspires to be the judge of good
history-writing, Croker is more at ease with the
memoirs of the eighteenth century, particularly
those of Horace Walpole. There is some ambivalence here. He lavishes eight articles on an
author whom he declares to be cold, heartless,
insincere, vain, selfish, misanthropic, sarcastic,
unamiable, and irreligious. The explicit justification for the interest in Walpole is to be found
not only in his historical importance, but also in
the qualities of his letters. These, though cold
and betraying a search for effect rather than the
truth, are at their best when witty and full of
gossip, and when gleams of good sense and feeling
shine through. Above all, Croker praises Walpole's
letters on stylistic grounds, admiring their epi-
grammatic and metaphoric cast (LXXXIII, June 1848,
124).

The problem of fascination and repulsion,
latent and manageable where Walpole and the
eighteenth century are concerned, comes to the
fore in connection with modern, and particularly
French, literature. Croker writes of Béranger:
'We confess that we feel some hesitation and difficulty in risking to offend the morals and the
taste of our readers, by alluding to the indecency
and impiety of the original passages...but such an
exposure is, we think, necessary to an understanding of the state of the public mind in France'
(XLVI, January 1832, 464).

Croker is especially fascinated by modern
French novels: 'We have upon our table before us
upwards of one hundred novels of this class published within the last five years...and there is
not in that number half a dozen...in which a lapse

of female chastity is not the main incident; there are not ten in which that lapse is not adulterous; - in not a few it is accompanied by incest and other unnatural profligacies; and in a majority it is attended by suicide and murder.' In these novels there are 'passages which swarm in every page, but which we trembled and shuddered to read, and which we dare not copy' (LVI, April 1836, 106). Croker is thus faced with the problem of justifying his interest in such immoral works, as well as the public discussion of them. He solves the difficulty in the following way:

> If...<u>ours</u> was the only channel by which the existence of such works could be known, no consideration would induce us to mention them; but when it is notorious that they are advertised in a thousand ways over the whole reading world - when we see them exhibited even in London in the windows of respectable shops - when they are to be had in circulating libraries - when we know, <u>as we do know</u> - that they find their way, under the specious title of '<u>the last new novel</u>,' into the hands of persons wholly or partially ignorant of their real character - nay, into <u>ladies' book clubs</u> - we feel that it is our <u>duty to stigmatize</u> them with a BRAND which may awaken the attention of those who, not condescending themselves to read what they may consider as mere harmless trash, might and <u>do</u> unconsciously permit these conductors of moral contagion to infect their dwellings (LVI, April 1836, 66).

In the eyes of one nineteenth-century critic, at least, Croker's technique of suppression-revelation was unsuccessful. E.M. Thompson commented in his copy of the edition of the letters of Lady Suffolk that Croker had been 'too squeamish in suppressing indecent words - for his <u>stars</u> often suggest a worse word than really occurs.'[5]

In his general defence of what he considers to be valuable, and when he is on quite safe ground, Croker employs a method the vigor of which quickly becomes severity and then brutality. He justifies such a transition in reviewing Maturin's <u>Melmoth the Wanderer</u>:

> On the occasion of Mr. Maturin's former novel, we veiled our disgust, and, out of

> respect for the clerical character, conveyed
> our censure under the appearance of irony; we
> endeavoured castigare ridendo, anxiously
> hoping by that lenient method of treatment to
> be spared the necessity of having recourse to
> the more violent remedies: - but we have been
> disappointed, and the new ravings of the
> unhappy patient exceed the old folly and
> indelicacy. Indeed, Mr. Maturin has con-
> trived, by a 'curiosa infelicitas,' to unite
> in this work all the worst particularities of
> the worst modern novels. Compared with it,
> Lady Morgan is almost intelligible - The
> Monk, decent - The Vampire, amiable - and
> Frankenstein, natural (XXIV, January 1821,
> 303).

Croker is, of course, perfectly conscious of his art. He calls himself with some justice 'the old flagellifer' (XLVII, March 1832, 270). An aspect of his vigorous method is a lack of chivalry towards women, such as Lady Morgan and Mme. D'Arblay. This is in marked contrast to the Whig courtesy of Jeffrey and Macaulay in the Edinburgh Review.
The instruments of Croker's severity include a pseudo-scientific classificatory method, as used against Lady Morgan's France: 'Bad taste - Bombast and Nonsense - Blunders - Ignorance of the French Language and Manners - General Ignorance - Jacobi-nism - Falsehood - Licentiousness, and Impiety' (XVII, April 1817, 264). Another instrument is the use of fragments snatched out of context, for example, in reviewing Hunt's Rimini (XIV, January 1816, 478). This was a technique perfected by Jeffrey. Croker also uses an unsubtle irony, as against Tennyson (XLIX, April 1833, 81ff.), as well as hyperbole, ridicule, and downright abuse. As an example of the last, he calls George Colman 'a poetical jack-pudding' (VIII, September 1812, 146), but his favourite words of condemnation are 'trash' and 'poison.' This last is applied to both Moore and Macaulay. However, the most re-fined point of abuse stings with an esoteric gal-licism. Croker writes of Macaulay as a 'badigeon-neur' (LXXXIV, March 1849, 602) and of Moore's 'polissonerie' (XCIII, June 1853, 292).
The underlying seriousness of Croker's atti-tudes has been stressed here, but it should be noted that both publisher and public welcomed his 'short, smart' articles because they added 'zest'

to the Quarterly Review. Croker himself believed that the public appetite craved 'a great deal of the piquant.' He wrote to Murray, quoting Touchstone: 'a fool "is meat and drink to me"...Pray help me to a fool and I will return him to you roasted, boiled, fricassied or devilled, as you may please' (Brightfield, pp. 336-37). One may note the combination of cannibalism and sensuality in the imagery here. It is unfortunate from the literary point of view that the fools thus cooked and eaten included Keats and Tennyson.

In conclusion, it must be acknowledged that Croker played an important role as a major participant in the influential periodical literature of the early nineteenth century. He wrote from a conservative standpoint, and he showed a real appreciation of scholarship, both historical and literary. However, he was perhaps more concerned with defending the status quo than with vindicating a Burkeian tradition. He flashed out with savage satire against radical and innovative writers. He betrays as he does so the elements of rancor and of ambivalence in his age. His is one voice in the expression of a wide spectrum of critical opinion, on whose range the formidable culture of nineteenth-century England burgeoned. The voice sounds shrill beside the urbanity of Jeffrey, the narrative power of Macaulay, and the mellowness of Scott.

NOTES

1. For a discussion of this neglected aspect of Croker's contribution see Hedva Ben-Israel, English Historians of the French Revolution (Cambridge University Press, Cambridge, 1968).
2. See his speeches, Parliamentary Debates, vol. 34 (June 1816), p. 1034, on the Elgin Marbles; vol. 10 (March 1824), on the British Museum.
3. Myron F. Brightfield, John Wilson Croker (University of California Press, Berkeley, 1940), p. 371.
4. It is interesting to see the admiration of the Quarterly Reviewers for the utilitarian Grote's History of Greece. Their attitude was shared by J.S. Mill who wrote more philosophically: Macaulay's 'object is to strike, & he attains it, but it is by scene painting.... What a difference between [his History] & Grote's Hist. of Greece, which is less brilliant, but far more

interesting in its simple veracity & because, instead of striving to astonish he strives to comprehend & explain,' <u>Collected Works</u>, ed. Robson (University of Toronto Press, Toronto, 1963-), vol. 15, p. 511.

    5. <u>Letters to and from Henrietta, Countess of Suffolk</u> (2 vols, Murray, London, 1824), volume in the University of Toronto Library.

PART FIVE. LOCKHART

My aim here is to present a sketch of the literary personality of John Gibson Lockhart, as the outcome of a survey of his printed works, and the commentaries on him. In his articles in Blackwood's Magazine and the Quarterly Review Lockhart made a contribution as a critic: this specific aspect of his work has been carefully examined by Gilbert Macbeth.[1] Lockhart also wrote the social satire Peter's Letters to His Kinsfolk and the novels Valerius, Adam Blair, Reginald Dalton and Matthew Wald. The achievement of these works has not been so thoroughly considered except recently and perceptively by Francis R. Hart.[2] Lockhart was also the biographer of Burns and Scott: here his work has also been fully investigated by Hart.[3] My intention here is not to rival the very thorough studies of Macbeth and Hart, but to bring together different facets of Lockhart's work, as far as this is possible within the limits of a short discussion. I hope to suggest that his writings show firm critical principles and literary skill, but that their unique quality is achieved by a combination of characteristics peculiar to the man himself. This element is perhaps captured in J.R. Hope Scott's biographical comment on 'that depth and tenderness of feeling which Lockhart...so often hid under an almost fierce reserve'.[4]

The lively surface of Lockhart's anonymous reviews in particular conceals solid principles linking orthodox religion and conventional morality with the spirit of nationality and a high estimation of the value of art, especially as expressive of the emotions. The combination of philosophical values with art and the emotions is not always an easy one for Lockhart to achieve either in his criticism or in his work as a novelist and biographer. A special tension arises out of the role assigned to the emotional and the role which the emotions insist upon playing. This combination and this tension which lie below the surface of Lockhart's ubiquitous anonymity will be discussed in the essay which follows. Stress on emotionality is a characteristic of the age, as we are discovering. Lockhart's special interest lies in the tension which the emphasis creates uniquely for him - but perhaps he is an example of the

'Caledonian antisyzygy' which G. Gregory Smith and others after him have observed.[5]

i

Lockhart vitually began his literary career in Blackwood's Magazine in 1817 and he contributed to that lively Tory periodical regularly until 1825, then much less frequently from 1828 until 1832, and occasionally in the following years. Beneath the varied, vivacious and (sometimes unpleasantly) bantering surface of Lockhart's criticism in Blackwood's there are present strongly held views of the desirability of a close relationship between literary genius and conventional morality firmly based on the Christian religion. For example, he pontificates in Southey's vein: 'That man must think lightly and erringly, who doubts the eternal union of the highest intellect with the highest virtue'.[6]

Lockhart in his articles in Blackwood's and in his work in general shows that he also believes strongly in the affinity between true genius and national spirit. This view coloured the Lectures on the History of Literature by Friedrich Schlegel, of which he published a translation in 1818. He illustrates the view in Blackwood's by particular reference to Cervantes and Scott as the true historians of their respective countries.[7] Lockhart further shows that the principle was very meaningful to him by translating Ancient Spanish Ballads (1823) and by translating from the 'Servian Minstrelsy' (1826).[8] In the same spirit, he edited Motteux' translation of Cervantes' Don Quixote (1822) and Scott's Poetical Works (1833-34), as well as preparing an abridged version of Scott's Life of Napoleon (1829) and himself writing the lives of Burns (1828) and Scott (1837-38).

Further, in Lockhart's view, the nationality of great literature gave importance to the national, that is, the public, response to it. This importance he asserted by direct references, for example, to 'the great judge - the public' (LXXVI, September 1845, 425): as well as indirectly throughout his career as critic in Blackwood's Magazine and as critic and editor of the Quarterly Review from 1826 until 1852, only two years before his death.

Moreover, it was natural for a man of

Lockhart's social position and conservative views to see the nation as comprised of several well-defined classes. Though his own career was marked by distinct professionalism, like Scott he preferred to consider literature as the product of the leisure of the educated gentleman or man of affairs. Such broad, basic principles of religion, morality, nationality and class led Lockhart into critical difficulties in considering his most fascinating contemporaries Byron and Shelley. Like other critics of the time, he had to combine moral deprecation with admiration of the aesthetic achievement of those passionately rebellious aristocrats. It was a relief for him to be able to turn from them to the objurgation of the supposedly underbred and blasphemous Leigh Hunt, who had led his superiors astray. He treated Keats, as Hunt's lackey, in a similar way. Through his outspoken Cockneyism, Hunt offered Lockhart - as he offered Croker - no cause for critical or satirical restraint.[9]

Such views sustained Lockhart through the main period of his contributorship to Blackwood's Magazine, and through the following years of hard work as editor and reviewer in the Quarterly Review. On the one hand must be set the sustained personal hostility to Hunt and the general severity of reaction to aspiring as well as pretentious authors, such as the young Tennyson. In this respect, Lockhart, unlike John Wilson, his old coadjutor of Blackwood's, did not admit that 'the Animosities are mortal, but the Humanities live forever'.[10] However, against this negative stance in relation to contemporaries can be put his eloquent praise of Johnson as the outstanding man of letters of the previous age. Lockhart admired Johnson because in him he found 'philosophy sublimed by faith' (XLVI, November 1831, 26). In these attitudes he is akin to his contributor Croker.

In Peter's Letters to his Kinsfolk (1819) Lockhart illustrated his preoccupation with the national culture by strafing Edinburgh society in what now seems a good-humoured way, though it shocked some contemporary readers. Lockhart shows at the same time that he possesses the moral purpose of the classical satirist. He argues eloquently for literature, especially the insufficiently appreciated poetry of Wordsworth, and he argues for national literature, as expressed in the popular work of Scott. When he criticises the

Edinburgh Reviewers he does so not merely to embarrass the dominant Whigs as political opponents, but more importantly because he feels that they are exerting too great a negative influence upon Scottish and indeed British culture in general. As the 'progeny of the sceptical philosophers of the last age', they are not only irreligious, but furthermore they lack 'reverence for Feeling'.[11] No wonder that Lockhart does what he can in this discursive work to further the cause of Wordsworth and Scott. The pity is that he himself, though reverencing humane feeling, did not articulate it more fully, more directly and openly in his own critical work in general.

ii

Indirection was the method natural to Lockhart:[12] he claimed that it was proper to literature itself. He agreed with Southey that reticence was a characteristic of genius which would not stoop to the nakedness of frank self-revelation: 'Few great men - none of the very highest order - have chosen to paint otherwise than indirectly, and through the shadows of imaginary forms, the secret workings of their own minds; nor is it likely that genius will ever be found altogether divested of this proud modesty, unless in the melancholy case of its being tinged, as in Rousseau, with insanity' (XXXV, January 1827, 164).

Lockhart worked anonymously himself as a reviewer of literature and life in Blackwood's Magazine and the Quarterly Review, and in Peter's Letters. In the busy period from 1821 to 1824 he followed Scott along the path of anonymous fiction, publishing Valerius, Adam Blair, Reginald Dalton and Matthew Wald. Like the reviews, these novels show an underlying concern with the issues of religion and nationality. At moments they also bring out vividly the tension between the moral and the emotional in Lockhart's work.

Valerius is a tale of Christians in Rome at the time of Trajan. Its stilted characters in contrived situations adopt at best the cold poses of neoclassical sculpture.[13] One is amazed and perhaps moved at the sudden outbreaks of emotion; for example, 'Athanasia presses the girl to her bosom, and made one struggle more - but it would not do - for her heart was running to the brim, and, at last, with one passionate sob, all the sluices gave way, and she was dissolved at once in a flood of weeping'.[14]

Critics agree that <u>Adam Blair</u> is the most successful of this group of novels. It is set much closer to home in time and space, since the action concerns a Scottish clergyman of the mid-eighteenth century. Here passion cannot be escaped, since it is at the core of the story: 'the bruised heart poured out all its luxury of tears'.[15] However, the climax of passion, which is that of love, is itself concealed typographically with asterisks like those of Sterne, though they are here used in full seriousness;[16] this technique will be used later in the far different context of the <u>Ballantyne-Humbug Handled.</u>[17] Moreover, in the development of the plot and psychology of <u>Adam Blair</u> the passion, which is that of adulterous love, though gratified, is severely chastised. The guilty woman dies, but the repentant clergyman hero is ultimately forgiven by her husband and received back into the bosom of his pious congregation. Thus Lockhart recognises the existence of passion, but he presents it in a moral and religious context which is destructive of it.

In his third novel, <u>Reginald Dalton</u>, Lockhart, still the fictional innovator, brings his attention to bear on the present, though he turns away from Scotland, partly under the influence of Wordsworth, in order to follow the adventures of his young hero from childhood in the Lake District to Oxford and beyond. Dalton is shown as the victim of imagination untempered by experience as he succumbs to the temptations of undergraduate life. He betrays his father's trust, but, unlike Adam Blair, he eventually enjoys redemptive love. The novel is brought to an end through an overreliance on machinery such as had been evidenced in <u>Valerius.</u> But Lockhart does succeed in presenting his favourite theme of repression of feeling, here between child and father and between lovers; for example in the staccato phrasing of 'he felt the trembling of the hand that was half seized, half surrendered - he felt the beating of the bosom that he strained to his with involuntary strength - he felt the eloquent blood rush into, and at the same breath desert again, the timid trembling lip - that lip had never touched before'.[18]

Because of such repression, evinced directly and also in the cumbersome structure of the novel, the outbreak of feeling when it does occur is all the more striking. For example, Ellen reacts to her lover: 'The blood rushed again over her cheek, brow, and bosom, and tears, an agony of tears, streamed from her fixed and motionless eyes'.[19] When Dalton challenges a rival to a duel, he knows that this means the end of his brief university career, but also that he must do what honour tells him. Lockhart's presentation of his turbulent state of mind is impressive, not the less so for suggesting his own affair of honour with John Scott, editor of the London Magazine. This had led to Scott's death at the hands of Lockhart's friend Christie in February 1821. Imprisoned, 'When daylight broke upon the dungeon, it seemed to [Dalton] as if it came to dash aside the blackness of one long terrible dream, in which every element of horror had been brooding over him - his sense of bodily pain, and all his confused remembrances of shame, and anger, and violence, and degradation, and scorn, and blood - all mixed up together in one inextricable chaos, with visions such as haunt the imagination of ruffians - the stalking phantoms of murdered men -the air-drawn dagger - and stripes, and chains, and gibbets'.[20] Here the elaborate syntax and even punctuation aid the expression of a turbulent psychological experience intimately familiar to Lockhart himself.

In Lockhart's final novel, Matthew Wald, the important interests of nationality and the clash between passion and moral repression (leading to guilt and final release) are weakened, because of the unusual twist which the author gives them. Lockhart further emphasises the melodrama to which as a novelist he is prone, weakening the national, moral and emotional interests. The story of fatal adulterous passion is related by the protagonist himself, who turns out to be insane, like Crabbe's Sir Eustace Grey.

iii

Lockhart's anonymous reviews and novels were based on firm principles, and were shot through with strong feeling. Though he published the Life of Robert Burns under his own name in 1828, the Memoirs of the Life of Sir Walter Scott (1837-38) did not have his own name on the title-page. In the Preface to the Life of Burns Lockhart disclaimed biographical and critical originality.

However, in the body of the work he did defend Burns 'the young and reckless satirist' in terms which might have been appropriate to himself,[21] and Scott at least was satisfied by his restrained treatment of what such contemporaries as Jeffrey and Carlyle regarded as the problem of Burns's morality. Lockhart asserted that part of Burns's undoubted greatness was due to his expressing the national spirit. He went further in his generous conclusion: 'whosoever sympathized with the verse of Burns, had his soul opened for the moment to the whole family of man'.[22]

Lockhart modestly called himself the editor of the <u>Memoirs of Scott</u>. He could do so freely, because he could allow Scott to speak in his own voice. In Lockhart's eyes Scott combined virtue with genius in an exemplary way which set him above, for example, both Dryden and Byron. This is by no means a purely individual matter, for Lockhart asserts that great art relies on public sympathy: 'high and sane art never attempts to express that for which the artist does not claim and expect general sympathy'.[23] Furthermore, Scott was a national poet, and at his best in his national novels. He possessed, and sought to express as the achievement of his work and life, a social ideal. Indeed, he achieved a work of great moral and political power.

Lockhart thus eulogises Scott, but he also sees a weakness in him. At one time he indicates a wellnigh perfect concordance in Scott's character between the artistic and the moral, between the man of letters and the gentleman. At another time, when he investigates more closely, this balance is shown to be lacking, partly for the general reason that the artist is doomed to live at one remove from everyday actuality. Scott is described as paying the price of artistic reverie: 'He must pay the penalty, as well as reap the glory of this lifelong abstraction of reverie, this self-abandonment of Fairyland'. He is described as 'the dupe of his own delusions'.[24] In a private letter, Scott's 'boundless energy of imagination' is seen to be too much 'under the sway of romantic association'.[25]

The desirable balance is lost again when Lockhart considers Scott as man of letters on the one hand and businessman on the other: this combination became even more of a stumbling block for Carlyle when he reviewed Lockhart's work. Somehow the artistic delusions which made Scott the master poet and novelist also sought expression in his secretive and over-ambitious commercial ventures, as he sought to realise an impossible dream, not in writing, but in life! Lockhart presents this tense situation, not in terms of art, but in terms of a personality which is more important to him than art. Scott paid the price for his delusions, but his biographer characteristically turns this defeat into a victory. The triumph is moral, the triumph of duty over inclination. Lockhart is proud that towards the end of the life of his father-in-law the moral spirit of the gentleman, indeed the Hero, survived the genius; he saw 'goodness, surviving greatness' (CXVI, October 1864, 472).

Perhaps a parallel can be drawn between Lockhart's twofold view of Scott the man as outlined here and his twofold critical appreciation of Scott's works. On the one hand, he admires a balance of qualities. This idealistic view is eloquently expressed in the remarks on <u>Waverley</u>:

> Loftier romance was never blended with easier, quainter humour, by Cervantes himself. In his familiar delineations he had combined the strength of Smollett with the native elegance and unaffected pathos of Goldsmith; in his darker scenes, he had revived that real tragedy which appeared to have left our stage with the age of Shakespeare; and elements of interest so diverse had been blended and interwoven with that nameless grace, which, more surely perhaps than even the highest perfection in the command of any one strain of sentiment, makes the master-mind cast in Nature's most felicitous mould.[26]

On the other hand, what Lockhart also admires is the interruption of the order suggested in such a passage as the above. He says elsewhere that such interruption is the highest quality of Scott's work in general and of the <u>Lay of the Last Minstrel</u> in particular. The allusions here seem apposite to Scott, but also to a lesser degree even to the writings and personality of Lockhart himself:

> For, in truth, what is it that gives to all his works their unique and marking charm, except the matchless effect which sudden

effusions of the purest heart-blood of nature derive from their being poured out, to all appearance involuntarily, amidst diction and sentiment cast equally in the mould of the busy world, and the seemingly habitual desire to dwell on nothing but what might be likely to excite curiosity, without too much disturbing deeper feelings, in the saloons of polished life? Such outbursts come forth dramatically in all his writings; but in the interludes and passionate parentheses of the 'Lay of the Last Minstrel' we have the poet's own inner soul and temperament laid bare and throbbing before us: - even here, indeed, he has a mask, and he trusts it - but fortunately it is a transparent one.[27]

The first quality which Lockhart admires in Scott's life and art, that is, his balance, characterises at a lower level of genius most of his own reviews, his novels and biographies. This order is not only of the surface in the manipulation of the materials under consideration, but also of critical principles beneath that surface: it is achieved with the most brilliant compression in Adam Blair.

The second admired artistic quality, of the interruption or 'sudden effusion', is naturally more elusive. In his work as reviewer especially, Lockhart, like Scott and Jeffrey, writes for the 'busy world', until even the critical spirit seems dormant, and the labour is at times relieved not by 'effusions of the purest heart-blood' but by outpourings of spleen or at best satirical indignation. The most liberating effusion occurs more freely at times in the novels, as I have tried to suggest. Vivacious feeling and Lockhart's underlying concern with principle are interwoven only occasionally in the reviews, perhaps most attractively in Peter's Letters, and also in the lives of Burns and Scott. The combination of feeling, principle, and 'almost fierce reserve' delimits Lockhart's literary achievement, but also gives it its unique quality.

NOTES

1. Gilbert Macbeth, John Gibson Lockhart (reprinted from Illinois Studies in Language and Literature, vol. 17, 1935).
2. Francis R. Hart, The Scottish Novel

(Harvard University Press, Cambridge, Mass, 1978), pp. 68-80.

3. Francis R. Hart, Lockhart as Romantic Biographer (Edinburgh University Press, Edinburgh, 1971).

4. J.G. Lockhart, Life of Sir Walter Scott, abridged (Black, Edinburgh, 1871), p. xi.

5. G. Gregory Smith, Scottish Literature (Macmillan, London, 1919), p. 4; C.M. Grieve (Hugh MacDiarmid), Selected Essays, ed. D. Glen (Cape, London, 1969), p. 56ff; Edwin Muir, Scott and Scotland (Routledge, London, 1936), p. 61.

6. Blackwood's Magazine, vol. 4 (October 1818), p. 2.

7. The same, vol. 10 (December 1821), p. 713.

8. The translation is identified as Lockhart's by Wm. Parker in Quarterly Review, vol. 289 (1951), p. 376.

9. In for example Blackwood's, vol. 7 (June 1820), p. 318, and Quarterly, vol. 37 (March 1828), pp. 402-26, review of Hunt's Byron.

10. Blackwood's, vol. 36 (August 1834), p. 273.

11. Peter's Letters, 2nd edn (3 vols, Blackwood, Edinburgh, 1819), vol. 2, pp. 128, 137.

12. Hart, The Scottish Novel, p. 71, uses the word "implication."

13. Valerius (3 vols, Blackwood, Edinburgh, 1821), for example, vol. 3, p. 179.

14. The same, vol. 3, p. 82f.

15. Adam Blair, ed D. Craig (Edinburgh University Press, Edinburgh, 1963), p. 69.

16. The same, p. 160.

17. Ballantyne-Humbug Handled (Cadell, Edinburgh, 1839), p. 47.

18. Reginald Dalton (2 vols, Blackwood, Edinburgh, 1823), vol. 2, p. 246.

19. The same, p. 99.

20. The same, p. 343.

21. Life of Robert Burns (Constable, Edinburgh, 1828), p. 65.

22. The same, p. 303.

23. Memoirs of the Life of Sir Walter Scott (7 vols, Cadell, Edinburgh, 1837-38), vol. 7, p. 398.

24. The same, vol. 6, p. 121; vol. 7, p. 407.

25. F.R. Hart, 'Proofreading Lockhart's "Scott",' Studies in Bibliography, vol. 14 (1961), p. 21f.

26. Memoirs, vol. 3, pp. 302-03.

27. The same, vol. 2, pp. 24-25.

Chapter Three

WESTMINSTER REVIEW: MILL AND POETRY

PART ONE. EARLY LIFE

This paper is the first part of a broadly chronological survey of the complex role played by poetry in the philosophical career of John Stuart Mill. Such a survey has not been undertaken before, particularly with a focus in the middle period on Mill's important contributions to magazines: the <u>Westminster Review</u>, the <u>Monthly Repository</u>, and the <u>London and Westminster Review</u>. Nor have attempts been made to draw material from the most diverse sources in the writings of Mill himself, as well as to suggest multiple analogies leading from Plato to I.A. Richards. The breadth of the undertaking, confined to a relatively small space, accounts partly for the mosaic-like character of the presentation, but this is also necessitated by the fragmentary nature of the evidence brought forth. The mosaic structure also reflects the complexity of the historical picture. I hope that all this constitutes a justification for the form and style of the paper. To achieve a broad picture I have deliberately gone beyond the many valuable books and articles on Mill's criticism where the approach has differed from mine. I am of course deeply indebted, especially to the work of J.M. Robson, Edward Alexander (both referred to in the text), and F. Marvin Sharpless.[1]

Some attention has been paid to John Stuart Mill's interest in poetry, but little consideration has been given to the varied and strong influences on him in early life which fostered this interest. It is the purpose of this paper, after an introductory survey, to indicate these influences, alongside the well-known negative factors which were at work on Mill as a child and young man. The poignance of their effect enriches one's appreciation of Mill's quite intense concern with poetry in his middle years and his cooler attitudes towards it later in life.

For Mill poetry was associated with feeling and feeling was associated with religion. So the absence of religion in his early life is significant, as well as the suppression of feeling in his relations with both parents. James Mill enthusiastically provided his son with an intense intellectual education, but the goal of this, paradoxically enough, was the development of a special moral and emotional attitude. Poetry itself had a part in the education. However, its most significant element, as counteracting the impact of its rigidity and allowing for the play of feeling as well as of mind, was the study of classical Greek culture, and in particular the works of Plato. For the Mills Greece was not only an historical fact to be intellectually understood, but also an ideal to be emotionally apprehended and striven after. The close study of Plato made Socrates especially a hero in young Mill's imagination. Moreover, he could not ignore the importance which Plato attached to poetry and the complexity of his attitudes towards it. He was made aware of the mysticism and the eloquence of Plato, and above all, of the Socratic method. Ironically, the training in the method which Mill received from his father freed him from the trammels of his father's intellectual dogmatism. To a degree it opened up to him many phases of experience, from the intellectual to the religious and the emotional, from the philosophic to the poetic. Through this Mill came to be called 'perhaps the greatest of the nineteenth century Platonists.'[2]

Thus the educational framework which James Mill established for his son was conducive to the poetic. He also established a supportive geographical setting for him. To both father and son the city (London) was the place of work. The Mills lived at its edge, able to enjoy the pleasures of nature. Young Mill certainly took advantage of this, intensively in his study of flowers and extensively in his enjoyment of visits to the West and South of England and to the South of France. All these experiences contained an emotional and poetic element which will be specified later. They were made available to him by his father. Finally, James Mill's own views of poetry received expression as part of the panoply of his

J.S. Mill

History of British India and Analysis of the Phenomena of the Human Mind. In these works, which greatly impressed his son, poetry has a place, but a restricted one. It occupies a similar confined place in the works of Mill's mentor, Bentham. It also has a place in the work of Plato, which both Mills closely studied. The poetic in Plato reemerges challengingly in the thought of the younger Mill.

As has been suggested in these introductory remarks, Mill's early religion, had it existed, would have been relevant to a discussion of his interest in poetry, because for him the emotional and poetic dimensions of religion are important. However, he 'was brought up from the first without any religious belief' (I, 41).[3] The reading of Dumont's Benthamite Traité de Législation in 1821 belatedly gave him a faith, he says. Doubts about this over the succeeding years yielded to personal worship of Harriet Taylor, affirmed after her death and declared through the later works, such as On Liberty, dedicated to her memory. Mill also became an adherent after his own fashion of the Comteian Religion of Humanity. The title of the posthumously published essay on 'The Utility of Religion' indicates the angle from which he persisted in regarding it.

Mill as a child had no religion, so its emotional and poetic aspects had no effect on him. Moreover, his emotional relationship with his parents was thwarted. As humanist philosophers, both Mill and his father recognised the great importance of the basic emotional relationship between mother and child. But this relationship seems to have been lacking, interrupted radically, or suppressed in Mill's own experience. In the Autobiography as published soon after his death he does not mention his mother. Indeed, he hardly mentions the rest of the large family of which he was the eldest.[4]

In the early version of the Autobiography Mill noted the incompatibility between his parents, and his own submission to the dominance of his father: awesome as he was, impatient, yet, like Plato in The Republic, contemptuous of 'passionate emotions' (I, 50). Yet in spite of his emotional limitations, there can be no doubt that James Mill succeeded in the incredibly concentrated 'intellectual education' of his son (I, 7), if one is to judge by the stature of its product. Relishing what he later called 'the perfect dependence of the child upon the parent,'[5] he wrote a few weeks after the birth of his son that he had 'a strong determination...to exert himself to the utmost to see what the power of education can do.'[6] Like his son, who appealed to Plato on this topic, James felt that education could perform wonders. He believed that its goal was happiness, though, writing on the topic in the Encyclopaedia Britannica, he admitted Socratically that he did not know what happiness was. He wrote with more conviction in the Analysis of the Phenomena of the Human Mind that the product of a 'Philosophical Education' was virtue, above all, the 'Love Of Mankind.'[7] Thus the hoped-for outcome of a severe intellectual training was an elevated, but rather mysterious, emotional state. With this as his goal, James surely succeeded with his son. However, the training left John with a sense of dissatisfaction and emotional incompleteness, for which poetry and the poetic provided a partial relief.

Of special significance in Mill's early education from the poetic point of view is his precocious exposure to Greek, and especially Plato. James Mill would have agreed with his son that Greece was 'a course of education' in itself (XI, 377). James thought of himself as a Platonist, as did his son, though it was on account of his use of the Socratic method, rather than for his acquiescence in 'poetic fancies' (I, 25). In his own account John emphasises the rigour of the method, but his friend Grote in his History of Greece (1846-56) points out that its aim was 'to create earnest seekers.'[8] The tone of this remark John would have endorsed. Grote interestingly compared James Mill's attitude towards his son to that of Socrates towards Theaetetus in Plato's dialogue of that name. According to Grote, Socrates aimed to evolve knowledge out of pregnant minds, though he did not succeed with Theaetetus. However, his negative method qualified 'the mind for a life of philosophical research.'[9] Such research meant that no dogma, including that of James Mill, could be left unquestioned, and no area of experience, including the emotional and the poetic, could be left unscanned.[10]

James Mill was also a Platonist in his admiration for the beauty of Plato's style, as well as for his presentation of Socrates as 'a model of ideal excellence' (I, 49). His son, using the word 'poetic' in characteristically broad fashion, described this last as 'poetic culture' in itself (I, 115).[11] He must have had in mind the educative function of poetry to show 'examples of self-control and fortitude on the part of famous men.'[12] The conflict within Plato, as Grote saw it, between scientific ethics and religious mission, between dialectic and dogmatism, was present still in John Mill, though not acknowledged by him. It is indicated by the positive and negative use of the word 'poetic' in the references above. With his father and Grote, Mill felt that he was on the scientific side, but to a certain extent he took up the challenge of the dialectic. The 'poetic' in the positive sense here involves delight in the persuasive use of language, the presentation of character through dramatic dialogue, and the impressive and magnetic nobility of that character and the ideas which he expresses. The poetic in such broad terms was made available to John Mill by Plato through his father.

Thus Mill associates poetry and the poetic with the feelings and their pleasurable expression. He did not enjoy such expression in his relations with his parents, and he only experienced it indirectly as part of his rigorous intellectual education, chiefly through the exposure to Greek. From this point of view, Mill's general physical environment and his response to it are significant. The utilitarians were theorists of modern British urban society, but if one considers London to be its nub, then Bentham and James Mill, with young Mill in tow, viewed it from the periphery. John was born in Pentonville in a modern house looking down over the City. From 1810 to 1813 the family lived further east in Newington Green, Islington, 'then an almost rustic neighbourhood.' Father and son walked together: 'with my earliest recollections of green fields and wild flowers, is mingled that of the account I gave him daily of what I had read the day before' (I, 10). In 1810 the Mills tried 'a pretty Gardenhouse'[13] in which Milton had lived. This belonged to Bentham who had devoutly provided it with a plaque, 'Sacred to Milton, Prince of Poets.'[14] Despite its character and associations, the house proved unsatisfactory, and Hazlitt moved in as the next tenant. He left under a cloud five years later, claiming that Bentham did not reverence the poet as the plaque indicated. In 1814 the Mills again became Bentham's tenants, moving into the house immediately adjacent to his in Queen Square

Place, happily called 'a kind of oasis in the heart of Westminster.'[15] They stayed there until 1831, when they moved further west to Kensington. In later life Mill became even more of a suburbanite as he enjoyed a romantic setting at Blackheath. This contrasted with the more remote beauties of Avignon in the south of France, where he lived in his later years, dying there close to the tomb of his wife. He was thus brought up and spent the rest of his life on the fringe of the city or outside it.

As a boy Mill went on walks through the fields with his father. Such situations made possible the experiencing of feelings, both pleasurable and aesthetic. In early childhood, he observes in a note to his edition of his father's *Analysis*, he experienced an 'intense and mysterious delight...in the colours of certain flowers.'[16] This delight merged with an enthusiasm for botany which developed after 1820. As a young man 'on country excursions' he 'would fill his pockets with sweet violet seed and scatter it in the hedges as he went along.'[17] Here we have a delightful instance of a desire to propagate the world not only with visual, but also with olfactory beauty, since this flower is 'highly prized for its fragrance.'[18] Flowers also entered later into Mill's own sexual life. In 1840 he concocted for Caroline Fox a botanical 'calendar of odours,'[19] and earlier he offered 'small flowers,' gathers in the New Forest, as a love-offering to Harriet (XII, 114). Here Mill shows a high degree of sensitivity, but with the sensitivity kept firmly under control.

In Mill's boyhood, the pleasure which both father and son took in nature, in however disciplined a fashion, led them further afield than the outskirts of London. Almost every year for ten years, according to Bentham's plan, they visited the sage 'at Barrow Green House, in a beautiful part of the Surrey hills.' In 1813 the three of them made an excursion to the West of England. On this occasion Mill acquired his 'first taste for natural scenery, in the elementary form of fondness for a "view".' From 1814 to 1817 the Mills also visited Bentham at Ford Abbey in Devon, and later John waxed eloquent over the 'poetic cultivation' which this provided (I, 57). He again uses the word 'poetic' in a broad sense, here to mean stimulating the imagination through the feelings in an aesthetically uplifting way.

William Gilpin had admired Ford Abbey at the

end of the previous century, but he was fastidiously upset by the contrast between its beauty and the supposed improvement of both building and grounds. It is noteworthy that for the young Mill the natural and the improved blended together most attractively. Unlike Gilpin, he was not bothered that 'Gothic walls' were 'adorned with Indian paper.'[20] On the contrary, his enjoyment must have been enriched, because the saloon was decorated in the manner of Inigo Jones. Moreover, the walls were 'hung with Mortlake tapestries in delicate shades of blue and green,' with designs based on the work of Raphael.[21] These peopled Mill's 'imagination with graceful and dignified forms,' so vividly that he recalled the experience in these terms many years later (XVII, 1661). Thus the young Mill's pleasure in nature, fostered by Bentham and his father, culminated in pleasure in medieval architecture, landscape gardening, seventeenth and eighteenth century interior decoration, and the painting of Raphael. Mill himself called this rich mixture 'a sort of poetic cultivation,' as we have just seen. The love of nature stayed with him, together with the biblical idealism of Raphael, a pictorial equivalent to the secular idealism which he admired in literature. Mill expressed enjoyment of the art of Raphael in his visit to Italy in 1855, and his dining-room at Blackheath contained a copy of a Madonna by him.

Mill's young imagination was stimulated further when in 1820 Bentham's brother invited him for a six months' visit to his home in the South of France. Though his diary shows this period to have been one of continued and extended study, Mill also found the visit a liberating experience. Thanks to the Pyrenees, mountains became for him his 'ideal of natural beauty' (I, 151); indeed, the views were 'fit for Salvator' (XIV, 260). Moreover, Mill enjoyed the 'free and genial atmosphere of Continental life' (I, 59), as opposed to what he later called the 'extreme incapacity for personal enjoyment' of the English (II, 171). In spite of this last comment, as a young man Mill himself did enjoy with his family summers spent in the countryside south of London. From 1830 they occupied 'a pleasant summer mansion' at Mickleham, near Dorking, not far from Barrow Green. According to Carlyle, the spot was surrounded by 'innumerable picturesquenesses.'[22] Another visitor, Henry Solly, also enjoyed the scenery. More loquacious than Mill himself on this topic, Solly remembered him for 'his domestic qualities, the affectionate playfulness of his character as a brother in the company of his sisters.'[23]

Much of this beneficent early environment, sketched in above, as well as the tightly controlled educational process, was arranged by James Mill for his son, with its poetic components, both specific and general. James's own attitudes towards literature and poetry in specifically verse form are revealed further in works which were published when John was a child and a young man. These were the History of British India (1817) and the Analysis of the Phenomena of the Human Mind (1829). John appreciated fully the qualities of both. At the beginning of the Autobiography he identified himself as the son of the author of the History, and he published an annotated edition of the Analysis in 1869.

In the History, whose distant aloofness distressed Hazlitt, Mill pays incidental attention to literature in its cultural context. He contrasts poetry characterized by exaggeration with historiography marked by exactness: though literature is the 'best friend' of historical knowledge, the latter is more useful. Mill admits the historical priority of poetry: 'The first literature is poetry. Poetry is the language of the passions, and men feel, before they speculate.'[24] But the tenor of the History shows Mill's certainty that in the progress of civilisation the authority of poetry has properly yielded to that of speculation. He contrasts the 'wild imagination' of the Hindus with the notions of truth to nature and an ordered art.[25] These latter qualities are characteristic of the superior literature of both medieval Europe and the Mohammedans. Thus Mill shows his appreciation of literature in using it as a criterion for assessing the cultural inferiority of the Hindus. This negative method is unfortunate, but it follows from Mill's enlightenment faith in progress and the triumph of reason.

In the History Mill presents a Hindu society that is pre-Greek in its primitivism. For him, as for Grote, who followed in his magisterial footsteps as the historian of Greece (also admired greatly by John), primitivism was marked, as we have noted, by the predominance of the feelings and of the medium which expressed them, poetry. Grote was more explicit about this than James Mill. He wrote that in early Greece 'a string of poetical fancies' were 'the governing realities of

139

the mental system.' Homer's epics affected their original hearers 'with the full weight and solemnity of history and religion combined, while the charm of poetry was only secondary and instrumental. The poet was then the teacher and preacher of the community, not simply the amuser of their leisure hours,' as, it is implied, he has properly become today.[26] Mill's History presented a formidable picture of a static primitive society, associated with the unbridled imagination and poetry. Grote was very impressed by this, though he showed the mythic, poetic stage of Greek society giving way to the historical and rational. John Mill was strongly influenced by the state of mind which informed these learned historical and geographical frameworks for a consideration of poetry. Neither framework leaves much room for poetry to play an important role in the modern, civilised world. Here the enlightenment tradition is very much in evidence.

James Mill's responsiveness to poetry is given more positive, though still limited expression in the Analysis of the Phenomena of the Human Mind. In discussing the imagination he emphasises that the poet's ideas are 'of all that is most lovely and striking in the visible appearances of nature, and of all that is most interesting in the actions and affections of human beings.'[27] The poet's train of ideas is an end in itself, at the same time as the product of poetry is pleasure. Mill puts it almost sensuously in the Fragment on Mackintosh (1835), where he observes that the 'pleasures of imagination' terminate 'in delightful contemplation.'[28] His son saw the value of this emphasis.

In discussing the sublime and the beautiful in the Analysis, Mill relies almost entirely on Alison's associationist account, but in a way which his son would endorse he adds the moral to the beautiful in considering the attraction of a bust of Socrates beside the Venus de Medici. In his notes to this section John goes significantly beyond his father's theory. Not only is there an 'element of direct physical and sensual pleasure' in certain kinds of beauty, but also the beautiful stimulates 'the active power of the imagination to rise above known reality, into a more attractive or a more majestic world.'[29] In the History James Mill fixed the living imagination and poetry in the geographically remote and the historical past. In the Analysis he gave them a position in his psychology, but a subordinate and a historical one. Both these presentations strongly affected John Mill, early and late.

Of course, Bentham's philosophical influence lies behind both James and John Mill. He wrote, as Mill well knew: 'the game of pushpin is of equal value with...music and poetry....between poetry and truth there is a natural opposition.'[30] However, Bentham did allow a place theoretically, as well as practically as we have seen, for the pleasures of imagination, of poetry, and of the landscape. John Mill asserted, and even Hazlitt admitted, Bentham's love of the arts. It must be added that, theory apart, Bentham with his family exercised a benign influence on the setting of Mill's early life.

For Bentham and James Mill the value and the role of poetry posed no problem, but they did threaten to become problematical for John Mill. Behind all three, as the Mills were certainly aware, loomed the massive classical figure of Plato, for whom the question was an important one. For example, in the Protagoras and the Apology Socrates is bothered by the elusiveness of poets. In the Republic their work is allowed a place in the education of the young, but, because of their emotionality, they are regarded as socially dangerous and in need of restraint. All the same, deliberately contrived fictions are necessary for the religious underpinning of the ideal state. All of these elements, except the aspect of control, are present in Mill's thought. The last element, the contrived fictions, emerges in his later comments on the utility of religion.

Mill's early life, here briefly surveyed, was more rich in influences themselves broadly poetic, or allowing a place for poetry, than many critics have allowed. He appreciated and benefited from the strenuous intellectual education which he received, though he came to regret the absence of genial emotion between his father and himself. He lamented also the absence of a sense of boyhood in himself as a child: '"I never was a boy," he said; "never played at cricket."'[31] However, James Mill made the further, though more indirect, contribution of providing his son with a congenial variety of geographical experiences, in England, in and out of London, and in France. The intellectual education which he provided had a stimulating historical and cultural dimension. Further, it was a matter not only of indoctrination, but also of intellectual stimulation. This was leavened by an element of poetry (as indicated by the names of authors in chapter one of the Autobiography), and above all by the inclusion of Plato, whose richness and complexity was to prove a continuous resource and challenge for the young Mill.

As a boy Mill knew poetry. Indeed, Bertrand Russell commented with pardonable exaggeration that 'James Mill caused John to read more poetry than was read by any other boy then living.'[32] Though Mill denigrated the 'poetic' as a quality in Plato, yet it was an attraction of Ford Abbey. He himself admitted, by way of a characteristic compromise, that he 'was very susceptible to the effect of all composition, whether in the form of poety or oratory, which appealed to the feelings on any basis of reason' (I, 73). He continued to be so.

In his account in the Autobiography of his intellectual development and role as Benthamite propagandist, Mill, with a typical movement towards compensation, asserts that he 'had obtained poetic culture of the most valuable kind, by means of reverential admiration for the lives and characters of heroic persons,' such as Socrates. He 'perpetually recurred' to the heroes of history, 'as others do to a favorite poet, when needing to be carried up into the more elevated regions of feeling and thought' (I, 115). 'Poetic culture' comes to Mill from historical writing, and elsewhere, as well as from poetry itself. However, in spite of his upbringing and its setting, despite the influence of Plato and James Mill, John came to recognise the absence in himself of 'the cultivation of feeling,' along with a neglect of 'Imagination' and 'an undervaluing of poetry' (I, 114). Poetry and the poetic had been valued, inculcated, and made available to Mill by his mentors, but not sufficiently. In the words of Abraham Hayward, Mill's obituarist in The Times, 'young Mill had a weakness for poetry, though he could not find its proper place in a perfect theory of human life.'[33]

NOTES

1. Robson is the general editor of Mill, Collected Works (University of Toronto Press, Toronto, 1963-), referred to in the following chapter by volume in Roman numerals. Alexander

edited Mill, Literary Essays (Bobbs-Merrill, New York, 1967). Sharpless is the author of The Literary Criticism of John Stuart Mill (Mouton, The Hague, 1967); he has also edited Mill, Essays on Poetry (University of South Carolina Press, Columbia, S.C., 1976).

2. Paul Shorey, Platonism (University of California Press, Berkeley, 1938), p. 231.

3. However, nothing is simple in Mill's life. He was baptised and as a little boy went to church. According to Alexander Bain, James Mill (Longman, London, 1882), p. 90, his father's religious (i.e., agnostic) views did not take final shape until 1808-10. M. St.J. Packe, Life of John Stuart Mill (Macmillan, New York, 1954), p. 25, dates the change 1816.

4. Mill's contemporary Carlyle also 'durst not freely love' his father, but he was devoted to his mother, as well as to his brothers and sisters: Reminiscences, ed. Norton (1887), vol. 1, p. 15.

5. Analysis of the Phenomena of the Human Mind, ed. J.S. Mill, 2nd edn (2 vols, Longman, London, 1869), vol. 2, p. 220. No doubt James Mill also submitted to what he called 'a grand governing law of human nature,' that is, the desire of power over others: essay on government in Supplement to Encyclopaedia Britannica, 5th edn (4 vols, Constable, Edinburgh, 1817), vol. 4, p. 494. He had what Alexander Bain admitted to be an 'overgrasping view' of education: Education as a Science (Kegan Paul, 1879), p. 3.

6. Mill News Letter (winter 1976), p. 11. Theoretically education can do a great deal, since its business is 'to make certain feelings or thoughts take place instead of others,' Supplement to Encyclopaedia Britannica (1817), vol. 4, p. 14.

7. Analysis, vol. 2, p. 278.

8. History of Greece, from 2nd London edn (12 vols, Harper, New York, 1857), vol. 8, p. 453. For Meno, in the words of Grote, the Socratic dialectic 'produced an immediate effect like the touch of the torpedo,' p. 448. Grote saw that Socrates created 'an uneasy longing after truth,' p. 449. As a mental midwife the philosopher scrutinised the offspring produced and if need be 'cast it away with the rigour of a Lykurgean nurse,' despite the feelings of the 'mother-mind,' p. 448. Some of the effect of the elder Mill is surely suggested here, as it is made explicit in Grote's

review of J.S. Mill's book on Sir William Hamilton, George Grote, Minor Works (Murray, London, 1873), p. 284.

9. Geaorge Grote, Plato (3 vols, Murray, London, 1865), vol. 2, p. 391.

10. Compare Mill himself to Carlyle in 1832: 'I was not crammed; my own thinking faculties were called into strong though but partial play; & by their means I have been enabled to remake all my opinions' (XII, 128). Note the word 'partial' and the emphasis Mill puts on his autonomy. Jonathan Loesberg, 'Fictions of Consciousness,' (Diss. Cornell, 1977, p. 61), quotes a similar passage in the Autobiography (I, 34), and comments acutely: 'James Mill is not the Gradgrind critics sometimes want to see him as. By demanding of Mill understanding, he makes the act of understanding the self, recognising what was lacking, possible, just as, by demanding thought rather then mere memory of fact, he gives Mill the method for constructing a new philosophy of self that would include emotion'. Loesberg makes the point again in Interspace and the Inward Spere, ed. N.A. Anderson and M.E. Weiss (W. Illinois University, Macomb, Ill., 1978), p. 99.

11. Mill surely shared Grote's admiration for Socrates' 'Colloquial magic,' History of Greece (New York), vol. 8, p. 449. Compare Richard Jenkyns, The Victoriams and Ancient Greece (Blackwell, Oxford, 1980), p. 231: 'Mill never outgrew this early hero-worship; throughout his life whenever he wrote of Socrates, his cool prose was suffused with feeling.'

12. Plato, Republic, tr. F.M. Cornford (Clarendon Press, Oxford, 1941), p. 77.

13. Edward Phillips, Life of Milton (1694), in Early Lives of Milton, ed. H. Darbishire (Constable, London, 1932), p. 71.

14. David Masson, Life of John Milton (7 vols, Macmillan, London, new edn, 1881-94), vol. 4, p. 420.

15. M. St.J. Packe, Life of John Stuart Mill, p. 16.

16. Analysis, vol. 2, p. 246n.

17. John A. Roebuck, Life and Letters (Arnold, London, 1897), p. 29.

18. Encyclopaedia Britannica, 11th edn (25 vols, Peale, Chicago, 1891-92), vol. 24, p. 241.

19. Caroline Fox, Memories, 2nd edn (2 vols, Smith, Elder, London, 1882), vol. 1, p. 166.

20. Wm Gilpin, Observations on the Western

Parts of England (Cadell, London, 1798), p. 277.
21. Jas Lees Milne, The Age of Inigo Jones (Batsford, London, 1953), p. 132, with an illustration facing p. 133.
22. Quoted by Packe, p. 206.
23. Workman's Magazine (1873), p. 385.
24. History, vol. 2, p. 33. This point of view is discussed by Wm Thomas, The Philosophical Radicals (Clarendon Press, Oxford, 1979), p. 112, cf p. 114f.
25. The same, p. 37.
26. History of Greece, edn cited, vol. 1, p. 351; vol. 2, p. 118. It is noteworthy that G.M. Young considered Grote's History 'the most conspicuous memorial of the Utilitarians,' Portrait of an Age, ed. G.K. Clark (Oxford University Press, London, 1977), p. 26.
27. Analysis, vol. 1, p. 242.
28. The same, p. 431.
29. The same, vol. 2, pp. 242n, 255n.
30. Works, ed. J. Bowring, reprint edn (11 vols, Russell, New York, 1962), vol. 2, p. 253.
31. Caroline Fox, Memories, edn cited, p. 163f.
32. Freedom and Organisation (Allen & Unwin, London, 1934), p. 140.
33. The Times, (10 November 1873), p. 6. Hayward is identified as the writer by Packe, p. 72.

J.S. Mill

PART TWO. MILL AND POETRY: THE CENTRAL YEARS

I hope I have shown that poetry and the poetic occupied an important, though restricted, place in Mill's early life and education. Poetry continued to be important in the central period of his life, from 1824 to 1840, what J.M. Robson has described as a phase of 'eclectic outreach and assimilation.'[1] In fact, poetry played a crucial role in enabling him to pass through his mental crisis. I wish to consider this period in relation to three phases of his public writing: for the Westminster Review (1824-28), for the Monthly Repository (1832-35), and for the London, then the London and Westminster Review (1835-40). Mill contributed to the first as an acolyte of his father and Bentham, although he already showed a more liberal view of literature than their's. The crisis in his personal life which took place at this time was similar to Coleridge's: he quoted Coleridge's poetry in describing it later. The crisis was also akin to the situation presented by Wordsworth in Book IV of The Excursion. As Mill later made clear, Wordsworth's poetry helped him to a recovery, because of its restrained emotionalism; but he could not accept its transcendental element. He did, however, yield momentarily to the broad influence of this kind exerted over him by Carlyle, his closer contemporary. He submitted finally to the influence of Harriet Taylor, though this was more sexual than philosophic or poetic.

Blossoming under such influences as those of Wordsworth, Coleridge, Carlyle, and Harriet Taylor, Mill developed theoretical views of the imagination and of poetry which he expressed clearly in the congenial setting of W.J. Fox's Monthly Repository. These accounts lacked romantic rapture, but they were full of humanity and feeling. Also Plato, a preoccupation since childhood, re-emerged through Mill's translations and commentaries in the Repository. In this genial, outgoing phase of his career he responded to Plato's idealist and poetic challenge.

In the final segment of this middle period, Mill himself established the London Review on a broader cultural base than that of Bentham's Westminster. He published in it warm accounts of Tennyson's poetry, of Carlyle's French Revolution, and the present state of civilisation, as well as the complementary accounts of Bentham and Coleridge. He combined ratiocination and feeling in these pieces. The poetic was present, in subject-matter and in mood, but as with the articles on Plato in the Monthly Repository, Mill did not quite fully respond to its challenge.

i

Mill began contributing to the Westminster Review as his father's enthusiastic henchman. In the second number (July 1826) he subjected the Edinburgh Review to a withering moralistic attack, in which both Shakespeare and Scott were involved. Mill made his onslaught in a spirit typical of the Westminster in its partisan early numbers. However, the prospect broadened in a speech probably of 1827 on the subject of historiography. Here he rather clumsily identified 'that nobler knowledge of human nature which consists in a knowledge of the outward signs by which the stronger passions display themselves and which gives to the dramatist all his power over our emotions and to poetry itself the greater part of its charm.'[2] He included history in this category of knowledge. It was important because it showed the few examples of great men who, on account of their 'sublime virtue,'[3] deserved that love on which human happiness depends. History indeed might be a better medium for conveying moral truth than poetry, because of its concern for truth, rather than for exciting emotion. It is noteworthy that James Mill's History of British India (1817), whose monumental character his son fully recognised, had not met the criteria put forward in Mill's speech. In his view of India no great men emerged to satisfy his son's moral, emotional, and aesthetic criteria.

Mill came to feel that the personal demands underlying these criteria had not been met in the course of his upbringing. The sense of something lacking in that crucial phase of his life became most acute at the time of his mental crisis, beginning in 1826. Significantly, despite the comparison of himself to a Methodist smitten by the 'conviction of sin' (I, 137), and thus ready to receive what John Galt called 'a cast of grace,'[4] he made no specific religious response to the crisis, as he described it in the Autobiography (published posthumously in 1873). Instead, he called up the crisis with references to the poetry

147

of <u>Macbeth</u> and Coleridge's 'Dejection.' Mill now thought of the analysis in which he had been trained as destructive of feeling, though he admitted at the same time that it made known 'the permanent sequences in nature' - which still needed to be 'imaginatively realised' (I, 141). He found immediate relief through reading Marmontel's moving account of his father's death, and he achieved an awareness of the need for a 'balance among the faculties' (I, 147).[5] His response to a sense of emotional deprivation was thus a thoughtful and positive one, and it led not to raw emotional expression, but to the cultivation of the feelings through the aesthetic. Especially, it led to an appreciation of the role of poetry and the poetic in this cultivation.

Mill's contemporary James Martineau recognised the power over young minds of the analytical psychology, derived from Hartley by James Mill. He drew a parallel between Mill's crisis and that of Coleridge. The poet had once felt, having read Hartley, 'that the sole practicable employment for the human mind was to observe, to collect, and to classify.'[6] This passage suggests James Mill's praise of classification as the essentially human, philosophical gift. Coleridge had written of his own release from such a narrow view thanks to the writings of the 'ignorant Mystics' who 'contributed to keep alive the heart in the head' and who gave him 'an indistinct...presentiment, that all the products of the mere <u>reflective</u> faculty partook of DEATH.'[7]

In contrast to this, the young Mill was unable to descend to the level of the mystics, but he turned instead to the poets, Coleridge himself and Wordsworth, and to Carlyle and the other thinkers named in the <u>Autobiography</u>.

Out of the expansion of Coleridge's philosophy arose his recognition of the importance of the 'shaping spirit of the Imagination,'[8] as well as his distinction between imagination and fancy. Coleridge's imagination extended much further than Mill could ever go, as far as God the creator. His fancy remained at the level of both James Mill and his son. As he put it in the <u>Biographia Literaria</u>, 'equally with the ordinary memory the Fancy must receive all its materials ready made from the law of association.'[9] Although Mill quoted Coleridge's poetry in describing his crisis, he could not follow the romantic poets' path of idealism and imagination.

However, in 1828 Wordsworth's poetry helped Mill escape from his crisis. What Hazlitt wrote of Coleridge almost applied to Mill: 'Poetry redeemed him from...spectral philosophy.'[10] Wordsworth appealed to Mill on account of his expression of 'states of feeling, and of thought coloured by feeling, under the excitement of beauty' (I, 151). Analysis had exposed 'the permanent sequences in nature' (I, 141). Now, in not quite parallel fashion, Wordsworth 'seemed' to show 'the perennial sources of happiness' (I, 151).[11] In line with this qualified affirmation of Wordsworth's power, Mill had to admit the relative character of the importance of this poet: that is, he was important to Mill himself in his own special, morbid situation. In general terms, he was 'the poet of unpoetical natures' (I, 153).

In the spirit of this rather devious response, Mill recognised that it was 'the crowning glory of Wordsworth...that he has borne witness' to 'the calm culture of reverence and love' (XIII, 474), but he also acknowledged the inappropriateness of Wordsworth's tranquil joy to the turbulent modern age. He declared the 'bad philosophy' of the 'Ode: Intimations of Immortality,' 'falsely called Platonic' (I, 153);[12] and he admitted that Wordsworth's 'talking of holding communion with the great forms of nature, his finding a grandeur in the beatings of the heart and so forth...is nonsense.'[13] The first phrase here suggests 'Tintern Abbey,' but more directly The Excursion, Book IV, significantly entitled 'Despondency Corrected.' At line 846 Wordsworth referred to 'The forms of Nature.' In the next paragraph he went on to describe the Greek belief in the existence of the gods in nature, a passage with which Mill would have had difficulty.[14] Later, Wordsworth wrote of the man who 'communes with the Forms/Of nature' (l. 1207). The Wanderer here 'contrasts the dignities of the Imagination with the presumptuous littleness of certain modern Philosophers.'[15] He ends his 'eloquent harangue' like 'an Indian Chief' (ll. 1276, 1279). After all, Mill stood on the side of the 'modern Philosophers' and against the 'Indian chief.' The imagination as presented by Wordsworth in The Excursion, like Coleridge's imagination in Biographia Literaria, was beyond his ken.

Mill enjoyed Wordsworth's poetry and like Arnold experienced his 'healing power.'[16] However, he did not appreciate his basic religious and philosophical message. Just as he enjoyed the landscape, but had no sense of its spiritual presence, or of such a presence looming through it. He had expressed a negative view of nature in The Republican (1823): and the feeling re-emerged explicitly in a letter of 1850 where he referred to nature's 'tyranny & iniquity' (XIV, 53) and again in the essay 'Nature' (1853-54). Harriet's lament was his: 'what an iron despotism we live under.'17

In spite of the reservations implied and stated above, in his other public statements in the years after his crisis Mill identified Wordsworth as the greatest poet of the age. Wordsworth's influence remained very much with him.18 In 1841 he wrote to a correspondent a passage which deserves to be quoted at length because it is so much infused with the spirit of the poet:

> the <u>great</u> simple elemental powers & constituents of the universe have however inexhaustible capabilities when any one is sufficiently fitted by nature & cultivation for poetry to have felt them as <u>realities</u>, that which a poet alone does habitually or frequently, which the majority of mankind never do at all & which we of the middle rank perhaps have the amazement of being able to do at some rare instants when all familiar things stand before us like spectres from another world - not however like phantoms but like the real things of which the phantoms alone are present to us or appear so in our common everyday state. That is truly a revelation of the seen, not of the unseen - & fills one with what Wordsworth must have been feeling when he wrote the line 'filled with the joy of troubled thoughts' (XIII, 469).

Francis E. Mineka suggests that Mill here might be misquoting from 'Tintern Abbey' (l. 94f). Mill quoted the same poem in discussing the Platonic ideas in his review of Grote's <u>Plato</u> a quarter of a century later. Here he wrote that to the 'contemplative mind,' such as Wordsworth's, 'all the objects of sense' suggest beyond themselves a 'something far more deeply interfused' (XI, 421). This was the poet's phrase in 'Tintern Abbey' (l. 96). Mill's 'splendid vision' (XI, 422) recalls the phrase in the 'Ode: Intimations of Immortality' (l. 73). For Wordsworth as for Plato this vision existed; but in Mill's eyes their's were only attempts 'to let in light on a dark subject' (XI, 421).

Thus Mill partly assimilated and partly fended off the influence of the great romantic poets. In 1831 he met their successor Carlyle. Carlyle's early writings seemed to Mill as to his father 'insane rhapsody,' 'a maze of poetry and German metaphysics' (I, 169, 181). However, he came to value Carlyle's work, 'not as philosophy to instruct, but as poetry to animate:' and Carlyle himself as 'one of the noblest spirits of our time' (I, 329), 'a poet...a man of intuition' (I, 183). He thus allowed Carlyle a position which Wordsworth had not been able to win.

Such great admiration caused Mill to praise Carlyle's French Revolution in the London and Westminster Review (1837), 'as an epic poem; and notwithstanding, or even in consequence of this, the truest of histories.'[19] So much for his father's attempt and for Mill's own earlier distinctions! In the course of their correspondence when the relationship between the two men was alive Mill could doubt with Carlyle 'whether Poetry is a thing that Science can define.'[20] He could see himself as providing the logical commentary which Carlyle the poet needed, like others and especially Harriet later: 'I can do homage to poetry. I can...make others...understand it in proportion to the measure of their capacity.' He continued, 'I believe that such a person is more wanted than even the poet himself' (XII, 163). Mill wrote to Carlyle again of art and science in balance: 'Have not all things two aspects, an Artistic and a Scientific; to the former of which the language of mysticism is the most appropriate, to the latter that of Logic?' 'One might almost say,' Mill continued, again giving emphasis to what he took to be his own role, that 'in these days' the latter is the 'necessary condition' of the former (XII, 219). However, doing the work of both poet and interpreter in one phase of Mill's thought at this time was the as yet unnamed comprehensive philosopher, never fully realised intellectually, but actualised in his own life in the person of Harriet Taylor.

Though Mill turned away from Carlyle's proferred leadership, with its mystical vision, as well as threatening racist and totalitarian aspects, he admitted that art in the modern age had to be 'polemical-Carlylean' (XIII, 446). He recognised, with Carlyle, the unsuitability of poetry (such as Wordsworth's) for the modern age.

Very soon the unitive figure greater in Mill's eyes than Carlyle and Wordsworth came along, possessing the desired 'balance among the faculties' (I, 147), lacking in both Mill himself and his literary mentors. This was Harriet Taylor, with whom he became intimate in 1832-33. Harriet enabled Mill to judge his contemporaries and to find them wanting. He praised her gift of imaginative sympathy; on account of her 'strength of noble and elevated feeling' he compared her favourably with Shelley (I, 195). Of course she became a 'predominating influence' in his life (I, 234). More than the poets and Carlyle, Harriet caused a broad flourishing of Mill's feelings, his sense of beauty, his moral idealism, and even his religious sense. As he later acknowledged, he owed to her 'poetic culture,' and by such culture he meant 'that my faculties, such as they were, became more and more attuned to the beautiful and elevated in all kinds, and especially in human feeling and character and more capable of vibrating in unison with it' (I, 623). Thus Mill admired the work of Wordsworth and Carlyle, but he turned away from them, unable and unwilling to follow the paths of nature and the ideal. He found a solution himself, not intellectually but personally, in his relationship with Harriet.

ii

It was through the independently minded unitarian W.J. Fox that Mill had met Harriet. In the congenial setting of Fox's <u>Monthly Repository</u> Mill elaborated his views on genius and on poetry in general (1832-33). At this stage of his career, and in this literary environment, poetry was so important to him that he discussed it, not only in terms of individuals, but, as he would be inclined to do temperamentally, in the abstract. In particular, Mill developed a concept of the imagination which took him beyond his father's quite generous discussion in the <u>Analysis</u>, though of course he did not go as far as his great romantic precursors Wordsworth, Coleridge and Shelley. Mill came to feel that 'imagination' had been neglected in his own upbringing. His faculty of analysis had been developed, to the degree that he was able to recognise 'the permanent sequences in nature' (I,

141), but he failed to realise them in his imagination. This demanded a sympathetic outgoing of mind of which Harriet was supremely capable. Mill also came to admire Shelley, especially through Harriet, but Shelley's eloquent argument on behalf of the broad utility of poetry through the exercise and development of the sympathetic imagination in the Defence of Poetry, though a reply to the satire of Mill's colleague Peacock (1820), did not appear in print until twenty years later.

In the light of the developing recognition of what he himself had lacked, Mill wrote in the article on genius in the Monthly Repository (1832) that imagination was a 'kind of self-observation' (I, 332). Further, it was another name for originality. By imagination Mill also sometimes meant pleasurable feelings and states of mind which possessed a degree of autonomy which separated them from our knowledge of the external world. He also meant the active sympathetic imagination which was a leading characteristic of both Shakespeare and Harriet. This sympathetic imagination on the part of the artist also somehow resulted in 'consistency and keeping' in the work of art.[21] It was furthermore a characteristic not only of creative, but also of what he called conceptive genius. Thus it was a mark not only of the poet and historian, but also of the reader and critic. This was the role of interpreter that Mill sought to play himself in his essays on particular writers of genius, for example, Carlyle and Tennyson.

In his article on Sedgwick (1835), Mill rejected the view of an historical decline of the role of the imagination, coinciding with a rise in the sway of reason. This Whiggish view had been expressed by his father in the History and popularised by Macaulay. On the contrary, young Mill now asserted that poetic imagination 'flourishes equally with reason' (X, 571). He defended Locke for not discussing imagination in Of Human Understanding, because 'with the imagination in its own province, as a source of enjoyment, and a means of educating the feelings, Locke had nothing to do' (X, 49). Mill himself here indicated that the autonomous and educational roles of the imagination were both important. Unfortunately, he did not pursue this, but in a note added in 1859 he allowed for another meaning of the term according to which imagination was the 'instrument of Reason' in 'keeping before the mind a lively and complete <u>image</u> of the thing to be reasoned about' (X, 50). The comment on the imagination in the text of the article was that of the young Mill, but in the later note he reverted to a more old-fashioned utilitarian position.

Reassessing Bentham in 1838 Mill allowed for an aesthetic aspect of <u>all</u> actions which appeals to the imagination (X, 1$\overline{12}$). This was an unusually sweeping view, appropriate to its ground-breaking context. It was later appreciated as a concession to the intuitionists by James Martineau and by Leckie. In fact Mill was living through a phase in which he could make such a concession. The yielding was not acknowledged in reference to Wordsworth and Coleridge, but it was present in the letters to Carlyle and in subsequent comments. However, the movement into this position was a rapid and brief one, and Mill gradually withdrew from it.

The sense of unity as crucial in the aesthetic experience remained with Mill, although he did not identify it with the imagination; rather, the late eighteenth century concepts of the sublime, the beautiful and the picturesque lurk at the back of his phrases. In letters to Harriet from Italy in 1855 he wrote of the 'infinite quantity of details subordinate to one coup d'oeil,' and of 'the vast multitude of distinguishable places & objects which the eye takes in at once, while one feels lifted out of all the littleness of it & conscious of a beauty which seems lent to it by something grander' (XIV, 286, 382).

Some of the comments in the edition of his father's <u>Analysis</u> (1869), bring us back to a much narrower base. Here Mill referred to 'mere imagination' and to the importance of memory as opposed to imagination. However, he also wrote characteristically that the beautiful appeals to the higher parts of our nature, stimulating 'the active power of the imagination to rise above known reality, into a more attractive or a more majestic world.'[22]

It was apparent that over the years from 1832 Mill developed a complex notion of the imagination. At one stage he rejected the view that it was no longer a dominant mental power, and also that its function was merely image-making and as such subordinate to that of the reason. He felt with Coleridge that the imagination was active generally. It was especially active both in the artist and in the spectator or critic. It manifested itself in the aesthetic experience and in the unity of the work of art. The imagination was autonomous, and also sympathetic. It had an educational function, in elevating the feelings above the level of the coarsely mundane. However, in spite of this frequently acknowledged importance, the imagination did not play a major role in Mill's later, more elaborated writings. It did not become of vital importance to him, as it had been for the romantic poets, Wordsworth, Coleridge and Shelley.

Mill gave some of the credit for sparking his own earlier discussions of poetry to James Martineau. Martineau began as a Benthamite; he himself said that 'though at times [he] was driven to disaffection by the dogmatism and acrid humours of [Bentham and James Mill, his] allegiance was restored and brightened by literary and personal relations with the younger Mill.'[23] A Unitarian, Martineau published articles on Priestley in the Monthly Repository (January-April 1833). Mill's connection with him is another indication of the kind of person he was now mixing with and being influenced by. The first instalment of Martineau's articles appeared in the same number with Mill's paper 'What is Poetry?' This was followed in February by Mill's article on Tennyson. Mill expressed his special debt to the conclusion of Martineau's articles, and he acknowledged their influence on 'The Two Kinds of Poetry,' which appeared in the following October. He also quoted Martineau and recalled his influence in the Logic. Here he paraphrased Martineau to the effect that 'in minds of strong organic sensibility synchronous associations will be likely to predominate, producing a tendency to conceive things in pictures and in the concrete, richly clothed in attributes and circumstances, a mental habit which is commonly called Imagination, and is one of the peculiarities of the painter and the poet,' as opposed to the historian and the scientist (VII, 481). It is piquant to observe that behind Martineau here lurked James Mill, whom Martineau praised in the article: before 'his gaze the most intricate and delicate of human emotions...are arrested.'[24] The distinction between synchronous and successive associations was James Mill's, but Martineau linked it to artistic and intellectual roles.

Responding to these various influences, in the Monthly Repository (January 1833), Mill himself sought to answer the question, what is poetry? He concluded that it was neither narration, nor description, nor eloquence. Rather than rhetoric to persuade the many, it was soliloquy, overheard by the few. It was 'the delineation of the deeper and more secret workings of the human heart' (I, 345).[25] In this view of the importance of psychological revelation Mill was close to the romantics, for example, Southey who had written a few years before: 'It is in verse only that we can throw off the yoke of the world, and are as it were privileged to utter our deepest and holiest feelings.'[26] In 1841, Mill, continuing this theoretical discussion in informal vein, admitted to G.H. Lewes: 'If we, more Germanico, call every idea a religious idea which either grows out of or leads to, feelings of infinity and mysteriousness...then religious ideas are the most poetical of all' (XIII, 466). He here extends the range of poetry from the psychological to the religious.

Mill took his analysis further in writing on 'The Two Kinds of Poetry' in the Monthly Repository (October 1833). Here he emphasised more the physiology, the legalism and the associationism of his utilitarian background. The last in particular was derived from James Mill and Martineau. Mill gave Wordsworth as the example of the lesser poet in whom thought is primary, as against the purer emotionalism of Shelley. He asked, 'What is poetry, but the thoughts and words in which emotion spontaneously embodies itself?' (I, 356). Poets were particularly concerned with 'unity of feeling,' achieved by the exercise of a 'fervid' imagination (I, 360). Mill admired Shelley's true passion, 'the exuberant outpourings of a seething fancy' (XII, 336), and he continued to do so throughout his life. Though he considered Macaulay 'an intellectual dwarf,' he singled out from his essays a passage praising Shelley, where he wrote, 'He turned atheism itself into a mythology, rich with visions' (XIV, 332). In 1870 Mill read the 'Ode to Liberty' aloud: 'he got quite excited & moved over it rocking backwards & forwards & nearly choking with emotion; he said himself: "it is almost too much for one!"'[27]

In connection with this emphasis on feeling, acutely verbalised publicly in the early 1830's, it is noteworthy that in an unpublished comment on Browning's 'Pauline' of 1833 Mill did not criticise the prominence of feeling in the poem, but the negative, egotistic character of the feeling displayed (I, 596f).

However, Mill concluded the essay on 'The Two Kinds of Poetry' by asserting that the poet can 'by culture, make himself a philosopher' (I, 363). In this essay Mill set forth the image of the 'logician-poet' (I, 364), associated with Milton and Coleridge, presumably a figure who transcended the positions of both Wordsworth and Shelley. He wrote on Tennyson that 'the noblest end of poetry as an intellectual pursuit [is] that of acting upon the desires and characters of mankind through their emotions, to raise them towards the perfection of their nature' (I, 414). And in 1841 he defined poetry as 'feeling expressing itself in the forms of thought' (XIII, 471). Much later, in 1865, he indicated approval of Comte's view of the poet's 'mixed appeal to the sentiments and the understanding, fitted [as he is] to educate the feelings of abstract thinkers, and enlarge the intellectual horizon of all men' (X, 324).

Though in these writings the poet was a central concern, he did not possess the imaginative fire which inspired the romantics. Without the transcendental element, he was the exponent of the aspirations of the merely human emotions and mind. Mill will turn unreluctantly from him in the direction of positive science.

In a kind of bold peroration to the essay 'The Two Kinds of Poetry,' Mill accounted for the abundance of conservative poets in the modern age. Their emotional sensitivity had made them receptive to the traditional values inculcated in them. Mill later defended De Vigny along these lines, and in doing so he evoked the 'pure untroubled spirit of Conservative poetry' in Southey and Wordsworth (I, 487). There was an elegiac character about these later critical comments as Mill made a case for the 'infinite longings' of the conservative poets in an alien modern world (I, 470).

In the <u>Monthly Repository</u> papers Mill emphasised the subjectivity and emotionality of poetry. Beyond Wordsworth, Shelley was his great contemporary example of these qualities. These elements satisfied Mill's own needs and related to the general conceptions of the post-romantic era in which he lived. Also Mill emphasised the elevating character of poetic feeling, in this expressing a demand characteristic both of himself and of the age. His views seemed to settle down, following a pattern typical of the mature thinker, into a recognition of the need, even in this art, of a balance, - a balance, not only between the emotional, the aesthetic and the moral, but also between feeling and thought, a unity of poetry and philosophy of which the greatest artist was capable.

    The influence of Plato through James Mill on the child John was significant. Mill thought himself 'beyond any modern man that I know of except my father and perhaps even beyond him, a pupil of Plato' (I, 24). Now, in this creative period of early manhood, Mill sent some of his notes on Plato, 'mostly written long ago' (XII, 218), to Fox for publication in the <u>Monthly Repository</u>. They appeared there in 1834-35. Mill wrote most expansively on the <u>Gorgias</u>. The comments here were suffused with the sense of the poetic which we have seen Mill developing. In an eloquent conclusion, he declared that the love of virtue was not to be achieved by argument, even on the part of Plato, 'but through the imagination and the affections.' We acquired this love 'from those we earliest love,' from the noble characters of history, and from the 'poets or artists' who 'can clothe [noble] feelings in the most beautiful forms, and breathe them into us through our imagination and our sensations.' It is for this last skill that 'Plato has deserved the title of a great moral writer.' In the final sentence of the article Mill completed the picture by emphasising the associational process which took place under the influence of Plato's writing: 'this dialogue makes the feelings and course of life which it inculcates commend themselves to our inmost nature, by associating them with our most impressive conceptions of beauty and power' (XI, 150). At this point the Socratic method was no longer for Mill a merely intellectual one, but emotive and aesthetic as well.

    This whole passage can be read as a kind of synopsis of Mill's broad development up to this time, with its admission of the limitation of the intellect and of the important role of imagination and affection; the reference to the need for early love, the importance of historical example, and the exaltation of the poet; the ethical emphasis, the reference to association, and the turning back to the Plato of Mill's infant reading, though finding in him qualities which could hardly have been observed then.

    In the <u>Monthly Repository</u> articles Mill

noted the 'extraordinary dramatic talent' (XI, 97) of Plato's dialogues, and he felt these qualities still when he reviewed Grote's Plato in the Edinburgh Review years later, in 1866. Through these qualities Plato constituted Mill's ideal, as a combination of philosopher, rhetorician and artist. Especially he clothed his doctrine in 'the most brilliant colours of his poetic imagination' (XI, 412f). And at the same time as he praised Plato's 'negative dialectics,' Mill admitted that negation was not enough (XI, 383). The dialectic process had a 'poetical and religious halo' for Plato, for through it he reached the 'divine essences' (XI, 406). The halo shone for Mill too, but he denied the value of its brightest light.

In this section, turning upon Mill's contributions to the Monthly Repository, we have seen his highly sympathetic appreciation of the nature of the imagination and of poetry itself. However, in the perspective of his career overall, this seems to be a concessive phase which leaves only a few traces in his later work. Nevertheless, these traces are clearly marked.

iii

Like his father, Mill felt the great importance of education in the narrowest as well as the broadest terms. The periodical was a means of education; poetry played an important part in education. Hence Mill's editorship of the London Review from 1835 was significant. It can be seen as an attempt to reach a wider audience on the basis of the theoretical views concerning poetry which he had developed in the Monthly Repository. Mill felt the need for such a review to erect what he called, using a new term, 'a Normal School of Literature' (XII, 210). Bentham, in founding the Westminster Review, had aimed to balance 'politics and morals' against 'flowery, literary insignificances.'[28] Mill's aim was loftier. He intended 'to develop the philosophy of society - of the human mind - of imaginative literature and ethics.'[29] He sought 'clear and comprehensive views of education and human culture,' on the basis partly of the evidence of the poets (X, 56).

In accordance with this ambition, in his article on Tennyson (1835) Mill analysed the character of the poet as such and offered a generous estimate of Tennyson in the light of it. He lauded Tennyson for his symbolisation of feeling, as well as of 'spiritual truths' (I, 417). He urged him to strive to achieve the spirituality and philosophical depth which mark the great poet.

Mill's aim in this characteristic article was not to judge, as Jeffrey had insisted upon doing in the Edinburgh Review, nor to ridicule, like Croker in the Quarterly, but to sympathise. He played the part of sympathetic reader which Wordsworth had desiderated and which was also appropriate to his own theory of the imagination. His aim was to reveal the qualities of the poetry which he was presenting, but it was also, in Coleridgean spirit, to apply philosophical principles which he himself had developed. Thus he wrote a warm, though not careless, appreciation of Tennyson, in direct reaction against and far different from the cold, sneering approach of Croker in the Quarterly. Mill appreciated the importance of the poetic function, and he felt that it was the pleasure and the duty of the critic to make the poet's work accessible to the reading public, as part of a process of propaganda and education.

In his London and Westminster Review article on the broad topic of 'Civilisation' (1836) Mill showed how much the regeneration of society depended upon literature and literary education. Education needed to include the study of the classics for their 'ennobling' tendency, as well as their power to engender toleration and sympathy; it should also include history, with modern literature, for its revelation of the 'infinite varieties of human nature' (XVIII, 145). Mill also more briefly recommended the study of the 'philosophy...of poetry and art' (XVIII, 146).

After his father's death in June 1836, Mill anticipated a broader role for the London and Westminster, in advocating a utilitarianism 'which holds Feeling at least as valuable as Thought, & Poetry not only on a par with, but the necessary condition of, any true & comprehensive Philosophy' (XII, 312). His ambition was to make the review 'an organ of real literary & social criticism' (XII, 314); he looked forward to a combination of 'philosophical & imaginative criticism' in its pages (XII, 319).

An example is Mill's own article on Carlyle's French Revolution (July 1837). The work he considered to be history and epic poem in one. It was poetry because, unlike Hume and Gibbon (and, one might add, James Mill) Carlyle did what the dramatists, particularly Shakespeare, had tried to do, that is, present sympathetically real human beings. Moreover, Carlyle presented the richly various feelings associated with historical events. He presented them in a unified form, and in a way to cause emotion in the reader, with a humour as well as a pathos 'which makes the heart too full for endurance.'[30] Thus Mill greatly admired Carlyle as an historical artist and the French Revolution as an effective work of art. At the same time, the old utilitarian and the new positivist rose in him as he recognised the necessity and value of scientific dissection and generalisation. Carlyle did not display 'the connected view of history' which Mill met with in Comte after this time (I, 219). Moreover, the 'natural supernaturalism' which permeated Carlyle's work was not understood by Mill.

Writing on Michelet in the Edinburgh Review seven years later, 1844, Mill put his review of Carlyle's French Revolution into a firm perspective which his father and Comte would have appreciated. Like a poet Carlyle had presented 'a living picture'[31] of the past, but he had not managed to construct the possible, necessary and desirable science of history.

After the death of his father, in the full tide of reaction, Mill in the London and Westminster (1838) stressed the incompleteness of Bentham as a thinker on society and as a man. He lacked the qualities which Mill doubted the power of in himself: sympathy, imagination, poetry. He was preoccupied with the moral aspects of human behaviour, as opposed to the sympathetic and aesthetic. This gap was filled by the compensatory portrait of Coleridge as thinker, published two years later. Yet the more purely poetic concerns were very much in the background here. Mill deplored the lack of imagination and appreciation for poetry on the part of Bentham. He himself acknowledged that action had a beautiful or aesthetic aspect which appealed to the imagination. On the other hand, he did not stress the poetry or the poetic qualities of Coleridge, though he believed that Coleridge belonged with those who possess the important sympathetic historical imagination. There is a sense of balance if one examines the two essays side by side, but not of dialectic. As with Wordsworth and Carlyle, there is an irreducible element in Coleridge as thinker and poet which Mill could not assimilate.

Edward Alexander writes that Mill's 'literary passion burned with a very subdued flame' after 1837.[32] It may not have been true, as Bowring asserted in 1840, that, with a newly-developed imagination, after reading Wordsworth Mill had 'been in a strange confusion... endeavouring to unite poetry and philosophy.'[33] But he settled down under the more than philosophical influence of Harriet Taylor. After a transitional period he reached what J.M. Robson calls a 'settled but not stagnant maturity.'[34] Mill came to regard Harriet as 'his one only source of good' (XIV, 43). He devoted the energies of the major part of his intellectual career not to the problem of the relationship between poetry and philosophy – or even the more urgent one of the relation between poetry and truth – , but to the examination of epistemology, logic and political economy, carried out in a humanitarian spirit. He moved on from a period in which he was directly engaged in the reading and evaluation of poetry, to one in which his interest became submerged in what for him were larger, more important, as well as more manageable concerns. Mill had first been interested in poems and poets. Now it became largely a question, insofar as it was a question at all, of aesthetics.[35]

NOTES

1. <u>Victorian Periodicals Newsletter</u>, no. 10 (1977), p. 124.
2. <u>Bermondsey Book</u>, vol. 6 (1929), p. 12f.
3. The same, p. 17.
4. <u>Annals of the Parish</u>, ed. J. Kinsley (Oxford University Press, London, 1967), p. 59.
5. It is noteworthy that the first break in Mill's mental crisis came through reading Marmontel. On this William James commented, 'Heaven save the mark!' <u>Varieties of Religious Experience</u> (Longman, London, 1902), p. 204. Marmontel was a favourite author of Macaulay: John Clive, <u>Macaulay</u> (Knopf, New York, 1973), p. 38; and also later of Ruskin: see for example <u>Letters to C.E. Norton</u> (2 vols, Houghton, Mifflin, Boston, 1905), vol. 1, pp. 6. 256. Carlyle commented on Marmontel's 'rose-pink romance-pictures' in celebration of the 'moral sublime,' <u>Critical and Miscellaneous Essays</u> (7 vols, Chapman and Hall, London, 1872), vol. 3,

p. 214.
6. *Biographia Literaria*, ed. J. Shawcross, vol. 1, p. 93.
7. The same, p. 97f.
8. A phrase in Coleridge's 'Dejection,' from which poem Mill quotes in his account of his mental crisis in the *Autobiography*.
9. *Biographia Literaria*, vol. 1, p. 202.
10. *Spirit of the Age* (Colburn, London, 1825), p. 70.
11. Jonathan Loesberg, 'Fictions of Consciousness' (Diss. Cornell, 1977), p. 62, comments on the repetition of the word 'seems,' as well as on Mill's 'always ambivalent' attitude towards Wordsworth, p. 190. This is illustrated by the passage which he quotes, p. 196, from 'The Two Kinds of Poetry' where Mill writes of 'that culture by which Wordsworth has reared from his own inward nature the richest harvest ever brought forth by a soil of so little depth' (I, 359).
12. Mill's reaction is the opposite of Keble's and Newman's. The latter quoted Keble and wrote of the 'noble philosophy' of the 'Ode': *Theological Papers* (Clarendon Press, Oxford, 1976), p. 74.
13. *Literary Essays*, ed. Alexander, p. 352.
14. Schiller's lament over the modern absence of 'The Gods of Greece' was quoted by Mill's friend Grote in the *Westminster Review* (1843), with the comment: 'Estimated by a poetical standard, the loss has been serious indeed,' *Minor Works* (1873), p. 133.
15. Argument of book iv, *Poetical Works*, ed. E. De Selincourt and H. Darbishire, vol. 5 (1949), p. 109. The second phrase in Mill's 1829 passage, 'a grandeur in the beatings of the heart,' comes from a section of *The Prelude* included in *Poems* (1815).
16. Arnold, 'Memorial Verses.'
17. F.A. Hayek, *John Stuart Mill and Harriet Taylor* (Routledge, London, 1951), p. 156. Compare Arnold on 'the iron age' in 'Memorial Verses.'
18. Though perhaps he hardly downed 'tomes of Wordsworth like medicinal draughts of stout,' Thomas M. Disch and Charles Naylor, *Neighbouring Lives* (Scribner's, New York, 1981), p. 38.
19. *Literary Essays*, p. 132.
20. Carlyle, *Collected Letters*, vol. 6, p. 404.
21. *Examiner* (3 June 1832), p. 358.
22. *Analysis*, vol. 1, p. 143; vol. 2, p.

255n.
23. Types of Ethical Theory (2 vols, Clarendon Press, Oxford, 1885), vol. 1, p. ix.
24. Monthly Repository, vol. 7 (1833), p. 85*. It is noteworthy that after this date Martineau went through his own intellectual crisis; this led him to a rejection of the utilitarian support for his unitarian faith.
25. 'The human heart' later became more coldly 'human emotion' (I. 345). Byron also had commented on the psychological function of poetry, using a striking metaphor: poetry 'is the lava of the imagination whose eruption prevents an earthquake,' Letters, ed. L.A. Marchand (Murray, London, 1973-), vol. 3, p. 179.
26. Sir Thomas More, 2nd edn (1831), vol. 2, p. 306. Also Keble had said: 'Poetry...is nothing else than each poet's innermost feeling issuing in rhythmic language:' Lectures on Poetry 1832-41, tr. E.K. Francis (2 vols, Clarendon Press, Oxford, 1912), vol. 2, p. 35. Ruskin opined in 1841: 'He is the best poet who can by the fewest words touch the greatest number of secret chords in his reader's own mind:' Works, ed. Cook and Wedderburn (39 vols, Allen, London, 1903-12), vol. 1, p. 441.
27. Amberley Papers, ed. B. and P. Russell (2 vols, Hogarth Press, London, 1937), vol. 2, p. 375.
28. Bentham, Works, vol. 10, p. 540.
29. Harriet Grote, The Philosophical Radicals of 1832, reprint edn (Franklin, New York, 1970), p. 10.
30. Literary Essays, p. 149.
31. Dissertations and Discussions (4 vols, Parker, London, 1859-75), vol. 2, p. 127.
32. Mill News Letter, vol. 5 (spring 1970), p. 16.
33. Caroline Fox, Memories, 2nd edn (1882), vol. 1, p. 216.
34. Victorian Periodicals Newsletter, no. 10 (1977), p. 124.
35. Cf I, xiv: 'it is probably best, in the over-all view, to say that where, before the mental crisis, he had been "theoretically indifferent" to poetry..., ever afterward he was theoretically in favour of it - still, however, almost entirely at the level of theory.'

J.S. Mill

PART THREE. MILL AND POETRY: LATER YEARS

Mill's mature phase began in the early 1840's. This was the period of his diverse major works: the <u>Logic</u> (1843), the <u>Principles of Political Economy</u> (1848), <u>On Liberty</u> (1859), <u>Utilitarianism</u> (1863), the commentaries on the philosophies of Sir William Hamilton and Comte (both 1865), the <u>Inaugural Address</u> delivered at St. Andrew's University (1867), the edition of his father's <u>Analysis of the Phenomena of the Human Mind</u> (1869), the <u>Autobiography</u>, begun 1853-54 but not published until after his death, and the essays on 'The Utility of Religion' and 'Nature' (1854) and 'Theism' (1868-70), also all published posthumously. Mill's concern in these later years is not so much with reflecting on the actual reading of poetry, as with incidentally incorporating his view of poetry in general as part of his view of art and the aesthetic into his broader presentations of human experience. In fact, he does not present a general view in his own terms, and the place of art in what he does write is a fluctuating and uncertain one. This will appear in the course of the ensuing survey.
    In the <u>Logic</u>, book three, Mill approvingly quotes Reid on the tendency of primitive man to find life in everything. Reid writes:

> When a few, of superior intellectual abilities, find leisure for speculation, they begin to philosophize, and soon discover, that many of those objects which at first they believed to be intelligent and active are really lifeless and passive. This is a very important discovery. It elevates the mind, emancipates from many vulgar superstitions.

Reid asserts that philosophy shows that nature is dead. Mill, aligning himself with this view, comments, with a powerful metaphor:

> The suggestions, however, of daily life continuing to be more powerful than those of scientific thought, the original instinctive philosophy maintains its ground in the mind, underneath the growths obtained by cultivation.... The theory against which I am

contending derives its nourishment from that substratum. Its strength does not lie in argument, but in its affinity to an obstinate tendency of the infancy of the human mind (VII, 358).

This tendency Mill would have found strongly exemplified, for example, in his reading of Wordsworth. He himself here rejects it.

In the passage quoted by Mill, Reid emphasizes the importance of language as an indicator of modes of thought. Mill himself, in book five of the Logic, allows the rhetorical value of metaphor, illustrating this, in his first edition, from Carlyle, but the value of metaphor, clearly a hangover from primitive modes of thought, is secondary in his view (VIII, 800).

In the final book of the Logic, 'on the logic of the moral sciences,' Mill presents an attitude which in outline might have been his father's, buttressed with the theory of Comte. He declares that there is a science of human nature, both static and dynamic. This science shows that society is progressive and that it has advanced from the stage of supernatural explanations to that of explanations according to natural law. The two stages had been juxtaposed by implication in James Mill's enlightened overview of Indian history, which his son endorsed. The same historical perspective is indicated more vividly in Mill's article on Grote's History of Greece in the Edinburgh Review (1846). Following Grote, he emphasizes the link between primitive beliefs, feeling and imagination.

This view lies behind the passages on the primitive and on metaphorical language which have just been discussed. In the Logic there is no place for poetry, associated with the primitive and the metaphorical, until one reaches the final chapter of book six. Here the broad category of the aesthetic does enter. At this point Mill turns from science or theory to art or practice. He emphasizes in a note of 1851 that he is using the word 'art' in the broadest sense (VIII, 943), not as denoting the poetic. But he himself says that science has to do with defining means, the end is a question of art. This certainly introduces art in the more special sense, because he defines the three departments of 'the Art of Life' as the moral, the prudent, and the aesthetic or beautiful and noble. These can all be subsumed under the utilitarian term 'happiness' (VIII, 951), which his father had been unable to define.[1] Perhaps sensing his own difficulty here, Mill refers in a note of 1865 to Utilitarianism, discussed below. Thus the emotional and the aesthetic, which Mill had fused in his earlier conception of poetry, emerge, but only at the conclusion of his discussion. He does not allow that, as aspects of the end, they might have qualified his earlier, long discussion of the means. The emotional and aesthetic problems which Mill was to recognize in terms of personal development in his account of his mental crisis of the 1820's in the Autobiography and which he had recognized in terms of philosophical description in the essays on Bentham and Coleridge seem to be present here, though unacknowledged. That is, there are gaps between the consideration of theory and that of practice, between means and end, between reason on the one hand and the emotional and the aesthetic on the other.

A surprising negative aesthetic note, which perhaps relates to the discussion of omission, even suppression, here, is sounded in an unpublished paragraph of the Logic, book four. Mill here asserts that 'good taste' keeps 'certain aspects of things as much as possible out of sight.' 'Close contemplation' of the 'mere mechanism of production' of agreable things 'diminishes their charm to the imagination' (VIII, 696). This reticence suggests Ruskin's and anticipates Mill's own comments on a much-admired painting by Perugino, his 'Descent from the Cross': 'one of the greatest pictures ever painted - all the disagreeable of the subject taken away & nothing but a beautiful dead body & the most beautiful feeling in the numerous gracefully grouped spectators' (XIV, 482).

What Mill would like to achieve in personal, social and aesthetic terms is a balance of values, at the same time as the expression of the suppressed, as well as its continued suppression! The expression is so difficult that Mill not only has to control it by means of the notion of balance, but also by the notion of cultivation and enhancement in order to make the suppressed a worthy factor in the equation. This is true of his presentation of the feelings in personal terms, as of the working class in social terms in the Principles, discussed below. The feelings, like the workers, can win a legitimate place, but only after a process of justification and ennoblement, of cultivation and education, - of beautification - has taken place.

Mill's difficulty on the political plane is indicated in his second major work, the Principle of Political Economy (1848). In book four he says that he would like to see a balance achieved between the currently dominant mode of competition on the one hand and cooperation on the other. Social progress furthermore can only be achieved by a change of character brought about by education. Mill's demand upon education is thus even greater than that of his father had been, since it requires an achievement not only intellectual, but in respect of the whole character. The progressive state about which conventional economists still tell us, and whose economy Mill himself has been analysing, will, when we consider ends (compare the conclusion of the Logic), become the stationary state. In economic terms, this society would be wealthier, and the wealth would be more evenly distributed. Moreover, at the cultural level, more people would be able 'to cultivate freely the graces of life.' It would be possible at last moreover, and this is a new element, to enjoy solitude 'in the presence of natural beauty and grandeur,' in places where the 'spontaneous activity of nature' still goes on (III, 755-56). Mill's actual social world is one of analysis and the sordid pursuit of wealth (III, 754), at best the 'delayed gratification'[2] of his father's utilitarian economic theory, as well as of Malthus's prudential population theory, both of which Mill broadly espoused. However, in the presentation in the Principles a picture of the ideal world is set beside the actual, though the two are hardly brought into alignment.

Mill's problem partly stems from the conflict between the utilitarian eschewal of happiness as an element in the means towards achieving the utilitarian goal and the fact that the goal itself is happiness. The problem also arises from his evident difficulty, like that of his father, in appreciating and in analyzing the nature of happiness as an actual experience in depth. Mill does courageously confront the basic teleological questions in a climactic position in his arguments, at the conclusion of book six of the Logic and of book four of the Principles, but the presentation in these crucial sections is at odds with the drift of what has gone before.[3]

J.S. Mill

In the <u>Logic</u> Mill analyzes one human intellectual tool, and in the <u>Principles</u> he uses it in analyzing one field of social endeavour. In both places he declares the exact boundaries of his subject-matter, though he recognizes the importance of the ends for which logic and political economy are employed, both social and personal. Mill extends his view in the two essays of 1854, 'Nature' and 'Utility of Religion.' Throughout he has used the Benthamite criterion of usefulness. The tool of logic is examined, so that more efficient use may be made of it, and the same is true of the field of political economy. The criterion of utility had been restricted to such areas by Bentham and James Mill, but Mill now extends it questioningly to the wider spheres of nature and religion.

Nature is indifferent or hostile to man, to be used by him for the advancement of his individual and social culture. Mill contrasts what nature is with what ought to be, the province of art in the broad sense. In spite of nature, the goal of man is, through civilization, the careful achievement of what ought to be. Thus the polarization between the actual and the ideal, indicated in the different spheres of the <u>Logic</u> and the <u>Principles</u>, persists strongly in this essay.

Like his predecessors, Mill in the essay on the utility of religion rejects the supernatural basis of religion, but he considers it primarily from the individual, rather than the social standpoint. He recognizes the needs of the individual in the light of his own experience, at this time being analyzed by himself in the first draft of the <u>Autobiography</u>. These needs are in the areas of emotional, aesthetic and spiritual cultivation. The individual possesses a sense of the infinite, which comes to him through the just now despised nature. The individual also retains the eighteenth century sense of the sublime and the beautiful, as well as possessing a sense of the moral ideal. These can be gratified through the imagination. The imagination itself is put to work by poetry and religion. Mill doubts the efficacy of the religious mode because of the obstacles which are raised by its insistence on the alignment of imaginative gratification with fact. The way of poetry Mill acknowledges the importance of, as he does in the <u>Autobiography</u>, but he turns away from poetry to take over from Comte the less than fully satisfactory Religion of Humanity. Thus Mill here appears to be making room for the feelings, imagination, poetry and some kind of religion in the post-utilitarian Comteian intellectual personal world which he is trying both to live in and to create.

Despite the theoretical stand-off between nature and man presented in the essay 'Nature,' Mill's epistolary accounts of his travels in Italy in 1855 show the continued power of his aesthetic sensibility in his day-to-day experience of both nature and art. He noticed both the beautiful and the sublime, and the contribution towards them made by historical and literary associations. At Naples he found beauty 'a perpetual feast': 'now in this bedroom by candlelight I am in a complete nervous state from the sensation of the beauty I am living among' (XIV, 325, 322). His notes in The Phytologist (1841-62) are those of a scientific observer, but in 1860 he waxed eloquent there over the beauties of the flowers of England. He writes of 'the elegant white Potentilla Fragariastrum, the starry Stellaria Holostea, the fragrant Ground-ivy..., the cheerful Mercurialis perennis, [and] the bright-eyed Germander Speedwell,' and then of the furze and broom 'which by their masses of deep yellow, convert many of our spring landscapes into the likeness of Turner's pictures.' In the conclusion of the article Mill turns enthusiastically to 'the true South,' with places which are 'the paradise of the botanist, as they are of the lover of Nature,' in particular, the hills outside Rome, with the crowning attraction of classical and religious associations:

> we climb through woods abounding in Galanthus nivalis and Corydalis cava, to that summit which was the arx of Jupiter Latialis, and to which the thirty Latian cities ascended in solemn procession to offer their annual sacrifice. The place is now occupied by a convent, under the wall of which I gathered Ornithogalum nutans, and from its neighbourhood I enjoyed a panoramic view, surely the most glorious, in its combination of natural beauty and grandeur of historical recollections, to be found anywhere on earth.[4]

Harriet Mill died in 1858, and according to her husband England lost with her its 'greatest mind' (XV, 601). On Liberty, published in the following year and Mill's most celebrated work, was intended as a memorial to her. The individual, of importance in 'Utility of Religion,' is of course central here. Mill argues that individual liberty is the highest value of social life, and that society should be so arranged as to protect it. Perhaps he goes furthest when he uses the phrase 'individual spontaneity.' He insists that what he wants is not just individuality of the understanding, but organic individuality of the 'desires and impulses' as well. Yet this demand loses some of its boldness when the phrase 'individual spontaneity' is set beside the authority of Humboldt's definition to which Mill appeals. Humboldt declares that 'the end of man, or that which is prescribed by the eternal...dictates of reason...is the highest...development of his powers.' Here 'individual spontaneity' has to submit to a supernatural standard. For Mill individuality becomes not an end in itself; but he values it when it is disciplined for the sake of the individual and also for the sake of others. Indeed, liberty is 'the only unfailing and permanent source' of general improvement (XVIII, 261, 263, 272).

Thus individual realization is the social goal, yet at the same time it should be pursued for the sake of others and for the sake of social progress. This circularity of argument marked Mill's discussion of the pursuit of happiness in the Autobiography. The injunction there is: do not seek happiness for yourself, seek it for others. If the enquirer is interested in finding out just what happiness is, and whether it is worth seeking for anyone's sake, he is not helped by the recommended procedure. He needs to look elsewhere, for example, to 'Utility of Religion' and Utilitarianism.

Alan Ryan at the conclusion of his book on Mill (1970) emphasizes the aesthetic personal ideal towards which On Liberty is moving, but the ideal is hardly defined and described as such in the work itself - except at a crucial point in the argument where he writes of human beings becoming 'a noble and beautiful object of contemplation' (XVIII, 266). The further critical comment has interestingly been made that 'the weight of Mill's analytical argument' in On Liberty is supported by the 'metaphorical assertion of feeling and imagination.'[5] However, metaphorical support is not enough to give the argument conviction, as Mill himself would acknowledge.

The gap with regard to the prized aesthetic element in individual life which perhaps exists in On Liberty may partly be filled in Utilitarianism (1861). Here Mill shows that he recognizes the need for a richer definition of individual happiness, his and the utilitarian goal, certainly in the light of popular misunderstandings in general, and perhaps also in that of the narrow focus in this respect of On Liberty. For Mill it is not enough to understand happiness in terms of qualitatively undifferentiated pleasures. Happiness becomes the exercise of the 'higher faculties' (X, 212)[6] and of sympathy, carried to the point of self-sacrifice for the sake of others. Here we may have escaped from the Benthamite view of the sensuality of most men and a simplistic view of happiness. However, we are still on the Benthamite plane of the exacting morality of the few. Tantalizing glimpses are provided of the role that the feelings, poetry and religion may play. The essay is written in the spirit of 'Utility of Religion.'

Perhaps Arnold had this work in mind when he commented in 1863 that Mill, beyond the rest of what he considered to be his sterile school, recognized the need for 'joyful emotion' in connection with morality. However, for Arnold Mill's recognition was not powerful enough.[7]

In the Examination of Sir William Hamilton's Philosophy and Auguste Comte and Positivism, both published in 1865, Mill moves away from the social and the personal plane into critiques of two powerful philosophies of the day. He attacks the intuitionism of Hamilton and the overstrained positivism of Comte, but in his response in both cases he allows room for the modulating influence of poetry and art.

In the Examination Mill continues to emphasize the priority and the centrality of human experience. As with the Logic and the Principles there is a crucial turn towards the conclusion which falls outside the general spirit of the book. He seems to contradict his earlier views of nature as a machine (the Logic) and as the dour antagonist ('Nature'). Hamilton conventionally associates ignorance with wonder and science with the annihilation of that experience. In reply Mill asserts that wonder is indeed an appropriate response to nature. At the same time moreover he declares that there is an 'irreducible residuum' in the world which will forever remain unknown to science (IX, 481). It is ironical that for the perseverance of the sense of wonder when faced with nature, marked by this residuum, Mill evokes the authority of the two poets Wordsworth and Goethe.

In discussing Comte and Positivism, Mill accepts Comte's analysis of historical development from theological through metaphysical to scientific: this had been the point of view adumbrated in the Logic over twenty years before. At the same time, Mill sympathizes with Comte in yielding a place to art and poetry in his scheme of things, although a subordinate one: 'He not only personally appreciates, but rates high in moral value, the creations of poets and artists...deeming them, by their mixed appeal to the sentiments and the understanding, admirably fitted to educate the feelings of abstract thinkers, and enlarge the intellectual horizon of people of the world' (X, 324). Later, Mill also expresses his admiration for Comte for seeking to develop his philosophy into a religion. As he does so, one experiences the shift of point of view which has been identified elsewhere, only the shift here is less abrupt. It is as though the trajectory of progress, indicated in the Logic (VIII, 913), is turning back into a Viconian orbit. The spectre of religion is making its presence felt yet again, in human history as in Mill's own personal life. Mill is also seen to be struggling to get beyond the dichotomy between egotism and altruism which he had himself set up, for example, in Utilitarianism and the Autobiography. He rejects, as he had done in On Liberty, the Calvinistic or Carlylean either-or. Yet the intermediate step which he himself takes is a very delicate one, here as elsewhere: 'The moralization of the personal enjoyments we deem to consist, not in reducing them to the smallest possible amount, but in cultivating the habitual wish to share them with others' (X, 339).

The uncharacteristic satire which marks Mill's presentation of the Religion of Humanity perhaps indicates his sensitivity. It seems that Comte presents an exaggerated version of Mill's own problems. Having built up a system intellectually, Comte's social ideal becomes to subordinate the intellect wholly to the feelings. He makes an important generalization, the seed of which had been present in Mill's own response to his mental crisis: 'Art, which calls the emotions into play along with and more than the reason, is the only intellectual exercise really adapted to human nature' (X, 355). Comte feels the dryness of the purely intellectual or scientific account of the world, and he calls in feeling, education and art in order to fill the gap.

> It would be an excellent thing, M. Comte thinks, if science could be deprived of this sécheresse, and directly associated with sentiment. Now it is impossible to prove that the external world, and the bodies composing it, are not endowed with feeling, and voluntary agency. It is therefore highly desirable that we should educate ourselves into imagining that they are (X, 363).

This is quite different from Mill's own opinion, as expressed in the Logic, appealing for support to Reid. Mill satirically comments: 'This stuff, though he calls it fiction, he soon after speaks of as..."perfecting our unity...by supplying the gaps in our scientific notions with poetic fictions, and developing sympathetic emotions and aesthetic inspirations"' (X, 364). Here Mill seems to be ridiculing Comte for trying to do in terms of a philosophical view what he himself had sensed the need of and tended to draw back from in his own thought and writings. Witness 'Utility of Religion' and later the Inaugural Address and 'Theism.' Moreover, Mill himself in the contemporaneous Hamilton brought forward Wordsworth and Goethe as supplying such gaps as Comte indicated.

Though art evidently has but a tentative place in Mill's own thinking, he gives it a major one in the educational process at large. In the Inaugural Address delivered at St. Andrew's (1867) he declares that the aim of the university is to provide 'general culture.' In a super-utilitarian way, of which his father would have approved, he particularly endorses the teaching of the classics, and the literature of the classics, for its historical value, its wisdom and its artistic perfection. Classical literature is more perfect, but less psychologically profound than the modern. It is more perfect, and yet its beauty is always subservient to sense. Mill says that there are three kinds of education: intellectual, moral and aesthetic. The last is 'the culture which comes through poetry and art, and may be described as the education of the feelings, and the cultivation of the beautiful.' This needs to be emphasized because in England the power of poetry has not been recognized, thanks to the dominance of business and puritanism. We need to 'sustain ourselves by the ideal sympathy of the great characters in history, or even in fiction, and by the contemplation of an idealized posterity: shall I add, of ideal perfection embodied in a Divine Being? Now, of this elevated tone of mind the great source of inspiration is poetry, and all literature so far as it is poetical and artistic.' And the power of poetry is in 'calming the soul' as well as in elevating it. 'There is, besides, a natural affinity between goodness and the cultivation of the Beautiful.'[8] The craving for perfection, which Ruskin also recognized, is both moral and aesthetic. Mill even acknowledges that it has a religious dimension.

In 'Theism' (1868-70) Mill allows that the notion of immortality expresses a profound hope in man, and that the hope needs to be fed and should be fed through the exercise of the imagination. He invokes in passing the high conceptions of poetry and art. But the overall picture is one of unassimilable fact and Comteian ungrounded hope, the latter nourished by imagination, the idealisms of poetry and art. What we are left with is cultivating 'the graces of life,' in the bleak phrase of the <u>Principles</u> (III, 755).

One of Mill's last publications was, fittingly, an edition of his father's <u>Analysis of the Phenomena of the Human Mind</u> (1869). In reprinting and annotating his father's book, Mill endorses it and only amplifies it to a degree. He comments that James has provided a 'sufficient theory of the intellectual element of the feelings,' but not of the animal. On the sublime and the beautiful Mill endorses his father's Alisonian associationism, but he notes that there is an 'element of direct physical and sensual pleasure' in music and in colours. John defends the associationist theory of beauty against Coleridge, and he slyly brings forward Ruskin as 'an unconscious witness' to its truth.[9] As with Wordsworth years before, though very perfunctorily here, Mill thinks that he can benefit from Ruskin's views, without endorsing their transcendental underpinnings. This is what I.A. Richards later tried to do with Coleridge in his denial of 'the phantom aesthetic state,'[10] as well as of mysticism. Mill also enlarges upon his father's presentation of the imagination.

This part of my chapter has sought evidence of concern for poetry and the poetic in Mill's later writings. One concludes the survey agreeing with the nineteenth century opinion of John Morley and Frederic Harrison that he unites 'stern science with infinite aspiration.'[11] Or perhaps one senses an attempt on Mill's part to achieve this unity, and a failure to do so resulting in a wide range of fruitful contributions which show the extent of the elements which such a unity must embrace. Poetry and art are amongst them, but their place is unfixed by Mill. It is most interesting in Mill that, although advocating attitudes that appear to have become dominant in the modern world, scientific and analytical in character, he recognised the limitations of the philosophy which he inherited from Bentham and James Mill. He saw the need to expand it; he saw areas that it did not embrace and that these included not only the experience of religion, but that of poetry as well. This tentative vision is evident through all his work. This is its value, from the point of view of the student of literature and art, as he looks back to the writing of the early nineteenth century and as he reflects from this perspective on the situation as it is today. Now the expansion which Mill sought after and the more than tentative vision that eluded him are more than ever urgently needed.

NOTES

1. Supplement to Encyclopaedia Britannica (1817), vol. 4, p. 18. On the topic 'Education:' 'Wherein does human happiness consist? This is a controverted question; and we have introduced it rather with a view to show the place which it occupies in the theory of education, than that we have it in our power to elucidate a subject about which there is so much diversity of opinion.'

2. This is the phrase of Bruce Mazlish, James and John Stuart Mill (Basic Books, New York, 1975), p. 100.

3. Is this an example of the 'unconscious shifts' which C.B. Macpherson observes in Bentham? The Life and Times of Liberal Democracy (Oxford University Press, New York, 1977), p. 31.

4. Phytologist (October 1860), pp. 290-95.

5. David R. Sanderson, 'Metaphor and Method

in Mill's _On Liberty_,' _Victorian Newsletter_, no. 34 (fall 1968), p. 25.

6. At least, 'A being of higher faculties requires more to make him happy.'

7. _Complete Prose Works_, ed. R.H. Super (11 vols, University of Michigan Press, Ann Arbor, 1960-77), vol. 3, pp. 134, 136.

8. _Literary Essays_, pp. 224-52. Mill even goes on to say that 'ideal Beauty' in art is 'to be eternally aimed at.'

9. _Analysis_, vol. 2, pp. 223, 242, 252.

10. _Principles of Literary Criticism_ (Kegan Paul, London, 1925), title of ch. 2.

11. John Morley, _Fortnightly Review_, nos. vol. 13 (1873), p. 671; Frederic Harrison, _Nineteenth Century_, vol. 40 (1896), p. 489.

INDEX

Addison, Joseph 17, 26, 65-68, 113
Akenside, Mark 36, 100
Alexander, Edward 132, 162
Alison, Archibald 8, 10, 24, 29, 31, 36, 41, 140
Arnold, Matthew 149, 172

Baillie, Joanna 17, 26, 100
Bentham, Jeremy 107, 134, 136-138, 141, 146-147, 154-155, 159, 161, 167, 169, 176
Boswell, James 64, 66, 77, 79, 111, 113
Bowles, William L. 100, 107
Brougham, Henry 43, 52, 55
Bunyan, John 65-66
Burke, Edmund 69-70
Burney, Fanny 65-66
Burns, Robert 4, 7, 13, 29, 33, 44-49, 53, 60-61, 71-72, 75, 77-78, 100, 122-123, 128, 130
Byron, Lord 7, 11-12, 46, 60, 62-63, 66, 71, 75, 77, 82, 86, 89, 91, 97, 99, 101-102, 107, 111, 124, 128

Campbell, Thomas 10, 62, 78
Carlyle, Jane W. 9, 40-41, 49, 54-56
Carlyle, Thomas xii-xiv, 12, 40-62, 65, 67-68, 70-73, 82, 84, 105-107, 110-111, 128, 138, 146, 148, 151-154, 160-161, 166
Cervantes 66, 123
Chaucer, Geoffrey 89, 97, 101
Clive, John xi-xii
Coleridge, Samuel T. 3, 12, 17-18, 22, 24-27, 29-31, 35, 47, 62, 78, 83-84, 89-91, 97, 99, 102, 107-108, 110, 146-149, 152, 154-155, 157, 161, 167, 175
Collier, Jeremy 65, 67
Comte, Auguste 157, 161, 165-166, 169, 172-174
Congreve, William 62-63, 65
Cowley, Abraham 67, 72
Cowper, William 3, 5, 15, 17-18, 89, 97, 100, 102

178

Index

Crabbe, George 3-5, 7, 11, 18, 111, 127
Croker, John W. xiii-xiv, 85, 111-121, 124, 160
Cromwell, Oliver 68, 72

Dante 67, 71, 95
Dickens, Charles xii, 115
Donne, John 3, 67, 102
Dryden, John 2, 5, 17, 26, 63-65, 71, 75, 79-81, 87, 89, 96, 99, 102, 111, 128
Dumont, Pierre 64, 67, 69, 134

Edgeworth, Maria 82, 87, 114-115
Elliott, Ebenezer 52, 60, 95

Fichte 43, 46
Fielding, Henry 81-82, 84, 115
Fox, William J. 146, 152, 158
Frederic the Great 63, 69-70
Froude, James A. 42, 44

Galt, John 112, 147
Gilpin, William 137-138
Goethe, Wolfgang von 40-42, 48, 53, 60, 173-174
Gray, Thomas 17, 100
Grote, George 135-136, 139-140, 150, 159, 166

Hamilton, William 165, 172
Hastings, Warren 63-64, 69
Hayden, John O. x-xii
Haywood, Abraham 115, 142
Hazlitt, William 8, 29, 31, 50, 90, 109, 114, 136, 139, 141, 149
Hemans, Felicia 10, 44
Heraud, John 95, 98
Homer 78, 99, 140
Hood, Thomas ix-x
Hume, David 43, 48, 64, 76, 106, 160
Hunt, Leigh 50, 54, 79, 111-114, 119, 124

Jeffrey, Francis xii-xiv, 1-58, 65, 72-73, 77-78, 81-82, 84-85, 88-89, 92, 101-102, 115, 119-120, 128, 130, 160
Johnson, Samuel 3, 62-63, 66, 68, 78, 84, 111, 113, 124

Keats, John ix, 9-10, 14-16, 18, 31, 93, 101, 109, 112-114, 120, 124

Lamb, Charles xii, 3, 105, 109
Landor, Walter S. 90-91, 93-95, 98
Locke, John 40, 107, 153
Lockhart, John G. xii-xiv, 22, 61, 76, 79, 107, 122-131

Macaulay, Thomas B. xii-xiv, 16-17, 42, 51-52, 59-74, 81-82, 89, 92, 99, 105-106, 111, 113, 116, 119-120, 153, 156
Machiavelli 63, 68
Marmontel, Jean 64, 148
Martineau, James 148, 154-156

Index

Maturin, Charles R. 78, 83, 118
Mill, Harriet T. 134, 137, 146, 150-154, 162, 170
Mill, James 133-136, 139-142, 147-148, 155-156, 158, 161, 166, 169, 175-176
Mill, John S. xiii-xiv, 84, 111, 132-177
Milton, John 2, 17, 26, 41, 63-66, 68, 72, 78, 80, 87, 89-90, 92, 95, 97-98, 100-101, 106, 136, 157
Mirabeau 67, 69
Molière, Jean-Baptiste 79-81
Moore, Thomas 44, 119
Morgan, Sydney 111, 119

Napier, Macvey 50-52, 59, 61
Nesbitt, George L. xi-xii
Novalis, Frederick 47, 53

Petrarch, Francis 67-68
Pitt, William 63, 69-70
Plato 41, 107, 132-136, 141-142, 146-147, 150, 158-159
Pope, Alexander 3, 5, 17, 80, 85, 89, 99-100, 102, 105, 111-113

Reid, Thomas 165-166, 174
Richards, I.A. 132, 175
Richardson, Samuel 81-82
Richter, Jean Paul 42, 60, 62
Robson, J.M. xiv, 132, 146, 162
Ruskin, John 167, 175
Schiller, Frederick 3, 42-43
Scott, Walter xiii-xiv, 11, 15, 17, 64, 71, 75-88, 93, 100, 105, 107-108, 110-111, 114-116, 120, 122-125, 128-130, 147
Shakespeare, William 2, 5, 8-9, 17, 26, 29, 31, 41, 63, 66, 80, 87, 89-90, 92, 95, 97, 100-101, 111-112, 147, 153, 161
Shelley, Mary 79, 115
Shelley, Percy B. 82, 86, 88, 91, 93, 102, 107, 113-114, 124, 152-153, 155-157
Smollett, Tobias 76, 84, 115
Southey, Robert xiii-xiv, 3-4, 11-12, 17-18, 24, 26, 37, 64, 89-110, 113, 123, 125, 156-157
Spenser, Edmund 66, 89-90, 92, 97-98, 101
Sterne, Laurence 115, 126
Swift, Jonathan 67, 75-76, 79-81, 87, 111, 113-114

Tacitus 62, 64
Tennyson, Alfred xii, 112-113, 119-120, 124, 146, 153, 155, 157, 159-160
Thomson, James 36, 100
Townshend, C.H. 91, 98

Voltaire, François de

Index

42, 47-48, 53, 64, 70, 114

Walpole, Horace 67-68, 113, 115, 117
Wellek, René 2, 89
Wilson, John 9, 124
Wordsworth, William xiii, 2-9, 11-12, 14, 17-18, 22-40, 47, 61-64, 66, 72, 75, 77-78, 80, 84, 86-90, 92, 94-97, 99-102, 105, 107-108, 110, 124-126, 146, 148-152, 154-157, 160-162, 166, 173-175
Wycherley, William 63, 65